TRAUMA TREATMENT IN ACTION

Over 85 Activities to Move Clients Toward Healing, Growth and Improved Functioning

Varleisha D. Gibbs PhD, OTD, OTR/L
& Nikki Harley, MSOD

Published by
PESI Publishing
3839 White Ave
Eau Claire, WI 54703

Cover: Amy Rubenzer
Editing: Jenessa Jackson, PhD
Layout: Amy Rubenzer & Bookmasters

ISBN: 9781683733942

Printed in the United States of America

About the Authors

Varleisha D. Gibbs, PhD, OTD, OTR/L

As an occupational therapist, Varleisha has a passion for designing strategies to support individuals in their journey to live their most independent and fulfilled lives. In addition to being a licensed occupational therapist, she is an author, speaker, and expert in the areas of the neurological connections for self-regulation, sensory processing, trauma responsive care, and health and wellness. She is the author of *Self-Regulation & Mindfulness and Raising Kids with Sensory Processing Disorders.*

Varleisha's experience extends beyond her professional training, as her personal journey consists of various traumatic events that have shaped who she is today, including growing up in high-crime and low-income environment, contending with the absence of her biological father, navigating the death of various family members, and facing her own complex medical diagnoses. With her family's support, Varleisha flourished and found solace and relief from her physical and emotional pain through the arts. She played the piano, sang in choirs, studied theater, and eventually became a professional dancer. These experiences led Varleisha to develop a love for social service, philanthropic initiatives, and healing through the arts.

Learning to overcome these obstacles and heal holistically has helped Varleisha thrive in her multi-faceted professional career. She holds four degrees in psychology, occupational therapy, and health sciences and leadership, with a focus on health disparities in the autism community. After spending nearly a decade in community practice helping children and families with special needs, she eventually landed in academia and chaired the first occupational therapy program in the state of Delaware.

Varleisha subsequently became the first Black American woman to serve as the Scientific Programs Officer at the American Occupational Therapy Foundation. While still in leadership as a vice president at her national association, Varleisha continues to lecture internationally and has authored four books, one of which is a bestseller. She has dedicated her time to teaching professionals, parents, teachers, and others the importance of using rhythm and movement to promote health and well-being. Her desire is to help shift others toward growth and healing despite traumatic experiences, diagnoses, or suboptimal living conditions.

Nikki Harley, MSOD, MT (ASCP), is an award-winning organizational development practitioner, speaker, and consultant. With over a decade of practice in the areas of organizational culture, climate, and human performance development, her focus includes building organizational diversity, equity, and inclusion (DEI) capacity, conflict resolution, climate assessment, onboarding, training compliance, leadership development, organizational change management, and performance and well-being coaching. In the capacity of master alternative dispute mediator and trainer, Nikki has facilitated the examination and resolution of organizational conflict, successfully investigating and mediating hundreds of workplace disputes. She credits traveling globally as a part of the Department of Defense's coveted Executive Leadership Development Program as a career capstone experience.

Organizational development and well-being work is Nikki's calling and deep passion. She has had the honor of witnessing the positive impacts of organizational climates and cultures that are connected and aligned with their values, purpose, and passions. Her work examining the impacts of organizational trauma and toxic and hostile workplaces led to a desire to co-create organizational development solutions focused on both organizational and individual holistic well-being. A principal consultant and wellness coach at Imprint Wellness, Nikki has partnered with a wide range of clients, from Fortune 500 companies to governmental agencies and non-profits, in co-creating, optimizing, and sustaining harmonious and safe organizational climates and cultures. Nikki's approach to organizational development fosters whole-person alignment, where individual goal achievement is assessed through a mind-body-spirit lens rooted in heart-centered mindfulness. Nikki believes that art is a powerful catalyst for transformation. As a creator and artist, she uses art and creative expression to foster healing and well-being in both herself and her clients. Her vision and passion is cultivating sanctuary within, from the inside out.

Nikki earned a Bachelor of Science in Medical Technology from the University of Delaware and a Master of Science in Organizational Development and Knowledge Management from George Mason University. She is an avid transcendental meditation and vinyasa yoga practitioner. Nikki lives and works from her home base in Wilmington, DE. She spends her free time creating, going to the beach, hiking, gardening, and biking. *Trauma Treatment in ACTION* is her first book.

Table of Contents

Acknowledgments

Thank you to my husband and children, who are my rocks. You are always willing to allow space for me to feed into others seeking my guidance. Thank you to Nikki Harley for your willingness to support this work. As I placed my thoughts into the various chapters, my beloved grandmother, Thelma Freeman, passed away, further connecting me to this content. I dedicate this book to her and to all of my loved ones who have passed away since my last publication, including my grandfather, Allen Freeman, and mother, Vanest Freeman. They all provided me with love and guidance and taught me how to live even in the face of trauma and adversity. I must also acknowledge those who left this earth during the coronavirus pandemic that occurred in the midst of completing this book. Lastly, I thank my inner child, who continues to push my creativity and who reminds me of my dream to become a doctor to help people heal. While my path did not lead me to become a medical doctor, this career is truly an honor.

—Varleisha D. Gibbs

As a first-time author, I am inspired by the guidance of my grandmother, Rachel Harley, who tirelessly encouraged her grandchildren to make their mark on the world, and my mother, Cornelia Strickland Harley, whose unwavering love remains my inspiration. I would like to thank Dr. Varleisha Gibbs for the opportunity to explore my passion for all things organizational development and Angela Warren, MS, for her steadfast friendship and expertise. I am especially grateful for the advice and counsel provided by C. Shaw, MEd, whose guidance, support, and passion for living purposefully are unmatched. Lastly, none of this would be possible without those on whose shoulders I stand; I am my ancestors' wildest dream.

—Nikki Harley

INTRODUCTION

It is an unfortunate yet true fact: We will all experience trauma during our lifetime. Although some may debate this statement, let us provide you with some examples. We may experience vicarious trauma as a result of frequently watching or hearing of natural disasters or mass murders on the news. Likewise, we may experience trauma as a result of growing up in neglectful and impoverished living conditions in which we do not have all of our needs met, or we may be exposed to it via the community violence that characterizes the inner-city neighborhood in which we live. This type of repeated and prolonged exposure to trauma is known as *complex trauma,* which is associated with a range of more long-lasting ramifications. However, trauma can even happen as a result of an isolated incident, such as an accident or injury to ourselves or someone we know. When we experience trauma, it affects how our brain functions and how we interact with others and society as a whole. It alters how we view ourselves, our environment, and our surroundings (Guarino et al., 2009). We become more vigilant and anxious, and we may struggle to function on an emotional and physical level.

As unsettling as it may be, we cannot ignore the impact of trauma. We must acknowledge and accept trauma in order to allow for healing and improved functioning. Toward this end, this book is a call to action to encourage movement toward healing and growth. In particular, the activities and tools presented here support an ACTION-from-Trauma approach (Figure 1):

- **A**cknowledge and be **A**ware of trauma
- **C**reate growth from trauma
- **T**each neuroeducation and steps toward growth
- **I**ntergenerational factors
- **O**rganizations and systems re-traumatization
- **N**ow is the time to take ACTION to create growth from trauma

Figure 1. ACTION-from-Trauma Approach

We also present trauma as a dynamic and multifaceted condition through the Five Dimensions of Trauma Model, which is an integral aspect of teaching and providing neuroeducation on the multilayered nature of trauma (Figure 2). These five dimensions of trauma include:

- **Structural Trauma:** Exposure to trauma or frequent stress can result in changes at the brain level that impact neurological functioning.
- **Physical Trauma:** Trauma can hide in the body and manifest within one's sensorimotor system, leading some people to exhibit sensory issues with regard to touch, movement, food, and more.
- **Complex Trauma:** Frequent exposure to traumatic events or the experience of living in conditions of chaos can lead to behavioral dysfunction. This includes trauma experienced during the developmental stages of childhood; contextual factors, such as neglect by a caregiver; and environmental factors, such as impoverished or violent living conditions.
- **Intergenerational Trauma:** Trauma is passed down across generations through the role of epigenetics and vicarious trauma.
- **Social and Cultural Trauma:** Organizations and systems can affect trauma through the impact of racism, classicism, organizational trauma, implicit bias, and re-traumatization.

ACTION-FROM-TRAUMA APPROACH

THE FIVE DIMENSIONS OF TRAUMA MODEL

The condition of trauma is dynamic. An individual, population, or community can be exposed to various forms of trauma. Ultimately, the exposure and experience impacts neurological functioning. Hence, the model proposes that structural trauma (i.e., changes on the neurological level) occurs as a result of the other forms of trauma.

When there is more exposure to the various forms of trauma, the severity of structural trauma increases.

Each form of trauma has secondary conditions as revealed in the model. Acknowledgment of the complexity provides a platform for addressing the needs of the individual, population, or community.

BODILY PAIN/ ILLLNESS
SENSORY SEEKING
PHYSICAL TRAUMA
SENSORY AVOIDING
BEHAVIORAL DYSFUNCTION
COMPLEX TRAUMA
ENVIRONMENTAL TRAUMA
STRUCTURAL TRAUMA
Acute and Chronic Stress Responses
INTER-GENERA-TIONAL TRAUMA
HISTORICAL TRAUMA
ANCESTRAL TRAUMA
SYSTEMS RE-TRAUMATIZATION
SOCIAL AND CULTURAL TRAUMA
ORGANIZATIONAL TRAUMA

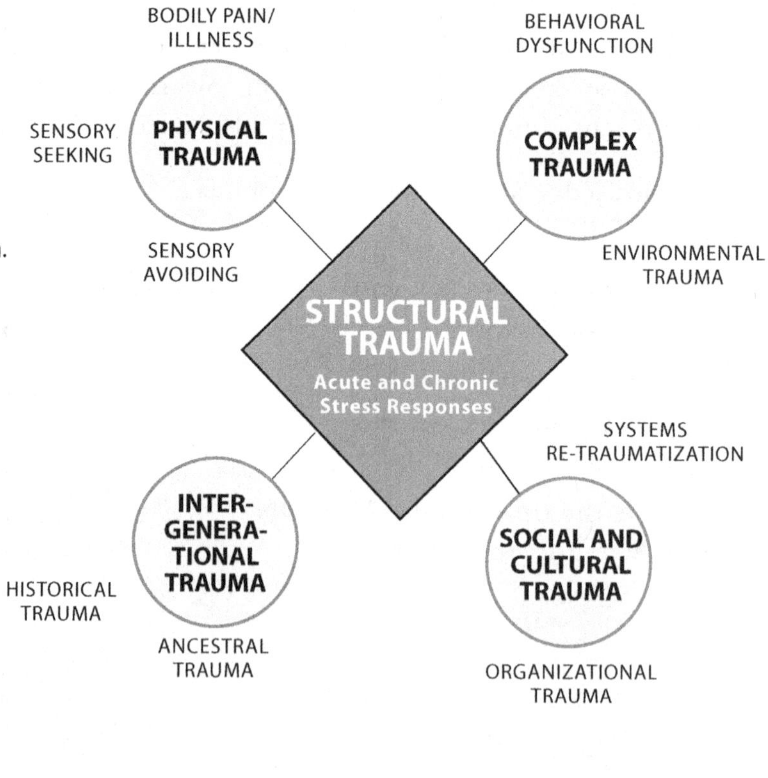

Figure 2. The Five Dimensions of Trauma Model

As these five dimensions illustrate, trauma has the ability to change the way we think and act, accumulates over time, transmits across generations if left unaddressed, and is further impacted by society and the organizations upon which we depend. By establishing dimensions or categories of trauma, we can gain clarity regarding the underlying factors of behavior and areas of dysfunction.

"NOT JUST FOR MENTAL HEALTH PROFESSIONALS"

This book is intended not only for mental health practitioners but for any allied health professionals who desire more tools to assist their clients with healing, including occupational therapists, rehab specialists, physical therapists, social workers, and counselors. Because trauma is so pervasive, the clients you serve may very well present with a history of trauma that can impact your provision of care and negatively affect their treatment outcomes. They may struggle to follow through with treatment recommendations, have poor session attendance, exhibit aggressive behavior, and lack trust in you as the therapy professional.

In order to be of support and provide effective therapeutic services, allied health professionals need to acknowledge the signs and symptoms of trauma. You must be able to identify and analyze the trauma that exists in your clients, even if your practice is not focused on mental health. You must understand trauma as a dynamic condition that presents in various forms. You must also recognize any trauma within yourself and the potential re-traumatization that you can unknowingly impose on those you serve.

WHY WE WROTE THIS BOOK

Dr. Varleisha Gibbs

As an occupational therapy student, entering into a full-time clinical experience was more than intriguing. It was my first summer of fieldwork, and I planned to learn everything it took to become a stellar clinician. In my mind, that meant helping heal those for whom I had the honor to provide treatment and care. I knew I wanted to work with children, yet I also had a desire to work with various age ranges. Regardless, there was a common denominator when it came to those I wished to serve: sensorimotor and neurological conditions. That summer, the curriculum required a mental health affiliation. I was able to enter into a fieldwork position at a mental health hospital for all age ranges, which included a pediatric department with a sensory gym. The patients had various diagnoses requiring sensory-based intervention. This was an area of practice in which I desired more hands-on experience, and my enthusiasm could not be contained.

My first day began with an intake of a young teenage female. She entered with a quiet and passive demeanor. While she spoke, my supervisor shared her chart for my review. I practically gasped out loud as I read about physical, emotional, and sexual abuse. As the young lady smiled and shared her story, I could not understand how she survived such horrible ordeals. Soon it became clear. As she began to discuss some of the events I read in the chart, I witnessed how disconnected she was from these experiences. Her narrative seemed to speak of someone else and not that of her own. She even laughed at some of the abuse as if it were normal. I did not know it then, but that was her sense of "normal." Those recurring acts were normal to her. With repeated abuse, neglect, and loss, she had learned to accept her trauma and, at the same time, had become an observer to it as opposed to the one who experienced it. I soon realized that her experiences had led to severe psychosis and hallucinations. Her ability to disconnect from the trauma had led her to disconnect from reality itself. Whether it was happiness, anger, or fear, there was little variation in her emotions.

Not long after, I completed an intake for a 3-year-old female who was wise beyond her years. Her story rang familiar. Her ability to move between laughing with the staff and attempting to cause physical harm was eerily similar to the adolescent female. I began to notice similarities with the various children in both the inpatient and outpatient units. Many of them were part of the foster care system. Most had experienced various traumatic events even before their birth, as their parents had struggled with addiction or been the victims of abuse during pregnancy. Other children lived with grandparents who attempted to keep them within the family despite an absent parent. The grandparents presented with that same disconnected demeanor.

In my undergraduate and graduate degree programs, I learned about mental health and psychosocial treatment models. However, nothing could have prepared me for the patient population at that fieldwork placement. Throughout the three months I spent at the site, I found myself crying in my car during lunch almost every day. What I witnessed was simply unexpected. Little did I know, it was in fact my own traumatic experience.

It is my desire to use my personal experiences and stories, not only of that summer I just described but of the various children and families I worked with over the years, to help other practitioners. It has been almost 20 years of encountering the unexpected impact that trauma has on the success of our treatment interventions. From working in schools in low-income areas of New York City to working with wealthy parents in affluent New Jersey towns who have discovered their child has a terminal illness, I have seen a lot. I decided to compile my clinical and research expertise to help other occupational therapists and rehab professionals. To expand upon this lens, Nikki Harley provides another perspective as an organizational development and conflict resolution expert.

Nikki Harley, MSOD

Having worked in the field of organizational development for over a decade, I approach holistic organizational transformation from a dialogic perspective, with a special interest in organizational culture and climate. I see value in examining the interface of human behavior and systems—specifically, the connection between organizational trauma and healing. This passion and interest were born out of witnessing the very real and serious impacts organizational trauma and dysfunction have on environments and individuals. Most of us have witnessed organizations with high turnover or challenges retaining talent. We have heard of spaces that are toxic or unpleasant to work in. We know of places rife with unresolved conflict or ineffective leadership. After assessing, investigating, and mediating hundreds of toxic and hostile workplaces, I have witnessed firsthand the influence imbalanced environments have on the minds, bodies, and spirits of individuals. My own experience with occupational burnout was a catalyst for personal reflection and transformation. My practice and personal experiences further demonstrated the importance of individual well-being within our organizational systems, leading me to acknowledge that growth and movement toward healing happens not solely at the individual level but at the organizational and system levels. Creating and sustaining safe, adaptable, and aware organizations is a critical strategic business imperative and is necessary for moving toward ACTION. These realizations, made urgent by the current impacts of social and cultural trauma, inform the whole-person-centric solutions created in *Trauma Treatment in ACTION*.

HOW WE DEFINE TRAUMA

Throughout this book, we do not define trauma solely based on diagnostic criteria because certain forms of trauma are not part of the fifth edition of the *Diagnostic and Statistical Manual of Mental Disorders* (DSM-5®; APA, 2013) or other clinical diagnostic manuals. Instead, we move past diagnosis by mapping out the signs and symptoms of common presentations we have encountered. There are various levels of stress and trauma that can impact a person's life. Not every individual will meet the threshold for clinical diagnosis, yet their actions and behaviors deserve our attention.

Trauma comes in many different forms, though all forms of trauma share some commonality. For the intent of this workbook, we define trauma as the impact that adverse experiences have on a person's mental, psychological, physical, financial, and overall well-being. Adverse experiences can include abuse, neglect, loss, physical assault, sexual assault, accidents, natural disasters, poverty, homelessness, imprisonment, and other potentially traumatic experiences. These adverse experiences can occur repeatedly throughout a person's life or be isolated to a specific event, and they also extend to the impact on the unborn child. In this respect, most individuals have experienced at least one adverse event in their lifetime (Felitti et al., 1998).

The detrimental effects of trauma are well-illustrated through the notable Adverse Childhood Experiences (ACE) Study, which helped to redefine trauma by connecting it to childhood experiences and not limiting it to the posttraumatic stress experienced by veterans of war (Felitti et al., 1998). In fact, the ACE Study found that trauma has a negative impact not only on mental well-being but on physical well-being as well. Specifically, individuals who reported at least two traumatic events in childhood were two to four times more likely to have a variety of negative health outcomes later in life, including chronic diseases and a reduced life expectancy.

These findings highlight the notion that trauma does not simply lead to social and emotional difficulties. It can also result in physical dysfunctions and behavioral challenges that, unbeknownst to you, have led clients to seek your services. They may exhibit heightened pain responses, hyperactivity, and aggression that are the result of adverse childhood experiences and past traumatic events. By reading this book, we seek to provide you with a primer in identifying the physical signs of trauma, unwrapping hidden trauma, and acknowledging the unconscious beliefs that influence the severity of trauma.

HOW THIS WORKBOOK CAN HELP

The word *trauma* can overshadow the individual. Hence, this book encourages providers to take a strengths-based approach in conjunction with acknowledging what happened to the person. There is also an emphasis on creating growth versus simply healing. Healing is vital but sometimes seems too far-fetched, produces additional stress, and may imply brokenness. Therefore, not only will this workbook unveil a trajectory of healing activities—such as screening procedures, body awareness mapping, grounding activities, breathwork, sensorimotor work, and early intervention strategies—but more importantly, it will discuss the use of autonomic rhythms, respect and empathy, gratitude statements, and tools to create growth. It provides igniting, life-changing principles that are easy for anyone to apply.

The book is separated into two parts: The first part is **ACT**. To act is to do or take action. The acronym ACT stands for: **A**cknowledge and be **A**ware of trauma, **C**reate growth from trauma, and **T**each neuroeducation and steps toward growth. The second part is **ION**. Just as ions are created by interaction, trauma does not happen in isolation for the individual. The acronym ION stands for: **I**ntergenerational factors, **O**rganizations and systems re-traumatization, and **N**ow is the time to take ACTION to create growth from trauma.

To capture the complexity of trauma, this workbook covers the entire lifespan and addresses all age ranges. In each chapter, we address how individuals may present with and experience trauma across the lifespan, ranging from childhood and adolescence to adulthood and older adulthood. We also include hands-on activities for clients, caregivers, and pediatric populations in particular. Throughout each chapter, we provide background information, screening tools, activities, case studies, and reflective practices. We also provide recommended age ranges for specific activities and screening tools. We strongly recommend that you read the supporting information before utilizing the tools and activities. You can also feel free to make copies of worksheets and activities for clients.

Whether trauma is a primary or secondary treatment condition, gaining knowledge and becoming familiar with trauma-informed intervention strategies is a must for any allied health professional. But more so, taking action is a much-needed next step. We must focus on areas of opportunity and begin to create growth for those living with trauma. It is our hope that this book guides you in helping your clients to heal and move toward a better quality of life... and for you to be able to do so as well!

PART ONE

ACT

CHAPTER 1

ACKNOWLEDGE AND BE AWARE OF TRAUMA

The first step in our ACTION-from-Trauma approach is to **A**cknowledge and be **A**ware. This step includes acknowledging how trauma presents, understanding the various risk factors for trauma, maintaining an awareness of the various categories and types of trauma, and learning the foundation of trauma-informed care. It also involves understanding the normal stress response so you can recognize the difference between function and dysfunction in response to acute stress. Finally, it involves examining your own readiness to care for those with trauma and learning how to use ACTION language that is trauma-informed.

In this chapter, we aim to justify the need to expand upon the current practices and employ ACTION steps toward healing through the following sections:

- ☐ A Call to ACTION
- ☐ Screening for Traumatic Experiences
- ☐ Complex Trauma Across the Lifespan
- ☐ SAMHSA's Trauma-Informed Care Approach
- ☐ Normal Stress Response
- ☐ Detecting Acute Stress
- ☐ Detecting Level of Self-Regulation
- ☐ Readiness to Provide Trauma Care
- ☐ From Trauma-Informed to ACTION Language
- ☐ Next Steps: Moving to the C in ACTION to Create Growth
- ☐ Case Scenario

A CALL TO ACTION

Before we start on our journey, we want to recognize the multitude of professions and variety of settings in which you may practice, as well as the many tiers of care that you may provide. As an allied health professional, you may work with at-risk individuals and families who present with challenging behaviors that impact your provision of care. You may also provide intensive trauma-specific care, such as exposure therapy, cognitive behavioral therapy, or other forms of psychotherapy. In making a call to action, it is not our intent to replace any intensive trauma-specific services you may already be providing. Rather, our ACTION-from-Trauma approach is intended to accompany those services and expand upon current trauma-informed practices so you can best support outcomes for your clients. Remember, trauma is complex and requires the support of an interdisciplinary team.

Although the ACE Study raised much-needed awareness regarding trauma, an unfortunate result of these efforts is that we have begun to define the individual by their trauma (Ginwright, 2018). By applying the label of a "trauma victim," we have impeded upon our lens to see the whole person. It has caused us to focus on people's deficits versus their innate capacity for resiliency (Leitch, 2017).

There is also a lack of specific guidance and recommendations when it comes to taking action in applying the now popularized model of trauma-informed care (Ginwright, 2018; Yatchmenoff, Sundborg, & Davis, 2017). It is time to shift the paradigm of trauma. Through our work, we want to reinvigorate the importance of looking at the person first as opposed to labeling the client by their pain. We want to shift the focus of our attention to well-being and growth versus the treatment of pathology. In doing so, we take a strengths-based approach and redirect our attention by looking at each person's strengths and detecting available opportunities for growth.

In addition, we need to revisit our trauma lens and expand it to include an individual's family, community, culture, organizations, systems, and societal experiences (Becker-Blease, 2017). That is because the experience of trauma is tethered to the community, policy, health care, child welfare services, the criminal justice system, and much more. It is for this reason that our ACTION-from-Trauma approach ventures into the Five Dimensions of Trauma Model to encapsulate the multitude of factors that can catapult us to the next level of care. We must address collective encounters of trauma and hold accountable those who impact an individual's experience of trauma.

SCREENING FOR TRAUMATIC EXPERIENCES

Individuals with trauma frequently utilize health and behavioral services. Therefore, the likelihood that you will encounter a client with trauma is high. In fact, certain communities and settings may have a universal spread of trauma among their members. Regardless of your practice setting or discipline, consider screening and assessing for trauma during the intake process and throughout your period of care. This is especially important when a client is overusing health care services, exhibiting difficulties with non-compliance, or presenting with overt signs of trauma, such as avoidance, detachment, or elopement. Being able to detect trauma early can facilitate successful treatment outcomes and promote growth toward healing. Therefore, be aware of the following trauma risk factors, and use the following checklist to identify those clients at risk for trauma.

Trauma Risk Factors Checklist

- ☐ **Minority status.** Those from underrepresented racial and ethnic groups are more likely to experience trauma.
- ☐ **Acute stress.** Exposure to ongoing stressful events and crises may diminish the ability to cope in the presence of trauma.
- ☐ **Childhood adversity.** Living in an impoverished or violent community, being exposed to domestic violence or parental neglect, experiencing a lack of cohesion within the family system, or growing up in a household characterized by parental physical or mental illness, parental stress, or parental substance abuse can all result in a child experiencing trauma.
- ☐ **Physiological characteristics.** Certain biomarkers, such as low heart rate variability and low cortisol levels, have been found to negatively correlate with the ability to cope in the presence of trauma.
- ☐ **Chronic or life-threatening health conditions** (experienced by the client or a loved one). Being diagnosed with a serious illness, such as cancer, or with a progressive neurological condition (e.g., amyotrophic lateral sclerosis or ALS) are stressful life crises that are also traumatic.
- ☐ **Low socioeconomic status.** Poverty is associated with chronic stress, exposure to violent and unhealthy environments, and lack of access to health care. It impacts the ability of parents to properly care for their children and can curtail growth and development.
- ☐ **Lack of education.** As a social determinant of health, education has a direct correlation with health outcomes, socioeconomic status, and life expectancy. These factors align with the trauma risk factors mentioned above.
- ☐ **Genetics and family trauma.** Some people are predisposed to trauma and have difficulty coping with secondary trauma due to intergenerational trauma, in which the effects of trauma are passed down across generations through epigenetic changes to DNA.
- ☐ **History of trauma.** Having prior exposure to trauma may increase the likelihood of future exposure to trauma, possibly due to the accumulation of stress and the resurfacing of symptoms from traumatic events.
- ☐ **Domestic violence.** Physical and emotional harm results in stress, anxiety, and fear, and it threatens one's safety. The chronic and persistent threat of domestic violence has long-term effects for the victim and for those witnessing the abuse.

While many of us can experience stressful situations, trauma can result in the development of posttraumatic stress disorder (PTSD) when it impacts someone for at least a month or more. The clinical symptoms of PTSD span across four main categories of symptoms (APA, 2013):

- ☐ **Intrusive thoughts and repeated memories, dreams, or flashbacks** of the traumatic event. These symptoms present challenges to various areas of life, such as sleep hygiene, social interaction, and the ability to care for oneself and others.
- ☐ **Avoidance of reminders of the trauma.** This may involve avoiding people, places, activities, or certain interactions that lead to unwanted memories or physical sensations that are reminiscent of the trauma.
- ☐ **Negative thoughts and feelings.** Symptoms can include negative self-appraisal, loss of interest in things previously enjoyed, shame, blame, loss of memory related to the trauma, or social isolation.
- ☐ **Hyperarousal.** Exposure to trauma leads to lack of concentration, challenges in modulating arousal levels, hypervigilance, impulsivity, aggression, and difficulty sleeping.

In the presence of PTSD, exposure to trauma can lead to biophysiological reactions that not only present themselves in the moment but also persist across an extended time frame. The fight-or-flight system remains in a state of constant activation, resulting in hyperarousal, anxiety, and avoidance. Individuals become stuck in the trauma, leading to problems with everyday activities, social interactions, and the ability to navigate life. Their perception of the world becomes framed by the trauma. Their focus becomes survival and protection, which limits their ability to see beyond the symptoms. This trauma lens limits people's vantage point by narrowing their view of the surrounding peripheral world, in turn making their world smaller. People are no longer able to see the full picture of events in their lives and instead have a more centralized view of the world, which poses a threat to their well-being (Figure 3).

There are various categories of traumatic experiences, including trauma that is expected versus unexpected, as well as trauma that is directly experienced versus indirectly experienced. To expand our view of the trauma landscape, we must review the complexity of trauma further by considering

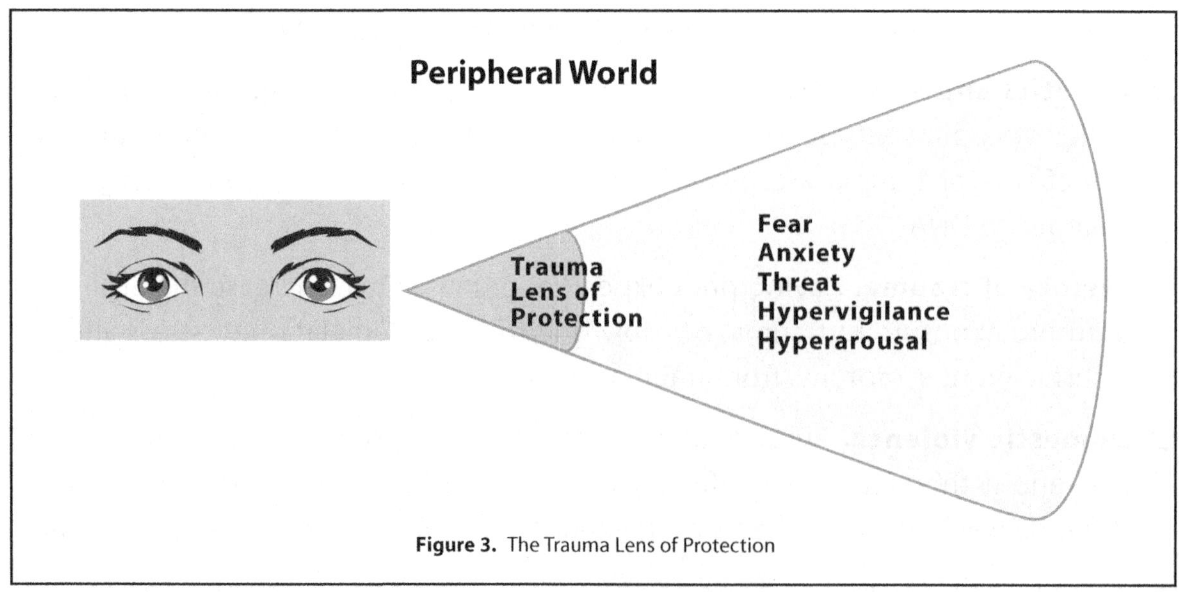

Figure 3. The Trauma Lens of Protection

the many dimensions of trauma (i.e., structural, physical, complex, intergenerational, social and cultural) that can fall within each of these categories. Utilizing the Five Dimensions of Trauma Model as a guide, we outline some specific factors to consider before you initiate a screening and assessment process. We also highlight the potential impact of traumatic experiences based on different categories of trauma and age ranges (Table 1).

Categorization of Traumatic Experiences*	Examples of Impact		
	Early Childhood and School Age	**Adolescence**	**Adulthood and Older Adulthood**
Expected (e.g., passing of a loved one who was ill)	An expected trauma may lead to significant **complex trauma**. For example, a child who is living in foster care and who is returned to their biological family as planned may respond with maladaptive behaviors, such as challenges with learning, sleeping, toileting, and engaging with others.	In adolescence, the passing of a loved one who was ill may lead to changes in personality, challenges at school, and difficulty engaging or socializing with others.	Expected trauma may greatly impact anyone regardless of their age. For example, a person with type 1 diabetes mellitus may be aware of a prognosis requiring a lower-limb amputation. Such an event can change how they socialize, challenge their ability to work, and impact their roles, such as caring for others.
Unexpected (e.g., sudden departure of a family member)	The unexpected passing or departure of a loved one due to incarceration can lead to maladaptive behaviors, such as detachment, aggression, and challenges in academics.	An unexpected move from an individual's childhood community secondary to parental divorce can lead to maladaptive behaviors, such as detachment, elopement, aggression, and challenges in academics.	Unexpected traumatic events may greatly affect well-being. For example, the sudden loss of employment can lead to anxiety, depression, substance use, aggression, and a poor outlook on life.
Isolated (single incident, such as a sexual assault)	Depending on the developmental stage, an isolated traumatic event, such as a car accident, can lead to changes in personality or behavior requiring intervention. **Physical trauma** may result, such as hypersensitivity, even if the effects are temporary.	An isolated traumatic event, such as a sexual assault, can lead to changes in personality or behavior requiring intervention. **Physical trauma** may result, such as hypersensitivity, even if temporary.	An isolated traumatic event, such as a home invasion for an older adult living alone, can lead to changes in personality or behavior requiring intervention. **Physical trauma** may result, such as hypersensitivity, even if temporary.
Pervasive (ongoing, such as repeated physical abuse or homelessness)	Pervasive trauma can have significant implications on development. For example, a child living in poverty or experiencing ongoing abuse may have **structural trauma** as a result, leading them to develop **complex trauma**.	This may be a form of **complex trauma** that has significant implications on an adolescent's outlook on life. For example, ongoing abuse or sex trafficking may result in **structural trauma** and lead to challenges with establishing future goals.	Adults may experience **complex trauma** in the form of ongoing domestic violence, which can cause **structural trauma** and interfere with their ability to establish future goals.
Intentional (e.g., neglect from a parent, physical or sexual assault)	Intentional trauma, such as neglect from a parent, may lead to social-emotional issues, such as lack of trust in and detachment from others. **Structural trauma** may lead to **physical** and **complex trauma**.	Adolescents who experience bullying by their peers may exhibit social-emotional issues, such as a lack of trust and risk-taking behaviors. **Structural trauma** may lead to **physical** and **complex trauma**.	Spousal abuse or caregiver abuse of an older adult may lead to social-emotional issues that manifest as acute anxiety, distorted expectations, and detachment from others. **Structural trauma** may lead to **physical** and **complex trauma**.

(*Continued*)

(*Continued*)

Categorization of Traumatic Experiences*	Examples of Impact		
	Early Childhood and School Age	Adolescence	Adulthood and Older Adulthood
Unintentional (e.g., natural disaster or pandemic)	Certain unintentional traumatic events represent a form of **social or cultural trauma**, such as pandemics or natural disasters, which can be very frightening to children due to a sense of loss of security. Feelings of helplessness and uncertainty can cause acute anxiety and stress, which can lead to PTSD if unaddressed. Children may display aggression, have problems sleeping, and exhibit difficulty concentrating.	Adolescents who experience unintentional forms of traumatic events, such as pandemics or natural disasters, can experience acute stress in response to the event. The effects of this type of **social or cultural trauma** may be revealed through changes in personality and behaviors, such as detachment, avoidance, and aggression.	Systematic and organizational culture and policies can result in re-traumatization. This may be revealed through changes in personality and behaviors. Adults may also experience feelings of insecurity, guilt, and shame in response to this **social or cultural trauma**.
Directly experienced (e.g., poverty due to loss of employment)	Directly experiencing abuse, neglect, or other traumatic events has very strong implications for child development. It can impact typical brain development, affect emotion regulation, and lead to dysfunction in sensory processing.	In adolescence, the direct experience of trauma, such as living in unsafe environments, experiencing abuse and neglect, or being exposed to a traumatic event, can negatively impact development and the establishment of future goals. The adolescent may isolate themselves, be aggressive, and have difficulty with academics.	There are several implications of directly experiencing trauma, including challenges in performing activities of daily living, practicing self-care, properly caring for others, and engaging in social interaction.
Indirectly experienced (e.g., shared experienced of a parent or observing the impact of injustices, such as unjustified killings)	**Intergenerational trauma** can impact children based on their caregiver's interactions with them. For example, a parent who experienced sexual abuse by a family member may reveal aggressive and overprotective behaviors toward their child in an attempt to prevent them from experiencing the same abuse. These behaviors are based on the caregiver's personal experiences and views.	**Intergenerational trauma** can impact an adolescent based on how their caregiver interacts with them. For example, a parent may reveal strict and aggressive behaviors toward the child secondary to their personal struggles with systemic racism and a history of violent attacks on family members. These behaviors are based on the caregiver's personal experiences and views.	**Intergenerational trauma** can impact one's experiences and interactions with the world. For example, adults may reveal certain fears grounded in stories or norms set by their family, which are based on historical events. Family members can pass on a lack of trust, shame, and anxiety to their offspring.

Table 1. Categories of Trauma and Their Impact

*There is the possibility of structural or physical trauma in all categories.

COMPLEX TRAUMA ACROSS THE LIFESPAN

In the United States alone, it is documented that more than 700,000 children experience abuse or neglect, though more than 3 million are suspected to have experienced abuse based on investigations by child protection agencies and services rendered (National Children's Alliance, 2019). In addition, four out of five times, the abusers in these situations are typically family members. This type of trauma during childhood can have detrimental effects on an individual's neurodevelopment and psychosocial well-being across the lifespan. It can result in what is known as complex trauma, which is a term used to describe "exposure to multiple traumatic events, often of an invasive, interpersonal nature, and the wide-ranging, long-term impact of this exposure" (National Child Traumatic Stress Network, 2017). In this book, we define complex trauma as the continued, long-term exposure to traumatic events that impacts a person at various biopsychosocial levels. These traumatic events can include continued violence, poverty, hunger, illness, and abuse that becomes intolerable. Such events are prevalent in minority populations, specifically those of low socioeconomic status.

The Substance Abuse and Mental Health Service Administration (SAMHSA) provides the following examples of complex childhood trauma (2014b):

- ☐ Psychological, physical, or sexual abuse
- ☐ Community or school violence
- ☐ Witnessing or experiencing domestic violence
- ☐ Commercial sexual exploitation (including sex trafficking)
- ☐ Refugee or war experiences in the military
- ☐ Family-related stressors (e.g., deployment, parental loss or injury)
- ☐ Neglect
- ☐ Life-threatening illness

We can expand upon these examples to also include:

- ☐ Maternal exposure to physical, mental, or emotional abuse
- ☐ Maternal malnourishment
- ☐ Racism and oppression
- ☐ Poverty
- ☐ Homelessness
- ☐ Being incarcerated as a minor
- ☐ Incarceration of a parent
- ☐ Living in the foster care system
- ☐ Intergenerational transmission of trauma (see chapter 4)

For such pervasive experiences of trauma, Dr. Judith Herman has suggested a diagnosis of complex PTSD given that the long-term implications of complex trauma are not captured in the traditional diagnosis of PTSD (Herman, 1997). According to Herman, those with complex trauma may require a different approach to care than those with the clinical diagnosis of PTSD. They may experience impulsive and aggressive behaviors and exhibit non-compliance or reduced participation in therapy, leading to poor treatment outcomes. They may also have other pathological conditions, exhibit challenges with personal relationships, and seek support through multiple visits to medical professionals. In addition, those with complex trauma may exhibit emotion dysregulation, musculoskeletal problems, challenges with sensory perception, poor self-care, and cognitive deficits (Gorman & Hatkevich, 2016). As result, they may struggle to perform basic and instrumental activities of daily living.

Practitioners delivering therapeutic services need to be aware of these behavioral, emotional, cognitive, interpersonal, and somatization difficulties accompanying complex trauma. For example, physical distance, emotional withdrawal, freeze, and aggressive behaviors can be mistaken for other diagnoses, such as attention-deficit/hyperactivity disorder (ADHD) or oppositional defiant disorder, or for non-compliance (Smith, 2010). Maintaining an awareness of these different manifestations of complex trauma can prevent against misdiagnosis and ill-informed treatment plans. This further supports our platform for the ACTION-from-Trauma approach.

Trauma, and particularly complex trauma, is a concern for early childhood development, as it can disrupt neural development associated with the ability to modulate stress and emotions. As a result, children may experience separation anxiety, poor eating habits, and nightmares. Those who are of school age may experience anxiety, fear, guilt, shame, learning difficulties, and poor concentration, while adolescents may present with secondary conditions, such as eating disorders, depression, substance use disorders, depression, loneliness, and risk-taking behaviors (SAMHSA, 2014b).

In addition, young children have not developed coping mechanisms to properly address life stressors, and they rely primarily on their parents and caregivers as a source of regulation. However, many children presenting with complex trauma may have caregivers who themselves have significant exposure to trauma, and they may struggle to manage stress, self-regulate, and interact with others. Indeed, individuals who were exposed to trauma in their earlier life stages frequently experience symptoms of depression and PTSD as adults (Dunn, Nishimi, Powers, & Bradley, 2017). It is for this reason that our ACTION-from-Trauma approach is for the lifespan. Trauma can start early in life and continue onward. Therefore, some of the age-specific approaches we present in this book are not for pediatric clients but for their caregivers.

To address complex childhood trauma, the **focus should be on restoring the child's sense of safety, increasing attachment, enhancing appropriate affect, and improving cognitive, behavioral, and social functioning** (Harley, Williams, Zamora, & Lakatos, 2014). To do so, we must take a biopsychosocial approach when it comes to awareness. First, society and medical professionals alike must acknowledge the neurological and physiological impacts of trauma. We must then consider the influence of the individual's culture, community, and family makeup. In addition, we must gain better awareness of symptomatology in terms of how trauma can manifest. Perhaps most importantly, though, we must attend to the child-caregiver connection. The bonds that children develop with their caregivers, including those involved in their education, are some of the most impactful. Caregivers play a huge role in detecting dysfunction that can impact a child's well-being. Therefore, successful treatment approaches for trauma require a two-person focused intervention that addresses the caregiver and child alike (Gibbs, 2017a). The onus is not only on the child but on all adults involved. When all these factors work together, it enhances the initiation of ACTION from trauma (Figure 4).

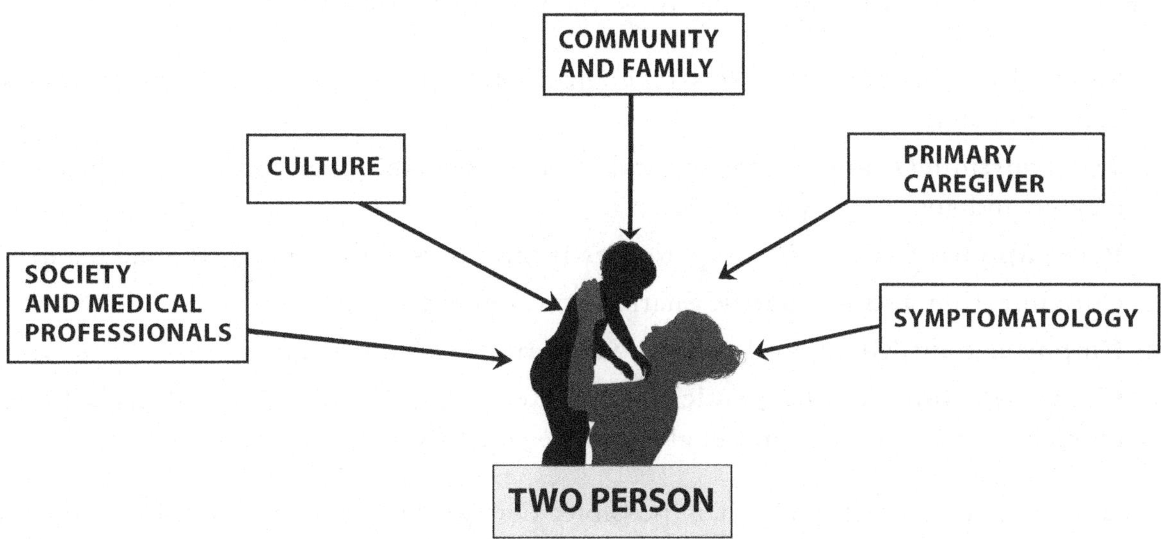

Figure 4. Biopsychosocial Approach to Awareness

SAMHSA'S TRAUMA-INFORMED CARE APPROACH

While we emphasize moving to more action-oriented approaches, it is crucial to provide information on trauma-informed care. The trauma-informed care approach serves as a starting point to apply the concepts we introduce in this workbook. Therefore, ensure you have a general understanding of trauma-informed approaches and principles before initiating any of the activities in this workbook.

The concept of trauma-informed care, which was first developed by SAMHSA, acknowledges that nothing is wrong with someone exposed to trauma. It shifts the focus from "What is wrong with you?" to "What happened to you?" We expand upon this definition of trauma-informed care to also consider the question "What do you need to grow from here?"

SAMHSA's trauma-informed approach starts with the three E's of trauma as a means of identifying and defining trauma: events, the experience of these events, and effect. At the most basic level, *events* represent what actually occurred. As stated in the DSM-5, the individual must be exposed to a traumatic event. This is a requirement of the diagnostic process, yet it leads to various debates about what events should be included. The individual's *experience of these events* goes deeper in acknowledging how the person interpreted the event. What did they feel? What meaning did the event have to them personally? As with most parts of life, we all have varying interpretations of lived experiences, and what we may label as "traumatic," another may not. Finally, the *effects* highlight the adverse impact of the trauma, including its short- and long-term effects on behavioral, psychosocial, and physical health (SAMHSA, 2014a).

Detecting trauma with the three E's is an initial step to the trauma-informed approach. Once trauma has been detected, there are four approaches and six principles that guide the subsequent care and intervention process. The four approaches involve *realizing* the widespread impact of the trauma and potential roads to recovery; *recognizing* the signs and symptoms of trauma; *responding* by integrating knowledge about trauma into policies, procedures, and practices; and *resisting re-traumatization* by identifying possible triggers and toxic environments for all involved. In addition, the following six key principles drive the process (SAMHSA, 2014a):

1. **Safety.** Ensuring physical and psychological safety at every level of the organization (e.g., client and staff)
2. **Trustworthiness and transparency.** Being open and transparent regarding decision making and goal development
3. **Peer support.** Sharing lived experiences from others with a similar trauma history
4. **Collaboration and mutuality.** Sharing power and decision making
5. **Empowerment, voice, and choice.** Supporting self-advocacy
6. **Cultural, historical, and gender issues.** Removing stereotypes regarding culture, race, ethnicity, sexual orientation, religion, gender identity, etc.

While recovery may be challenging, it is possible. Our workbook primarily focuses on trauma-informed care approaches versus specific treatment models. However, resilience and recovery depend on support from the various angles, levels, and systems of care. *You are part of that hierarchy*. In addition, we want to remove the strain of the word *healing* when it comes to recovery from trauma. Healing may lead to thoughts of brokenness or something being "wrong" with the individual. Instead, we approach care through the creation of growth.

How does that growth occur? As a result of trauma, the brain may develop neural connections that are grounded in persistent fear, stress, and anxiety. Luckily, we produce new cells and neurons each day, and the brain has the capacity to rewire itself and form new neural connections through a process known as *neuroplasticity*. Trauma-informed approaches, as well as current clinical practices, may support the brain's ability to heal itself, but we must go beyond current approaches and act with strategies focused on growth. We need to repackage our message to illustrate the possibility of growth on a structural level to enhance well-being in life.

NORMAL STRESS RESPONSE

The neurological changes that occur following trauma align with a variety of bodily changes that also occur in response to stress. To illustrate, we start with an examination of the universal stress response, which reflects a typical reaction to stress. It was once believed that unaddressed universal stress responses resulted in trauma. We now know that not everyone who is exposed to stress will experience trauma. It is the absence of recovery from the universal stress response that may lead to dysfunction. This universal stress response is governed by our body's autonomic nervous system, which is an internal alarm system we have in response to stress, threats, and the unexpected. While our body's alarm signals are mostly short-lived, they can persist in strength and frequency in response to stressful or traumatic events, which has long-term implications. But what defines a "normal stress" response versus acute stress or posttraumatic stress? Let us review to begin our **A**cknowledgment and **A**wareness of trauma.

Imagine that you have a trip planned. You have been excited for this vacation and can barely sleep. You finally close your eyes and drift off. Before you know it, it's morning. As you rise, you notice that your alarm did not go off, and you are now an hour behind your scheduled departure time. You race to pack your luggage and gather other items for your trip. After quickly calling for transportation to the airport, you grab your keys and quickly head outside.

Once you are in the car, you realize that you have neglected to grab your passport. You tell the driver to please wait as you run inside to obtain your necessary identification. This has now cost you valuable time! You then tell the driver that you are short on time. Of course, there is traffic on the highway, and it is taking you even longer to get to the airport. You finally arrive, but the line for security seems to be out the door. After you make it through, you run toward your gate, where the airport staff inform you that they have been calling your name and were about to close the doors. However, you made it just in time! You locate your seat on the flight and finally get to rest a bit after your ordeal. Unfortunately, it is hard for you to relax, and you still feel the racing of your heart and the labored breathing from your lungs. It seems as if it takes the entire flight to your destination for your body to calm.

While this example may seem dramatic, most people would not view it as traumatic. It reflects a common and universal stress response, which is known as the fight-or-flight response (Figure 5).

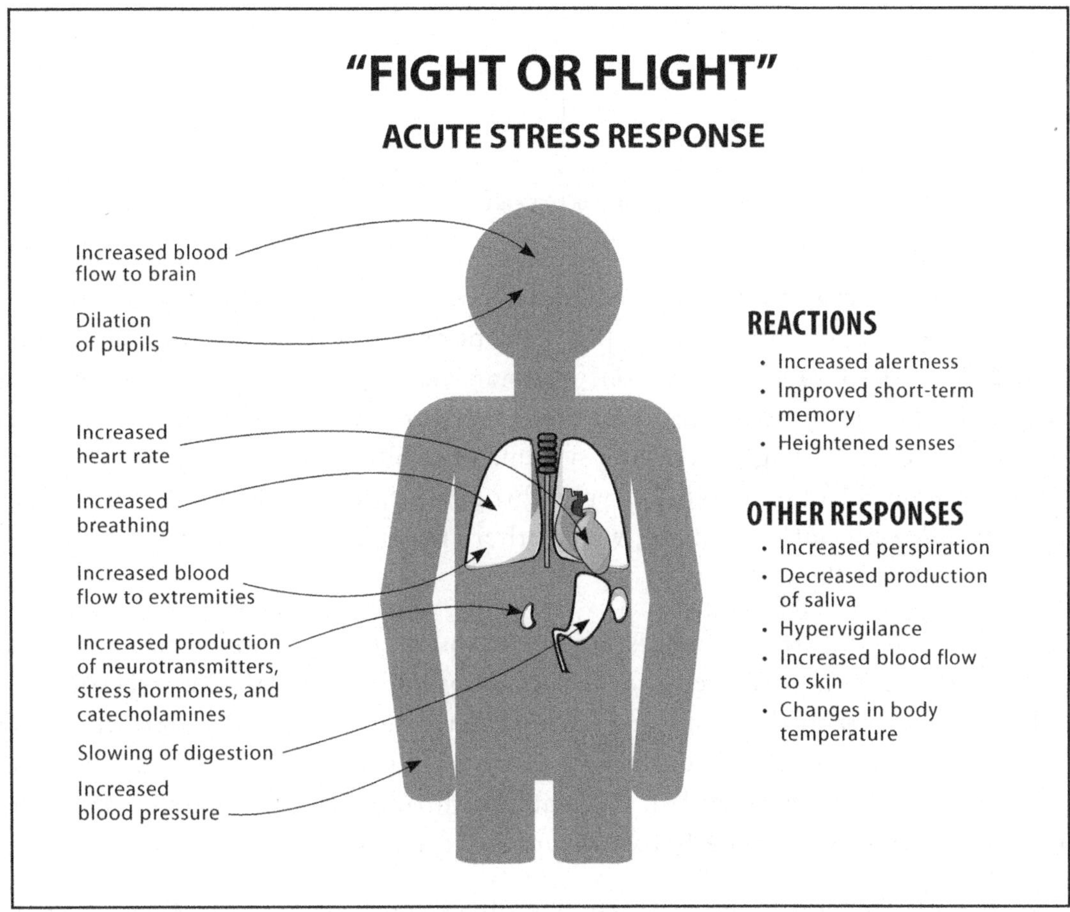

Figure 5. The Fight-or-Flight Response*

* Adapted from https://www.polar.com/blog/recovery-from-exercise/

In response to stressful or threatening situations, the brain sends out a signal that there is a problem, which activates the body's sympathetic nervous system, resulting in a release of stress hormones to the body that prepare the individual to fight back against the stressor (fight) or run away from it (flight). However, stressors do not solely involve negative events, as even positive events and experiences can cause stress. This is known as eustress. Distress is a term that refers to negative stress, which impacts our physiology in a more negative manner, whereas eustress refers to positive forms of stress (Table 2). These stressors can be internal, external, or a combination of both.

Examples of Distress	**Examples of Eustress**
Financial stressors Work-life imbalance Illness or death Divorce Abuse/neglect	Work needed to complete a desired degree Marriage/wedding planning Giving birth Caring for a loved one Creating, such as working on a desired project
Add your personal examples (consider both internal and external factors):	Add your personal examples (consider both internal and external factors):

Table 2. Examples of Distress and Eustress

The body's stress reaction was first identified by Hans Selye (1974), whose work on the stress response resulted in his identifying a three-phase response to stress called general adaptation syndrome (Tan & Yip, 2018). The phases consist of an alarm phase, a resistance phase, and an exhaustion phase. The *alarm* phase occurs when the brain perceives a threat or problem, resulting in the activation of the body's fight-or-flight system. Our blood flow increases, our heart rate accelerates, and our lungs dilate to increase oxygen throughout the body in the brain. Some people may experience feeling a bit out of control, while others may experience increased mental acuity as they prepare for fight or flight.

After the initial shock of the stressor wears off, we then enter the *resistance* phase, in which the body continues to mobilize the resources needed to adapt and cope with the stressor. Assuming the stressor finally abates, then the body's parasympathetic nervous system activates as a means of returning the body to baseline and regaining a sense of homeostasis. However, even after the events that triggered the stress have ended, the reaction throughout the body persists. The stress hormones may linger for several hours before returning to baseline.

If the stress is chronic, though, then the resistance phase can lead to *exhaustion* if recovery and relief do not occur. Because the body's resources are finite, they eventually become depleted, which potentiates the development of trauma. The following are signs and symptoms of the exhaustion phase that signal a trauma response, which providers need to be **A**ware of:

- ☐ Depression
- ☐ Frequent crying
- ☐ Feeling sick
- ☐ Numbness
- ☐ Flashbacks or vivid memories of the stressor
- ☐ Nightmares
- ☐ Negative thoughts, such as:
    - Shame
    - Guilt
- ☐ Avoidance of people, places, or things that remind them of the stressor
- ☐ Hypervigilance
- ☐ Hyperactivity
- ☐ Anxiety
- ☐ Detachment
- ☐ Aggression
- ☐ Confusion and difficulty remembering details of trauma
- ☐ Chronic physical pain and poor circulation
- ☐ Repetitive body movements
- ☐ Weight gain
- ☐ Illness and secondary health conditions

Trauma is unique to each individual and may present in additional ways not listed here. In addition, we have all experienced at least a few of these signs and symptoms, so how do you know if the universal stress response is headed toward exhaustion and a trauma response? It starts with analyzing your own reactions to stress. What does it feel like to you? Do you have coping mechanisms that allow you to recover from stress? Review the following **ACTION Personal Reflection: ABCs of the Universal Stress Response** worksheet to help guide you in a personal reflection. Feel free to use additional paper if you need to expand on your thoughts. You can use this worksheet with your clients as well.

PROVIDER WORKSHEET

ACTION PERSONAL REFLECTION: ABCs OF THE UNIVERSAL STRESS RESPONSE

The following activity will assist you in connecting to the universal stress response. Reflect on an experience that caused you to feel concerned, anxious, uncomfortable, nervous, or fearful. Write the details of what occurred before you began to feel stressed, what you felt at the moment, and how you recovered following the experience.

1. **Antecedent (Alarm Phase):** What was the stressor? Consider aspects of who, what, when, where, why, and how.

____

____

____

____

____

2. **Behavior (Resistance Phase):** How did you feel or react to the stress? Consider what you heard, felt, saw, smelled, and thought, as well as your initial reaction.

____

____

____

____

____

3. **Consequence (Recovery Phase):** What occurred after your reaction? Consider how long it took you to recover, whether your reaction was helpful or appropriate, and what actions you performed to feel better after the experience.

____

____

____

____

____

DETECTING ACUTE STRESS

The primary difference between a clinical diagnosis of PTSD and acute stress disorder (ASD) involves the onset and duration of the symptoms. While both disorders interfere with functioning, the symptoms of ASD are briefer in duration and do not exceed a one-month time frame. Most individuals will have an immediate recovery from ASD, but if the symptoms continue to persist after one month, then the diagnosis is revised to PTSD. Although some of the examples we share in this workbook may not meet the criteria for a clinical diagnosis of ASD or PTSD, both disorders deserve attention given their association with reduced health and well-being. Indeed, clients who have experienced acute stress may still require support and intervention to enhance their quality of life even if they do not meet diagnostic criteria. Therefore, practitioners should identify additional methods to detect dysfunction. The following checklist can initiate the screening process for acute stress that may perpetuate into more chronic stress:

- ☐ While formal assessment tools are needed to develop targeted intervention approaches for trauma, practitioners should first complete an informal screening process to determine whether clients require further assessment or referral. Be sure to adhere to the four approaches of trauma-informed care when conducting this screening: realize, recognize, respond, and resist re-traumatization.
- ☐ Our initial focus in the ACTION-from-Trauma approach is the detection of trauma. Given that acute stress can precipitate trauma, this is a place to start the screening process. Such a landing point allows you to attempt to curate an understanding of the client's experience without being too invasive, which addresses the first principle of trauma-informed care: safety. Continually prioritize safety and seek out immediate support for your client, or yourself, in the presence of potential harm or danger.
- ☐ Remember that the person is not their trauma. Seeing the person first is key! In addition to their history of trauma, they may bring strength, resilience, support systems, and coping mechanisms that work. Do not assume you have to "fix" the person while creating growth toward healing.
- ☐ Both ASD and PTSD can interfere with attendance and treatment adherence, and it may result in early termination of services. Start out by trying to build rapport, and be willing to share some of your life to connect. Prioritize learning about the person first before you delve into their trauma.
- ☐ Other diagnoses, such as depression or anxiety, may reveal similar symptoms. It is important to use proper screening tools and determine the required professionals who can best support your client.

The following is an informal acute stress screening tool for practitioners to consider when determining next steps with clients, as well as a scoring guide to help practitioners interpret a client's scores.

PROVIDER WORKSHEET

ACTION ACUTE STRESS SCREENING TOOL

Check all that apply to your client/caregiver following your session. Analyze your results to consider next steps based on clinical reasoning and tools within this workbook.

NAME:________________________

DOB: ________________________

DATE: ________________________

PARTICIPATION

THE CLIENT/CAREGIVER

- HAD DIFFICULTY RECALLING FROM MEMORY OR ANSWERING QUESTIONS
- APPEARED DETACHED/WITHDRAWN
- PRESENTED AS IRRITABLE OR HYPERVIGILANT

COMMUNICATION

THE CLIENT/CAREGIVER

- REPORTED INCREASED PAIN/DISCOMFORT
- SHARED RECENT STRESSORS OR TRAUMATIC EVENT
- REPORTED DISTURBANCES IN SELF-CARE SUCH AS SLEEP OR DIET

NONVERBALS

THE CLIENT/CAREGIVER

- STARTLED EASILY OR APPEARED UNCOMFORTABLE
- PRESENTED WITH REPETITIVE MOVEMENTS (E.G., TWITCHING, ROCKING, OR EXCESSIVE EYE BLINKING)
- PRESENTED WITH SENSORY SENSITIVITY OR SENSORY-SEEKING BEHAVIORS

PROVIDER HANDOUT

ACTION ACUTE STRESS SCREENING TOOL ANALYSIS

Practitioners can use the following scoring guidelines to interpret a client's scores on the ACTION Acute Stress Screening Tool. Based on your interpretation, consider the next steps to take as provided within each zone.

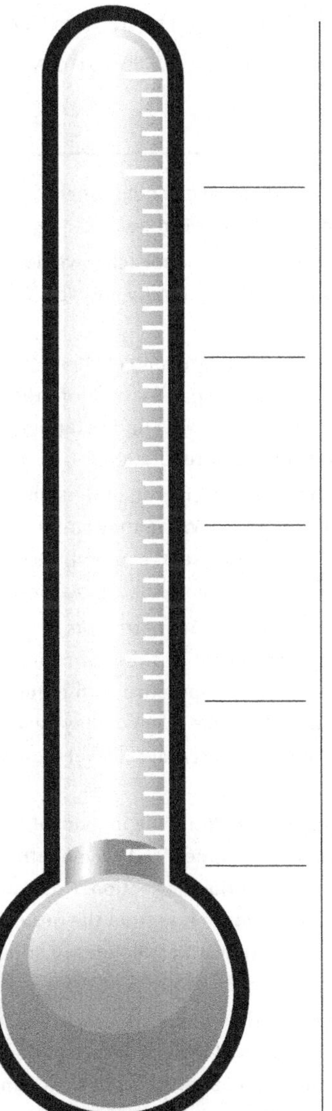

Critical: Suspected presentation of PTSD and/or harmful or dangerous behavior.

Next Steps: **Consider seeking immediate medical assistance if the client is a risk to themselves or others.** Document results and make the necessary referrals to specialists, and/or contact a mental health helpline to assist you in deterring the next steps in the absence of imminent danger.

Severe: Presents with six or more of the screening tool characteristics.

Next Steps: Document results and consider necessary referrals to specialists. If appropriate, incorporate treatment goals related to stress reduction and interventions to reduce symptoms. Consider your "readiness" to provide trauma care based on your scope of practice and training.

Moderate: Presents with three or more of the screening tool characteristics.

Next Steps: Document results and consider necessary referrals to specialists. Consider adding treatment goals related to stress reduction and interventions to reduce symptoms. Consider your "readiness" to provide trauma care based on your scope of practice and training.

Mild: Presents with one or more of the screening tool characteristics.

Next Steps: Document results and consider incorporating stress-reducing activities at the start of sessions and as part of a home therapy program.

Not present during encounter: Does not present with any of the characteristics from the screening tool.

Next Steps: Document results and rescreen when reassessing for service continuation.

DETECTING LEVEL OF SELF-REGULATION

Maslow's hierarchy of needs views motivation as a factor in growth and development (Maslow, 1943). In the presence of trauma, motivation becomes more in alignment with protection and self-preservation. When people are deprived of their basic needs due to lack of resources, abuse, or injustices, deficiency and dysfunction are the outcomes. Fear, anxiety, and stress emerge, which pose a challenge to self-regulation. The pyramid structure implies a hierarchy for growth, expanding upon the idea that people are not in a fixed state but are constantly developing.

In her book *Self-Regulation and Mindfulness*, coauthor Gibbs (2017b) developed a seven-level self-regulation and mindfulness hierarchy based on Maslow's hierarchy of needs (Figure 6). It presents a structure for caregivers and professionals to gain insight on individuals healing from trauma with regard to their self-regulation abilities (i.e., ability to adapt and adjust their arousal levels to meet the demands of the environmental and required activities; involves sensory processing, emotion regulation, and executive function). The hierarchy also provides guidance regarding their mindfulness skills (i.e., ability to be present, engaged, and self-aware). Starting from the bottom up, the first tier of the pyramid represents the foundation of *safety and preservation*. As individuals ascend to the top of the pyramid, they develop *reciprocal mindfulness*.

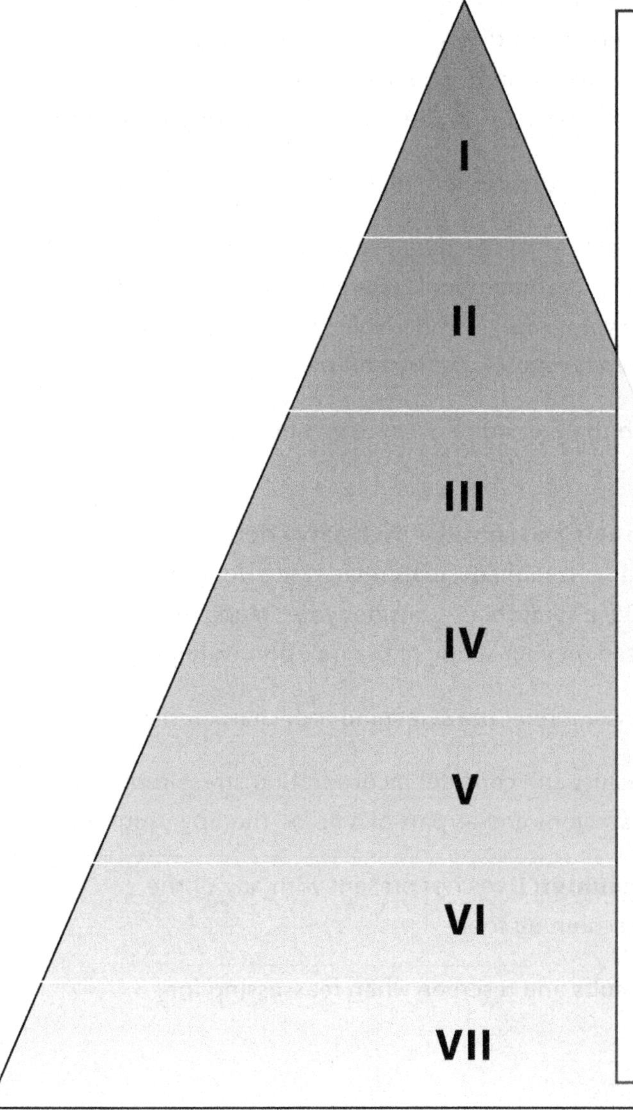

I. **Reciprocal Mindfulness:** The individual can help others understand their potential and ability to self-regulate.

II. Self-Actualized Mindfulness: The individual acknowledges their potential and frequently uses methods to identify and adjust their emotions and arousal.

III. Aesthetic Mindfulness: While still addressing challenges, the individual expresses compassion and an appreciation for others and the environment around them. They display an understanding of their ability to adapt and adjust their self-regulation.

IV. Cognitive Mindfulness: The individual has an understanding of their own challenges with self-regulation. While they continue to have difficulty, there is curiosity and a sense of exploration as they make occasional attempts to adjust their emotions and arousal.

V. Self-Esteem: The individual makes frequent attempts of engage with peers and others in their environment, yet they appear to have poor social skills. They lack a sense of competence with required tasks and have difficulty following the rules. Hence, they have challenges in adjusting their emotions and arousal level required for different activities.

VI. Belonging and Social Acceptance: While the individual may interact for short periods of time, they appear to lack empathy as revealed in challenges expressing emotions, affection, trust, and acceptance. The individual isolates themselves from the group or family system. The individual has significant challenges in adjusting their emotions and arousal levels.

VII. Safety and Self-Preservation: The individual is focused on protecting themselves from physical and mental harm and desires routines and familiarity. Elopement and aggressive behavior and present. Proper engagement with the environment and others is limited. Poor emotion regulation, high arousal, and stereotypical behavior may be present.

Figure 6. Seven-Level Self-Regulation and Mindfulness Hierarchy (Gibbs, 2017b)

When interacting with an individual living with the aftermath of trauma, you should have an idea of their general level of functioning as it relates to their self-regulation and mindfulness abilities. Reviewing the hierarchy may assist you in developing goals for the client and acknowledging gains they have made. When complex trauma ensues, you must realize that chronological age may not equate to the client's ability to self-regulate and to be aware of their behavior. In fact, some adults may present at the foundational and mid-levels of the hierarchy due to their history of trauma.

The following two checklists provide a method to determine the client's level on the hierarchy. The first checklist is intended for adults, whereas the second checklist is intended for caregivers to complete in relation to their child's level on the hierarchy. Review the purpose of the checklist and your intent for using the data. After completion, be sure to revisit each response with the client. This dialogue will allow you to clarify the items and make any necessary adjustments.

CLIENT WORKSHEET

SEVEN-LEVEL SELF-REGULATION AND MINDFULNESS CHECKLIST

Review each statement within the following checklist. Check all of the boxes that best apply to you.

I. Reciprocal Mindfulness:

- ☐ I have great relationships with others and get along with most people.
- ☐ I often help others in need and give them my advice.
- ☐ I recognize what people think of my behavior by reading their body language. I try to better understand their feelings by asking questions.

II. Self-Actualized Mindfulness:

- ☐ I know when I am anxious or feeling out of control (e.g., racing heart rate, sweaty palms, tight muscles) and have the ability to calm my body (e.g., slowing down my breathing).
- ☐ I often share my feelings and seek out the feelings of others to improve my behavior.
- ☐ I enjoy connecting with new people and can change my actions to better engage with them.

III. Aesthetic Mindfulness:

- ☐ Although I sometimes feel out of control, I am aware of my actions and my effect on others.
- ☐ I am aware of my emotions and challenges and try to make improvements.
- ☐ Even when upset, I am able to respect others in my surroundings and their property.

IV. Cognitive Mindfulness:

- ☐ I am easily upset by others but try my best to keep my emotions under control.
- ☐ I often feel anxious and/or out of control (e.g., racing heart rate, sweaty palms, tight muscles), and it takes a long time to calm my body.
- ☐ I often attempt to engage with others. However, I have difficulty making friends and being in long-term relationships.

V. Self-Esteem:

- ☐ I try my best and want to engage with others, but I frequently upset them, and my emotions are often out of control.
- ☐ Even though I try, I am unable to calm myself after becoming upset.
- ☐ I have difficulty finishing what I start, keeping a job, and getting along with others.

VI. Belonging and Social Acceptance:

- ☐ I occasionally spend time with others, but I lack trust in most people.
- ☐ I occasionally try new things, but it usually does not go well.
- ☐ I am often anxious, fearful, worried, and/or out of control around others.

VII. Safety and Self-Preservation:

- ☐ I do not try new things (e.g., food, change in routine, meeting new people) and am fearful of the unknown.
- ☐ I am aggressive at times and/or run away from things I do not like.
- ☐ I am often sick and/or tired.

CLIENT WORKSHEET

SEVEN-LEVEL SELF-REGULATION AND MINDFULNESS CAREGIVER CHECKLIST

Review each statement within the following checklist. Check all of the boxes that best apply to your child or the child you are caring for.

My child (or child I am caring for):

I. Reciprocal Mindfulness:

- ☐ Knows when they are in need or when others are in need (e.g., tells a teacher when their peer is upset).
- ☐ Frequently helps others having a challenging time (e.g., helps a friend needing a push on the swing or tries to help a friend calm down).
- ☐ Recognizes what people think of their behavior by looking at body language. They try to better understand others' feelings by asking questions (e.g., asking if a friend is angry with them).

II. Self-Actualized Mindfulness:

- ☐ Has awareness of what their body needs to finish tasks and engage with others (e.g., stating they need a break or expressing how they feel).
- ☐ Often shares their feelings and seeks out the feelings of others to improve their behavior.
- ☐ Always tries their best to follow directions and to improve interactions with peers.

III. Aesthetic Mindfulness:

- ☐ Sometimes has outbursts but is aware of their actions and their effect on others.
- ☐ Is aware of their emotions and challenges and tries to make improvements.
- ☐ Even when upset, will respect others in their surroundings and the property of others.

IV. Cognitive Mindfulness:

- ☐ Gets easily upset but tries their best to keep their emotions in control.
- ☐ Often seems anxious or upset, and it takes a long time for them to calm their body.
- ☐ Often tries to engage with others but has difficulty making friends.

V. Self-Esteem:

- ☐ Is frequently upset by others, and their emotions are often out of control.
- ☐ Attempts to calm themself when upset, but it does not work.
- ☐ Has difficulty finishing projects, keeping friends, and/or staying at the same school.

VI. Belonging and Social Acceptance:

- ☐ Occasionally spends time with others, but they appear to lack trust in most people.
- ☐ Occasionally will try new things, but it usually does not go well.
- ☐ Often seems anxious, fearful, worried, and/or out of control around others.

VII. Safety and Self-Preservation:

- ☐ Does not try new things (e.g., food, change in routine, meeting new people).
- ☐ Is aggressive at times and/or runs away from undesirable experiences.
- ☐ Is often sick and/or tired.

Review the checklist upon the client's completion. To identify the client's level, determine the section containing the most check marks. If there is more than one section with the same amount of check marks, select the lowest level on the hierarchy (e.g., if the *reciprocal mindfulness* and *self-actualized mindfulness* levels both have three checkmarks, the client falls at level II, *self-actualized mindfulness*). However, if a client has check marks within the higher levels, this indicates areas of potential and strengths to acknowledge. To better illustrate this process, we provide an example and analysis here. For guidance in applying the client's level into treatment planning, we also provide a chart connecting the seven-level self-regulation and mindfulness hierarchy to areas of consideration for intervention activities. Lastly, we present a treatment planning tool to synthesize the information gained from the checklist and other methods of assessment.

SAMPLE ANALYSIS OF RESPONSES

I. Reciprocal Mindfulness:

- ☑ I have great relationships with others and get along with most people.
- ☐ I often help others in need and give them my advice.
- ☐ I recognize what people think of my behavior by reading their body language. I try to better understand their feelings by asking questions.

II. Self-Actualized Mindfulness:

- ☑ I know when I am anxious or feeling out of control (e.g., racing heart rate, sweaty palms, tight muscles) and have the ability to calm my body (e.g., slowing down my breathing).
- ☑ I often share my feelings and seek out the feelings of others to improve my behavior.
- ☐ I enjoy connecting with new people and can change my actions to better engage with them.

III. Aesthetic Mindfulness:

- ☑ Although I sometimes feel out of control, I am aware of my actions and my effect on others.
- ☑ I am aware of my emotions and challenges and try to make improvements.
- ☑ Even when upset, I am able to respect others in my surroundings and their property.

IV. Cognitive Mindfulness:

- ☐ I am easily upset by others and try my best to keep my emotions in control.
- ☐ I often feel anxious and/or out of control (e.g., racing heart rate, sweaty palms, tight muscles), and it takes a long time to calm my body.
- ☑ I often attempt to engage with others. However, I have difficulty making friends and being in long-term relationships.

V. Self-Esteem:

- ☐ I try my best and want to engage with others, but I frequently upset them, and my emotions are often out of control.
- ☐ Even though I try, I am unable to calm myself after becoming upset.
- ☑ I have difficulty finishing what I start, keeping a job, and getting along with others.

VI. Belonging and Social Acceptance:

- ☐ I occasionally spend time with others, but I lack trust in most people.
- ☑ I occasionally try new things, but it usually does not go well.
- ☐ I am often anxious, fearful, worried, and/or out of control around others.

VII. Safety and Self-Preservation:

- ☑ I do not try new things (e.g., food, change in routine, meeting new people) and am fearful of the unknown.
- ☐ I am aggressive at times and/or run away from things I do not like.
- ☐ I am often sick and/or tired.

Although there are check marks at every level in this sample checklist, the person falls more into level III on the hierarchy, while progressing into level II. This gives the clinician the opportunity to acknowledge behavior below *aesthetic mindfulness* that the client can address while strengthening those at their identified level and above.

At each level of the hierarchy, there is a neurological connection that impacts functioning. Behavior provides an observable representation of what is occurring neurologically, and what we witness at the behavioral level represents a manifestation of the underlying neural dysfunction resulting from trauma. Secondary to trauma, it is vital to acknowledge the overpowering effect of lower-level, more primitive areas of the brain that are responsible for safety and self-preservation. By taking a bottom-up approach, we attempt to connect survival behaviors to the functions related to the brainstem, followed by emotion regulation to the limbic system, followed by higher-level executive functioning within the cortices of the brain.

An individual's ability to successfully engage and function with others and within the environment requires the various parts of the brain to work together. To this end, overactivity of lower-level structures may impair access to higher-order brain structures involved in self-regulation and mindfulness. This does not equate to a lack of intellect. It implies challenges in self-regulation and the presence of a trauma lens of protection. Therefore, when selecting activities and treatment interventions, it is crucial that you detect where individuals land in their ability to self-regulate and be self-aware. The following table assists in such analysis for all age groups.

Level	Neural Functioning	Considerations for Interactions and Interventions
Levels VI–VII: Foundational Level	**Brainstem Level Functioning:** Reactive versus responsive engagement with others and their environment **Body Signals and Actions:** ○ Protective flexion positions ○ Arms and legs close to the body ○ Eloping behaviors ○ Hiding (e.g., wearing a hooded jacket with head covered or sunglasses indoors) ○ Preferring specific clothing, food, and rigid routine ○ Unsafe risk-taking behavior ○ Aggression ○ Repetitive and stereotypical movements	Activities should be body-focused and less top-down. At this level, the person primarily utilizes neurological structures for arousal and safety preservation. Decrease environmental stimulation (including overuse of verbal directives), and consider using gestures or simple verbal cues to communicate. Provide sensory-rich activities, ensuring safe boundaries and exits due to eloping behaviors, and develop safe, comfortable spaces. **Provider/Caregiver/Educator Considerations:** At this level, it is difficult for the person to listen and follow directions, especially when other things are occurring in the environment. Try to decrease noise and clutter in the environment, avoid speaking too loudly, and don't offer too many activities. They may need your help to provide or identify sensory input to calm and engage. This may include input to the skin, deep pressure to the muscles, controlled movement, aromatherapy, rhythmic music, and activities. Be careful to set expectations and use open communication for scheduling and changes in plans.

(Continued)

(*Continued*)

Level	Neural Functioning	Considerations for Interactions and Interventions
Level V: Mid-Level	**Limbic System Level Functioning:** Challenges regulating emotions during social interaction; Difficulty with learning and memory; Increased detection and awareness of sensory stimuli but exhibits challenges with integrating multiple sensory stimuli for self-regulation; Challenges with executive functioning in the frontal areas of the brain **Body Signals and Actions:** ◦ May present with sensory-seeking or avoidance behaviors ◦ Has an awareness of personal needs ◦ Exhibits challenges with social engagement ◦ Responds well to routine ◦ May have poor eye contact ◦ Quickly changes emotions when presented with a trigger	Caregivers and providers should continue strategies from the foundational level while also exploring strategies to improve self-awareness and recognize reactions to sensory stimuli. Incorporate visual cues and sensorimotor activities to enhance body awareness. **Provider/Caregiver/Educator Considerations:** At this level, the person attempts to follow directions and engage with others, though it may be challenging at times. The use of visual aids, such as schedules and signs, may make it easier for them to follow directions. Set up the environment so it is organized, and have needed tools and resources readily available. Develop ways to schedule in sensory and controlled movement breaks.
Levels I–IV: Higher Level	**Cortical Level Functioning:** Increased responsiveness to others and the environment via activation of the frontal lobes (i.e., areas of the brain involved in executive functioning); Ability to adapt their level of arousal based on the environment due to integration throughout the nervous system **Body Signals and Actions:** ◦ Has an awareness of personal needs ◦ Responds well to routine ◦ Occasionally responds to emotional triggers ◦ Self-advocates personal needs	Caregivers and providers should continue strategies from the mid-level while also increasing top-down activities that incorporate self-regulation, sensory processing, emotion regulation, and executive functioning. Self-monitoring can assist in enhancing abilities to participate in daily activities. **Provider/Caregiver/Educator Considerations:** At this level, the person knows what to do and how to adjust arousal as needed, though they may need reminders and prompts to help maintain awareness of arousal and continue making the best choices. Work on self-monitoring of growth and positive interactions.

Table 3. Seven-Level Self-Regulation and Mindfulness Hierarchy Across the Lifespan

After completing the seven-level self-regulation and mindfulness checklist and reviewing the chart presented in Table 3, use the following plan to assist you in selecting areas to address when developing long-term treatment goals. Refer to the sample goals at the end of this worksheet for assistance.

PROVIDER WORKSHEET

SEVEN-LEVEL SELF-REGULATION AND MINDFULNESS HIERARCHY TREATMENT PLAN

Client's Name: ______________________ **Date:** ____________________________

Date of Birth: ______________________ **Re-assessment Date:** ______________

I. Clinical history and background information:

____

____

____

____

____

II. Self-regulation and mindfulness seven-level hierarchy level:

____

____

____

____

____

III. Assessment tools utilized (if applicable to your practice):

____

____

____

____

____

IV. Scores and results (if applicable to your practice—attach any additional information):

____

____

____

____

____

V. Long-term treatment goals based on assessment outcomes:

____

____

____

____

____

Sample Long-Term Treatment Goals

Client will:

- Use verbal cues to request a break when overwhelmed 80 percent of the time (within six months)
- Refrain from physically harming themself or others 100 percent of the time (within one year)
- Utilize a visual schedule to stay on task throughout the day 75 percent of the time (within six months)

READINESS TO PROVIDE TRAUMA CARE

This workbook provides strategies intended to guide the practice of allied health professionals in gaining techniques that support their scope of practice and that enhance their ability to address the needs of their clients and clients' families. Before introducing these concepts into your care approaches, though, it is necessary to assess your own readiness to provide trauma care. To do so, you can use the following Practitioner Readiness for Trauma Care Checklist (Cook, Newman, & The New Haven Trauma Competency Group, 2014). Revisit this checklist while reviewing, and after completing, this book.

Practitioner Readiness for Trauma Care Checklist

As a provider, I am able to:

- ☐ Tailor trauma assessments and interventions in a way that considers diversity in socioeconomic, organizational, community, population, and intersecting cultural identities
- ☐ Employ a biopsychosocial approach to care that considers the complex interactions of cognitive, biological, psychological, and social factors
- ☐ Understand the impact of traumatic experiences across the lifespan and between family members (e.g., pediatric providers have knowledge of the impact of trauma on the adult caregiver)
- ☐ Acknowledge short-term and long-term effects of trauma (e.g., comorbidities, housing-related issues) and person-environment interactions related to trauma (e.g., running away from home and being assaulted)
- ☐ Perform shared decision making with clients and focus on strength, resilience, and areas for growth
- ☐ Provide a sense of autonomy, safety, and security with an awareness of how trauma impacts an individual's and organization's sense of trust
- ☐ Understand trauma reactions and their implications for assessment and treatment (e.g., able to alter plans in the presence of avoidance behaviors or triggers)
- ☐ Acknowledge how society, organizations, and systems can result in the possibility of re-traumatization

- ☐ Effectively tolerate trauma-related content and the intense sharing of traumatic experiences
- ☐ Engage in self-care and self-reflection to protect against burnout and compassion fatigue
- ☐ Maintain self-awareness of my own personal experiences that can impact trauma treatment
- ☐ Utilize evidence-based interventions and strategies
- ☐ Work collaboratively with other disciplines and within my scope of practice to optimize care and enhance positive outcomes
- ☐ Communicate and translate assessment findings into tailored treatment approaches
- ☐ Acknowledge what stage the client is in as it relates to their trauma so I can pivot care and provide appropriate interventions

FROM TRAUMA-INFORMED TO ACTION LANGUAGE

Those who have experienced trauma experience it with each context of their lives. Therefore, it is crucial that practitioners have an awareness of how words can trigger and further complicate the patient relationship. Even if we don't intend to do so, our words and actions can reinforce clients' fear-based reactions, defensive responses, and avoidance behavior. However, there are direct methods we can intentionally use to avoid re-traumatization. In particular, Leitch (2017) suggests a resilience model that includes strength-based and protective questioning. This strategy empowers the individual and presents a respectful and empathic dialogue that decreases the opportunity for re-traumatization. Expanding on this approach, our ACTION-from-Trauma approach promotes the use of *respect and empathy language,* as well as *gratitude and growth statements.*

Respect and empathy language involves gaining permission from the client to discuss or address certain topics, which provides them with a sense of validation and acknowledges their lived experiences. Gratitude and growth statements involve making the individual feel appreciated and part of the process. These two styles of communicating provide positive reinforcement and strengthen the client-practitioner relationship, which leads to growth. Table 4 provides examples of each type of language, though you should always adjust this language to meet the intellectual and developmental needs of the client and/or caregiver.

Respect and Empathy Language	Gratitude and Growth Statements
Children	
◦ "What do you need?" ◦ "Do you need a break?" ◦ "How can I help?" ◦ "All done? Or do you need more?" ◦ "I want to help you." ◦ "What you experienced is not okay. What support do you need?"	◦ "Thank you!" ◦ "I like your hard work!" ◦ "Wow! Look at how you grew today by finishing your work!" ◦ "You have grown so much!"
Adolescents, Adults, and Older Adults	
◦ "That is really challenging, and I see you are upset. Can I suggest some strategies to assist with your anxiety?" ◦ "Would it be okay for us to discuss how that made you feel?" ◦ "While it may not have been the best choice, your response matches how you felt." ◦ "How can I help you grow from here?" ◦ "Did that make you feel uncomfortable? That was not my intent." ◦ "I see that may not have been the best way to phrase that. What I meant was..."	◦ "That was brave of you." ◦ "Your sharing shows your strength." ◦ "Look at all you have done since and despite of..." ◦ "That is tough to talk about. I appreciate your openness and trust."

Table 4. ACTION Language

Try to sandwich respect and empathy language with gratitude and growth statements so you can build trust and connect to the natural flow of our nervous system (Leitch, 2017). Here is an example of a parent-teacher conference to discuss a preschool child having tantrums and physical aggression:

> "I am glad you came in today. I know it takes time away from your work. I respect the dedication you have for your son. I want to discuss what happened in class yesterday. Would it be okay if I start? I appreciate your allowing me to share. Now I want to focus on how we can work with him to grow from here. What are your thoughts?"

This dialogue invites the parent to be part of the decision-making process as opposed to making them feel isolated or that their child is being punished. In addition, keep the following key considerations in mind when speaking with clients or their caregivers:

- ☐ Speak clearly and concisely, avoiding jargon.
- ☐ Do not make judgments or assumptions.
- ☐ Avoid labeling and re-traumatizing the individual by seeking too many details. The focus should be on emphasizing growth and identifying opportunities to develop action steps.
- ☐ While it is important to make appropriate referrals for clients who require additional support and direct trauma services, do not discount shared experiences. (Be sure to address any legalities regarding mandated reporting in your state.)

NEXT STEPS: MOVING TO THE C IN ACTION TO CREATE GROWTH*

Although this chapter is focused on **A**cknowledging and being **A**ware of trauma, there are several considerations that providers must take into account when screening for and assessing trauma prior to proceeding to the next step of **C**reating growth. At this step, you must address the second principle of a trauma-informed approach: trustworthiness and transparency. That is, you need to be open and transparent when it comes to decision making and goal development. This workbook is intended to support your practices, building upon your training and knowledge. Be sure to use your clinical reasoning and judgment moving forward. Note that there may be legal implications requiring mandated reporting of certain information based on your state. Figure 7 provides an algorithm to assist you in determining how to precede.

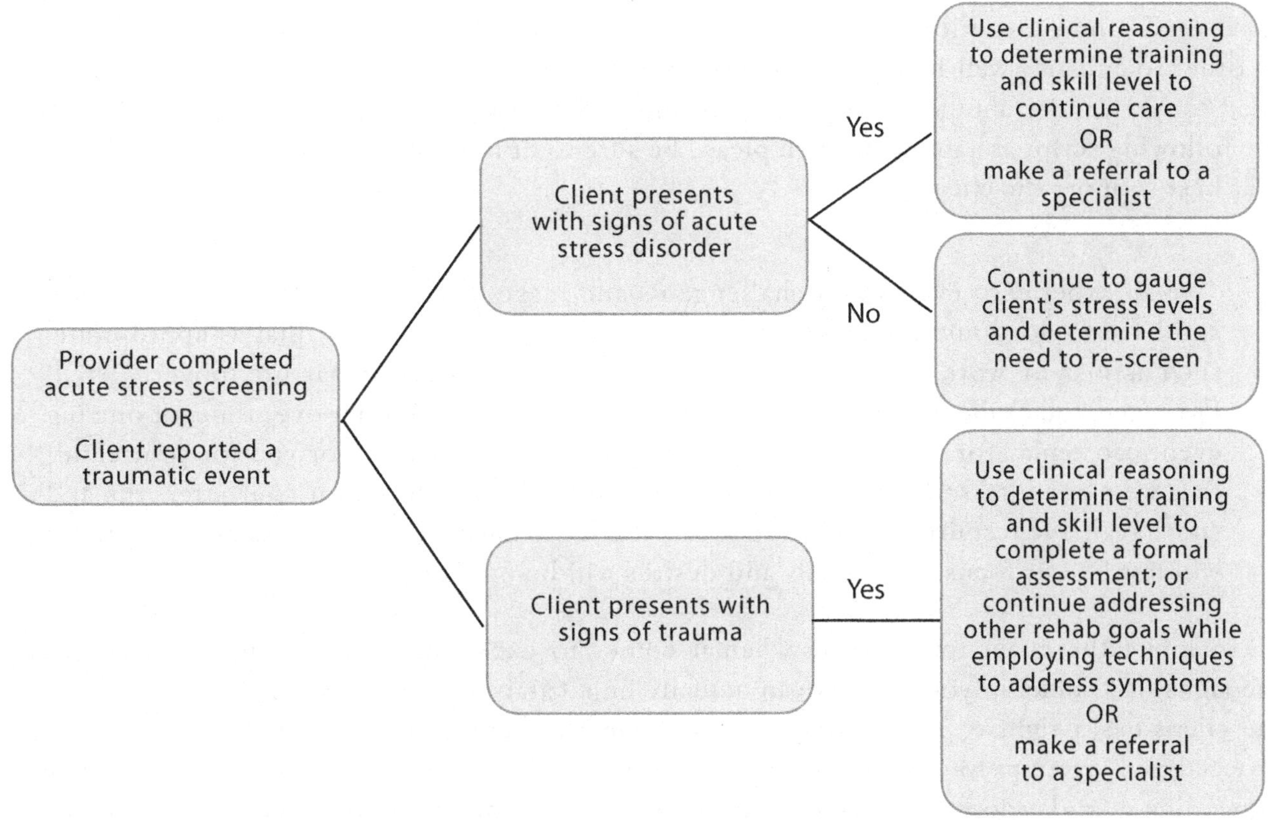

Figure 7. Algorithm to Assist Providers in Determining Next Steps following the Trauma Screening

If you determine that the client requires additional screening or a formal assessment, provide education and reasoning for the screening and assessment. First, ensure protection by providing a safe space. If possible, discuss areas of strength and a desire to expand upon such factors. For example, perhaps the client or caregiver has consistently attended sessions or meetings. You can highlight their commitment and willingness to continue working together. If it is a new referral, the intake process should begin with a focus on available resources, desires, and goals. This must

---

* Portions of this section are based off of the Substance Abuse and Mental Health Services Administration. (2014b). *Trauma-informed care in behavioral health services.* Treatment Improvement Protocol (TIP) Series 57. HHS Publication No. (SMA) 13-4801. Rockville, MD: Substance Abuse and Mental Health Services Administration.

precede discussions on trauma. For children in particular, you can build rapport by asking them to draw a picture of their world, including their family, things they enjoy, where they live, and so on. Use the images to identify areas of concern, and then discuss how you want to help those areas. For adolescent and adults, you can start by inquiring the following:

- ☐ How would you describe yourself?
- ☐ Who is in your life (e.g., friends, family members, social supports)?
- ☐ What are the areas that present as challenging?
- ☐ What do you want to improve?
- ☐ How can I help you grow?

After establishing a relationship, you can then share your desire to build upon the areas discussed. In order to enhance well-being and growth toward their goals (for themselves or their child), you need to learn more about their experiences and determine specific areas to target. You can use the following script as a guide, though please be sure to utilize language and communication skills that best support the client:

> "We all experience events that challenge us and make it hard to do the things we want and have to do. Some examples of challenges are ______________ [list as appropriate, such as loss of work, illness, loss of a loved one to death or departure, poverty, etc.]. For some, the challenges we face continue to build upon each other over time, or one big event can replay for us. I want to know if there are any barriers for you [or your child] that we can address and remove to create growth. We will focus on your strengths and some available resources to address them. While we must first identify challenges, these will not be our focus. Your goals and desires will be our focus."

Next, invite the client to the table when it comes to exploring their trauma history. Ignoring the signs of trauma in your clients can actually be a catalyst to ignite such behaviors. However, the client has a right to not participate in a formal screening or assessment. If they desire to proceed, only attempt to collect necessary information that relates to your treatment practice and impending goal development. Try to acknowledge statements or actions that may be triggers for the client and acknowledge their reaction. Take a sensitive approach in proceeding, and anticipate that your actions can re-traumatize the client. Be sure to gain permission to initiate a formal evaluation and assessment, sharing each step of the process before beginning. Invite the client or caregiver to verbalize their perception of the process to ensure that they are not misinterpreting your communication.

Before beginning with the assessment, make sure that you provide a safe context and a comfortable environment. Ensure there is proper space to allow distancing if you are in a face-to-face environment, and assist the client in selecting a preferred seating position. Modulate your tone of voice to provide a supportive and comforting tone. Always be aware of cultural, literacy, or linguistic barriers that you need to address before proceeding.

In addition, form an emergency plan to address red flags and possible triggering of emotions during the assessment. For example, have necessary contact information on hand so you can report abuse to welfare services, have a variety of calming techniques readily available to address anxiety and stress, and make sure you have non-violent self-protection training in the event of aggressive outbursts. Remember to provide support and praise where appropriate, and check in periodically to ensure that the client or caregiver understands the process (e.g., "I want to make sure that I'm clear and that I don't move through things too quickly. In your own words, what did you hear me say?").

When conducting an assessment, it is necessary to use valid and reliable standardized assessment tools. As an allied health professional, consider your scope of practice, licensure, and clinical skills, given that not all allied health professionals can administer such tools. In that case, it is necessary to make an appropriate referral to a licensed professional. Valid and reliable assessment tools provide a formalized structure to the evaluation process. They also highlight areas of need across various contexts and areas of life. Based on our ACTION-from-Trauma approach, the assessment should reveal strengths to utilize in treatment. Before administering any assessment, review the guidelines for each tool and the time required to administer. Here are some available tools to consider:

- ☐ Clinician-Administered PTSD Scale for DSM-5 (CAPS-5)
- ☐ PTSD Symptom Scale Interview for DSM-5 (PSS-I-5)
- ☐ Structured Clinical Interview for DSM-5 (SCID-5)
- ☐ Strengths and Difficulties Questionnaire (SDQ)
- ☐ VIA Character Strengths Survey
- ☐ Mini-Mental State Examination (MMSE) or Folstein test
- ☐ Child and Adolescent Needs and Strengths (CANS)
- ☐ Family Needs & Strengths (FANS) Assessment
- ☐ Childhood Trauma Questionnaire (CTQ)
- ☐ Pediatric Emotional Distress Scale (PEDS)

Although conducting a complete interview and history taking is necessary to gain an understanding of your client, you should avoid requesting specific details that can be overwhelming and traumatic to revisit. Be sure to not place labels on their behaviors, as doing so can indirectly place a negative connotation on what they share. If possible, it is best to utilize a self-report tool so clients can write down their experiences. The following are some options available through the Centers for Disease Control and Prevention, though be sure to address your client's preferred language and health literacy level:

- ☐ Adverse Childhood Experiences (ACE) Questionnaire: https://www.cdc.gov/violenceprevention/acestudy/pdf/BRFSS_Adverse_Module.pdf
- ☐ Family History and Health Appraisal Questionnaires (see "Study Questionnaires" tab): https://www.cdc.gov/violenceprevention/childabuseandneglect/acestudy/about.html

Depending on your practice setting, this assessment can be part of your intake process with all clients and families. The following pages contain a modified version of the Adverse Child Experiences (ACE) Questionnaire, as well as the Pediatric Adverse Experiences Questionnaire, which you can give to clients.

CLIENT WORKSHEET

THE ADVERSE CHILD EXPERIENCES (ACE) QUESTIONNAIRE*

I'd like to ask you some questions about events that happened during your childhood. This information will allow us to better understand problems that may occur early in life and may help others in the future. This is a sensitive topic, and some people may feel uncomfortable with these questions. Please keep in mind that you can skip any questions you do not want to answer. All questions refer to the time period before you were 18 years of age.

While you were growing up, during your first 18 years of life:

1. Did you live with anyone who was depressed, mentally ill, or suicidal?

   ______ Yes ______ No

2. Did you live with anyone who was a problem drinker or alcoholic?

   ______ Yes ______ No

3. Did you live with anyone who used illegal street drugs or who abused prescription medications?

   ______ Yes ______ No

4. Did you live with anyone who served time or was sentenced to serve time in a prison, jail, or other correctional facility?

   ______ Yes ______ No

5. Were your parents separated or divorced?

   ______ Yes ______ No

6. Did your parents or other adults in your home often or very often slap, hit, kick, punch, or beat each other?

   ______ Yes ______ No

---

*Adapted from https://www.cdc.gov/violenceprevention/acestudy/pdf/BRFSS_Adverse_Module.pdf

7. Did a parent or other adults in your home often or very often hit, beat, kick, or physically hurt you in any way? Ever hit you so hard that you had marks or were injured? (Do not include spanking.)

______ Yes ______ No

8. Did a parent or adult in your home often or very often swear at you, insult you, or put you down?

______ Yes ______ No

9. Did an adult or person at least five years older than you ever touch you sexually?

______ Yes ______ No

10. Did an adult or person at least five years older than you ever try to make you touch their body sexually?

______ Yes ______ No

11. Did an adult or person at least five years older than you ever force you to have sex?

______ Yes ______ No

Now add up your "yes" answers. This is your ACE score.

CLIENT WORKSHEET

PEDIATRIC ADVERSE EXPERIENCES QUESTIONNAIRE

I'd like to ask you some questions about your child. Some of these questions are sensitive. You do not have to answer if you are uncomfortable. This information will assist in gaining clarity of your child's needs and can provide areas to address when we develop a treatment plan.

Has your child experienced any of the following?

1. Problems with sleep, such as difficulty falling asleep, difficulty staying asleep, restlessness, nightmares, or bedwetting?

   ______ Yes ______ No

2. Changes in behavior, such aggression, increased attachment, detachment, or increased sadness?

   ______ Yes ______ No

3. Challenges with eating, such as loss of appetite, eating quickly, overeating, or other significant changes in eating habits?

   ______ Yes ______ No

4. Verbalized feelings of hopelessness or feeling unsafe?

   ______ Yes ______ No

5. Gut issues, such as constipation, bowel movement accidents, or soiled underwear (encopresis)?

   ______ Yes ______ No

6. Urinary accidents (enuresis)?

   ______ Yes ______ No

7. Major changes in the homelife (e.g., death of family members, parent leaving the home, changes in the family structure)?

______ Yes ______ No

8. Any events that may cause sadness, fear, or increased stress?

______ Yes ______ No

In what areas would you say you and your child need assistance?

____

____

____

____

____

Once you complete the assessment and additional screening tools, address what has happened to the client since the trauma. The perception of trauma is extremely unique. Some may recover from a traumatic experience without professional intervention, while others may require support and treatment along their healing process. Highlight where the client has showed signs of strength after the trauma, such as being brave or resilient to even share the experience.

In addition, explain how you plan to utilize the information you have gleaned, including your plans (with permission) to share any findings with other professionals involved in the client's care, such as the health care or education team. When appropriate, use visuals to share feedback, such as drawings, graphs, and scores. Relate the client's lived experiences with your results. Some clients may not be aware how the traumatic events they reported are connected to their behaviors, and they may be unclear of the services required to address these behaviors so they can best reach their treatment goals. Highlight a few key points and areas to initially address, and provide brief education on common themes and trauma symptoms.

It is also crucial that you follow up on any assessments by checking in with the client and/or caregiver to ensure they are not overwhelmed before departing. Ensure that they are alert and oriented by doing an environmental check-in. For example, ask them to identify objects in the environment, or ask if the temperature in the room is comfortable. If you witness any signs of discomfort, acknowledge it to the client, and consider using somatosensory approaches, such as deep pressure, breathing exercises, or stretches (see chapters 2 and 3). Before they leave, share your intent for the remainder of your day, and ask them what plans they have for the rest of the day. If they do not appear prepared to depart, invite them to stay longer to address any emotions that remain.

Know that trauma screening and assessment is ongoing and, in general, should be revisited throughout the treatment process. The timing and emotional state of the client can greatly impact the results, which can lead you to miss or misinterpret shared information. Some clients may also withhold information until they gain a feeling of trust for the practitioner.

Finally, take a client-centered approach when it comes to treatment planning, goal setting, and intervention objectives by ensuring that you collaborate with the client or caregiver. Invite your client to assist in developing a plan of care. They must be fully involved in this process to avoid re-traumatization and enhance trustworthiness and transparency. Be open and answer their questions with basic terminology. Check in to assure their understanding of your interpretation and to gain assurance of your accuracy. Additionally, acknowledge the presence of comorbid conditions or diagnoses that need to be addressed. Be sure to take an interprofessional approach to meet the client's needs that reach outside of your scope of practice.

CASE SCENARIO*

Review the following case study. Then use the worksheet to apply some of the ACTION approaches discussed in this chapter.

Name: Stephanie
Setting: School-based
Age: 11

I first met Stephanie when she was in the sixth grade. I was working as a school social worker at her middle school. She was 11 at the time and was living in an urban, low socioeconomic status environment with her mother and two brothers. The whereabouts of her father were unknown.

Prior to transitioning to middle school, Stephanie had attended three different elementary schools between the second and fifth grades, all of which were spread throughout the state. Her kindergarten and first-grade school experiences were unknown because our district was not able to secure those school records.

During her sixth-grade year, Stephanie was not known as a "highflyer," meaning that she was not a student who consumed a vast amount of our school's resources. The school administration and team members only issued Stephanie a total of seven office discipline referrals throughout that entire school year. Referrals ranged mostly from classroom disruption to defiance of school authority. She was absent only four days, tardy a total of nine days, and her final grades were in the A–B range. Relatively speaking, she was not a student of concern within our building. In fact, I do not have record of or even recall providing Stephanie with any intervention support that school year.

Stephanie's seventh-grade year was starkly different from her sixth-grade year. She went from requiring little to no support to needing various intervention supports. I recall her teachers describing her as irritable, loud, argumentative, disruptive, defiant, and both physically and verbally aggressive. She received out-of-school suspension a total of 13 days and was suspended in school for a total of 4 days. Stephanie also received 48 office discipline referrals for major offenses, 20 referrals for minor offenses, and was sent to our school's time-out room 43 times. She was absent a total of 37 days, tardy a total of 49 days, and failed four classes.

The school decided to refer Stephanie to our problem-solving team, and the Communities in Schools (CIS) site director and I were tasked with implementing intervention supports. Fortunately, throughout her sixth- and seventh-grade school years, our school psychologist engaged our staff in a professional development series educating us on the negative impact that adverse childhood experiences can have on brain development. We learned that negative experiences can actually stunt a child's cognitive and social-emotional development as a result of constantly living in a fight-or-flight state.

Based on this knowledge, we began to view Stephanie's behavior changes through a different lens, and instead of thinking, "What's wrong with her?" we shifted our thoughts to "What happened to her?" We also realized that in order for us to implement effective supports, we had to first gain a better understanding of the experiences that seemed to cause the changes in her behavior. Gathering details was a challenge—Stephanie's attendance was inconsistent, and attempts to connect with her mother were unsuccessful due to nonworking telephone numbers and failed home visits—but we were able to gather that Stephanie and her family had lost their housing and had been forced to live between family members' homes and a shelter.

The intervention supports we decided to put in place were focused on strengthening Stephanie's resiliency by establishing positive relationships with school staff and by providing her with structure, consistency, and skill-building opportunities. We intensified a well-known and evidence-based intervention called Check-In/Check-Out (CICO). Stephanie connected with either the CIS director or me three times a day: morning, midday, and afternoon.

During the morning check-in, we assessed both her mental and physical preparedness for school while helping her set behavioral goals and identify strategies she could use to help her achieve those goals. We then checked in with her midday to see how her day was going, and during the afternoon check-out, we helped her reflect on her day. We cheered successes and problem solved around any difficulties she experienced in an effort to decrease the likelihood of their reoccurring. Stephanie's teachers were also expected to provide her with regular constructive feedback as a means of developing a relationship and skill building with her.

We discovered that the fidelity of the intervention's implementation greatly depended on the staff member's mindset and the lens through which they viewed Stephanie's behavior. Staff members who still tended to think, "What's wrong with her?" were less likely to correct Stephanie's behavior using a problem-solving approach that would preserve the integrity of the relationship they were trying to build with her. Instead, their use of punitive corrective measures either sustained or escalated her challenging behavior. On the contrary, staff members who shifted their mindset and began to approach Stephanie in a way that conveyed "I'm here and care about you" were less likely to experience negative interactions with her, and they were more likely to successfully deescalate her during times of challenging behavior.

---

[*]Case study by Adriane L. Simpson, MSW

PROVIDER WORKSHEET

CASE ANALYSIS

In this chapter, we have reviewed the background information on the various dimensions and types of trauma. After reading through Stephanie's case, see if you are able to connect her trauma to her functioning. Use the following worksheet to analyze the case.

Task #1: What were the red flags that Stephanie had experienced a trauma? What would have been your next steps after she began to have challenges at school? List your thoughts here.

____

____

____

____

____

Task #2: What level of the seven-level self-regulation and mindfulness hierarchy would you expect Stephanie to be on? What were some of Stephanie's strengths, resources, or opportunities?

____

____

____

____

____

Task #3: How could you utilize ACTION language with Stephanie? Provide some example statements.

____

____

____

____

____

CHAPTER 2

CREATE GROWTH

The second step in our ACTION-from-Trauma approach is to **C**reate growth. To do so, we present tools to monitor growth at the individual level rather basing a client's growth on external comparisons (e.g., other children within the school setting). Although we offer a variety of activities in this chapter, they are not intended for everyone. Some activities could actually be a trigger. Breathwork, for example, is an activity that you must present carefully given that many individuals with a trauma history hold tension in their bodies that poses a challenge to deep breathing. Forced breathing can even trigger a fight-or-flight reaction. Therefore, it is critical that you engage in an exploration of each client's history prior to enacting these recommendations.

In this chapter, we aim to justify the need to expand upon the current practices to employ action steps toward healing through the following sections:

- ☐ Creating a Growth Contract and Needs Plan
- ☐ Grounding Activities and Practitioner Check-Ins
- ☐ The Sensory Connection
- ☐ Contextual Sensory Investigation
- ☐ ACTION Creating Growth Tools
- ☐ Case Scenario

CREATING A GROWTH CONTRACT AND NEEDS PLAN

When addressing trauma, information gathering is important, but there is the need to go beyond information (Leitch, 2017). We also need to better understand and gain knowledge of what to *do* for clients. While healing is the ultimate goal, it should not be the focus. We have found that such language is a trigger for clients because it insinuates brokenness. If clients invite a discussion on healing, that is fine. However, growth is more achievable, and you can help clients obtain it in the small steps they take each day.

In order to create growth, you must start by decreasing stress and anxiety, forming a professional relationship, and learning more about areas for growth. Determine what the individual needs rather than assuming. *And always ask permission to perform activities, particularly those that include touch.*

The onus is not solely on the client. Remember, as the practitioner, you play a major role. The following worksheets can serve as a starting point to support you in assessing a client's needs and developing a plan to **C**reate growth. The first worksheet helps you to perform a client needs assessment, while the next two worksheets allow you to create a plan that can best support the client in expressing their needs in a way that supports autonomy and safety.

PROVIDER WORKSHEET

ACTION NEEDS ASSESSMENT

Age Range: All

Objective: To acknowledge trauma and identify areas of need and resources to support treatment planning

Directions: The first step toward growth is not instant healing. It is acknowledging where the person and family are in the given moment. Are they able to acknowledge their trauma? Do they look through a trauma lens, impeding their ability to acknowledge areas of strength and resilience? Are there necessary supports and resources you can assist in obtaining? Upon re-assessment, return to this worksheet to determine growth.

Client Name: ______________________________ **Date:** ___________________________

Date of Birth: ____________________________ **Re-assessment Date:** ____________

Acknowledgment of strength, resilience, support, and available resources	**Acknowledgment of the trauma** List all types and categories of trauma, as well as what support is needed	**Interdisciplinary team** Who is needed to move toward balance?

PROVIDER WORKSHEET

ACTION CREATING GROWTH: WHAT I NEED PLAN

Age Range: Children

Objective: To develop a method to communicate needs that supports the client's progress toward growth

Directions: Following a screening or assessment, it is crucial to have a plan to provide safety, set boundaries, and develop autonomy. Use this checklist to identify sensorimotor activities, mindfulness practices, or other methods that best support the child's arousal and that facilitate their participation in required tasks, treatment sessions, and engagement with others. Work with caregivers, and the child as appropriate, to develop these activities. Highlight a way to communicate needs through specified statements or nonverbal options. (Gestures are especially useful for young children.) This should be a starting point for continued strategizing to expand methods of communication.

Desired Action	Key Words, Phrases, or Strategies
End a task	☐ Say "Stop please" ☐ Use pictures with a stop sign ☐ Signal with gestures
Share needs	☐ Say "I need..." or "I want..." ☐ Say "Give me" ☐ Use pictures of desired items to select ☐ Signal with gestures
Express feelings	☐ Use "I feel" statements ☐ Use pictures of emotions ☐ Signal with gestures

PROVIDER WORKSHEET

ACTION CREATING GROWTH: WHAT I NEED PLAN

Age Range: Adolescents and adults

Objective: To develop a method to communicate needs and promote a feeling of safety that supports the client's progress toward growth

Directions: Following a screening or assessment, it is crucial to have a plan to provide safety, set boundaries, and develop autonomy. To do so, you can establish a safety contract that highlights ways clients can communicate their needs through specified statements or nonverbal options. This is a contract that clients can sign with you as the provider, as well as with their educator, caregiver, or any other key individuals. The following is a sample template you can adjust based on policies, regulation, and the specific needs of the client.

Provider/Educator: I agree to try my best to listen to your needs. When you say ________________ (e.g., "I need a break; a walk; to stop"), we will take a moment to stop. We will work together to help you grow. To help you relax and feel safe, I will ________________ (e.g., list preferred and available activities, such as "assist you in meditation" or "perform a yoga or movement break").

Client: I agree to try my best to share what I need. When I say (or do) these things, it means I am upset, overwhelmed, or need to stop: ________________ (e.g., "I need a break; a walk" or I gesture to stop). To help me relax and feel safe, I need ____________ (e.g., list preferred and available activities, such as "to meditate" or "to take a yoga or movement break"). I will let you know when I am in need.

GROUNDING ACTIVITIES AND PRACTITIONER CHECK-INS

Grounding activities are a great place to start with any care for trauma because they facilitate present-moment awareness. Clients who have a history of trauma frequently experience dissociative symptoms, such as flashbacks and intrusive memories, that cause them to reexperience the trauma as if it were still occurring in real time. By using grounding techniques, clients can reorient themselves to the here and now, which can decrease dissociative symptoms as they become more aware of the moment and acknowledge being safe.

One simple grounding technique involves asking clients to make self-awareness affirmations, in which they simply state information about themselves based on orientation to time and space (e.g., "I am [name]" and "I am at [location]"). You can use similar techniques with children by asking them self-awareness questions, such as "What is your name?" and "How old are you?" and "What is this [point to familiar object from the environment]?" In the following sections, we will explore several other types of grounding techniques, including mindfulness activities, sensory awareness exercises, and breathwork, and we will present activities and tools you can use with clients in each of these categories.

Grounding Activities: Mindfulness

Mindfulness is the quality of fully immersing yourself in and being aware of the present moment. It involves purposefully focusing all of your attention to whatever it is you are doing at the moment. Clients do not need to schedule extra time to practice mindfulness but can incorporate it into their everyday activities. For example, they can take a mindful walk with bare feet and connect to the sensations they feel on the ground, or they can practice mindful eating at their next meal by eating slowly and describing the characteristics of the food, such as the color, texture, smell, and taste. Clients can also set aside time for formal mindfulness practices by engaging in meditation. These practices can be guided or independent. You can also use the following activities with clients to promote mindful awareness.

IN-SESSION ACTIVITY

MINDFUL FINGER COUNTDOWN

Age Range: Children

Objective: To reorient to the present moment with touch and mindful counting

Directions: Have the child hold up their hand with their fingers separated. As you demonstrate the movements, ask them to imitate you. Take your thumb and second finger, and touch the pads together. With each breath, you will have the child touch the pads of the remaining fingers as described in the script below.

Provider Script: State out loud "four." Take a deep, purposeful breath and have the child do the same. Move to your next finger, touching the pads of your thumb and third finger. State out loud "three." Again, take a deep, purposeful breath and have the child do the same. Continue with the remaining fingers, breathing in between and having the child imitate. Count down to one, repeating the process if needed.

IN-SESSION ACTIVITY

MINDFUL FINGER COUNTDOWN

Age Range: Adolescents and adults

Objective: To reorient to the present moment with touch and mindful counting

Directions: Use the following script while demonstrating the activity to the client.

Provider Script: Hold up your hand in front of your face. What do you see? Notice the creases on your fingers. Increase your focus, and look at the front and back of your hand. Now, with your fingers separated, identify five things in your environment. What do you see? After you identify five things, flex your thumb into your palm. You should now have four fingers raised. Next, name four things you feel, such as the temperature in the room, your clothing, the floor, or the chair you're sitting in. Flex your pointer finger into your palm. Now you have three fingers extended. Next, name three things you hear in your environment. After, flex your middle finger into your palm, leaving two fingers extended. Name two things you smell in your environment. After, flex your ring finger into your palm, leaving one finger extended. Finally, name one thing you would like to taste that makes you feel happy.

IN-SESSION ACTIVITY

A-G-E BREATHING*

Age Range: All

Objective: To practice narrowing and expanding the focus of mindful awareness

Directions: Use the following script with your client.

Provider Script: Envision the following figure is an hourglass. Just like an hourglass expands at the top, narrows in the middle, and expands again at the bottom, you will follow three steps to widen the focus of your attention, narrow it, and then widen it again. Start by bringing your attention to the present moment. Broaden the focus of your attention to acknowledge anything you are experiencing in this moment, including any thoughts, sensations, or feelings (*awareness*). Next, narrow the focus of your attention by bringing your awareness to your breathing. Focus on the inhale and exhale of each breath (*gathering*). Finally, expand the focus of your attention once more and become aware of your whole body, recognizing the sensations throughout your body, face, and head (*expanding*).

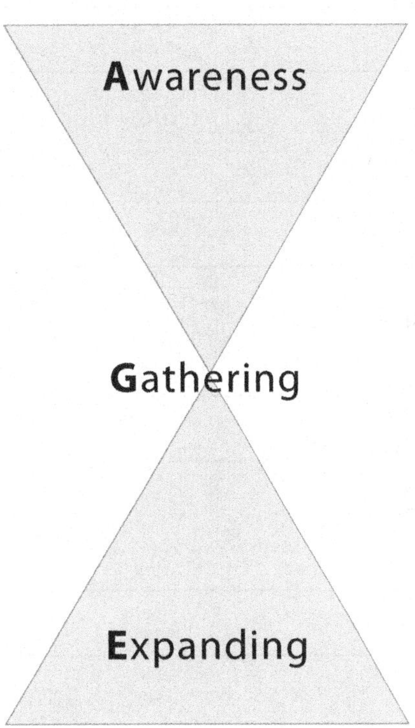

*Adapted from *Mindfulness-Based Cognitive Therapy for Depression: A New Approach to Preventing Relapse* (Segal, Williams, & Teasdale, 2001)

CLIENT ACTIVITY

MINDFUL EATING

Age Range: All

Objective: To become present and practice mindfulness through touch and taste

Directions: Choose a preferred snack. Before eating, use your senses to explore the food. Take your time to scan the food and smell it, using your hands to feel its texture and temperature. Place a small portion of the snack in your mouth, and allow it to sit on your tongue for a bit. Slowly begin to move it around your mouth and begin to chew it slowly. Once you are finished, answer the questions below.

Note: For smaller children, an adult must be present to assist with the activity and to ensure the food is safe and appropriate for the child to consume. Place it in front of them to first explore with their hands.

1. What color is it?

____

____

2. What does it smell like?

____

____

3. What does it feel like in your hands?

____

____

4. What does it feel like to chew it?

____

____

5. How does it taste?

____

____

IN-SESSION ACTIVITY

GUIDED MEDITATION

Age Range: Adolescents and adults

Objective: To bring the attention to the body and become aware of the present moment

Directions: Find a comfortable space for the client to sit, and have them place their body into a comfortable position. Ask them to close their eyes and envision the following scene as you read the script aloud to them. (Give them permission to keep their eyes open if they desire.)

Provider Script: You are walking through a wooded area. You can feel the leaves crumble under your feet and the branches snap with every step you take. It is a hot summer day, and you feel the heat from the sun. A welcome cool breeze blows against your face. You look around and see the birds flying above and hear them chirping to one another. As you slowly make your way through the woods, the light begins to get brighter as you move to where the trees are spaced farther apart.

You come upon an open space. It is a beautiful field with soft grass. You decide to take your shoes off to feel the blades beneath your feet. In the air, you smell the flowers that provide this scenic landscape. As you continue to walk, you hear people laughing and playing in the distance. As you get closer, you see a body of water. It is a lake. You decide to place your feet in the water. It is cool and clear. You can see all the way to the bottom. You decide to sit in the water, allowing it to cool your body. You place your arms behind you and look up to the sky. You feel a sense of relaxation and renewal as you take a deep breath through your nose. Then you slowly exhale through your mouth. You do this a few times, taking three deep breaths. Now, wiggle your toes and your fingers, and begin to move your feet, hands, arms, and legs. Slowly open your eyes and return.

CLIENT ACTIVITY

OPPOSITE HAND USE

Age Range: All

Objective: To bring your focus to the present moment through movement

Directions: Choose a familiar task, such as writing, brushing your teeth, combing your hair, or pouring a simple glass of water, and perform the selected task with your nonpreferred hand. If you are right-handed, use your left hand. If you are left-handed, use your right hand. When you are finished, answer the following questions.

1. How did you perform the activity compared to when you use your preferred hand?

____

____

2. Was it more challenging to complete the task? In what ways?

____

____

3. Where was your focus during the task?

____

____

4. What emotions did you experience (e.g., frustration)?

____

____

Grounding Activities: Brain Rhythm and Body Awareness

The brain loves rhythm and repetition (Gibbs, 2017b). In fact, several bodily functions rely on or produce rhythm, such as our heartbeat, circadian rhythms, and breath rate, as well as the sucking reflex. Because rhythm and repetition have an inherently soothing quality, those with trauma may present with repetitive behaviors and actions, such as hand-flapping or body rocking, in an attempt to self-regulate. When they perform such sensorimotor actions, a synchronous rhythm occurs that decreases external stimuli and provides a self-regulatory function. However, clients may not always implement the most efficient or appropriate methods. For example, some children may perform self-stimulatory behaviors that are harmful in nature, such as head-banging, whereas adults may seek out risky behaviors and addictions, such as heavy alcohol use and compulsive sexual behavior.

As practitioners, we can provide specific methods to enhance preferred responses in the brain that utilize rhythmic activity. For example, it can be helpful to use a metronome with clients during specific tasks, such as writing, reading, or deep breathing. Metronomes are readily available via smartphone apps or online videos, or you can purchase an actual device. In addition, you can help clients reground themselves through rhythm by offering activities that involve a level of repetition, such as mandala drawing, rhythmic breathing, and marching, dancing, or drumming exercises. The following section offers several of these activities that you can introduce to clients.

CLIENT ACTIVITY

MANDALA DRAWING AND COLORING

Age Range: All

Objective: To enhance focus, attention, and mindful awareness of the senses involving vision and movement

Directions: Obtain a sheet of paper and pencil. Place a dot on the paper to indicate your starting point and, using a compass, make various size circles on the paper in a preferred pattern. This could involve overlapping the circles and choosing different starting points for each. You can also make circles by tracing a circular-shaped object or attempt to draw freehand. Be creative. Use a ruler to add different shapes around and through your circles, such as triangles or hexagons, similar to the example here. Follow by coloring the mandala as desired. For younger children, you can use a pre-printed design for them to color or paint. You can also enlarge the design and use it as a pattern to fill with various colors of modeling clay or dough.

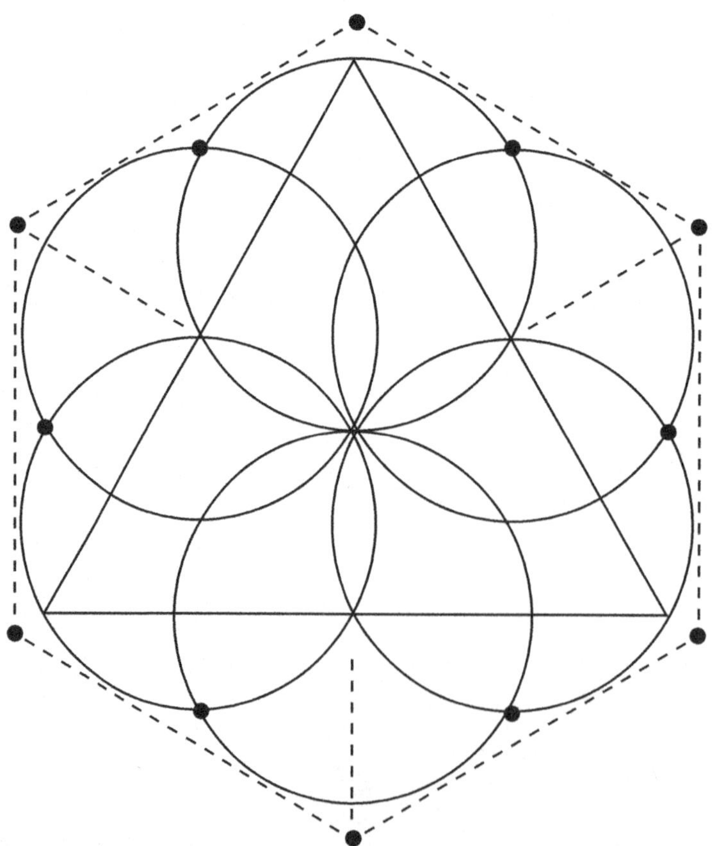

IN-SESSION ACTIVITY

RHYTHMIC BREATHING

Age Range: All

Objective: To enhance focus, attention, and body awareness through breathing

Directions: You can choose to perform the following activity with a metronome sound, with music (e.g., slow drumming sounds), or with chimes. The client may be seated or lying on their back. Use the script that follows.

Provider Script:

1. Become aware of your breath.
2. Slowly inhale through your nose.
3. Gently exhale through your mouth.
4. Allow your breath to flow naturally.
5. Begin to notice the rhythm of your breath.
6. Notice the rhythm of the sound around you.
7. Continue breathing, allowing your breath to join the rhythm of the sound being played.
8. If desired, you can count to yourself to highlight the rhythm. For example, inhale 2-3-4, exhale 2-3-4. (Note to provider: This is especially useful with younger children.)

IN-SESSION ACTIVITY

MARCHING TO THE DRUM

Age Range: All

Objective: To enhance focus, attention, and body awareness through movement and sound

Directions: You can choose to play music over the speakers (e.g., drumming music), or play a small drum you can hold, such as a bongo. If a drum is not available, you can use a large coffee can with a plastic lid or other available items (e.g., the bottom of a small tin paper waste bin). Allow the client to sit or stand, and read the script that follows.

Provider Script:

1. Play a slow beat on the drum. (Note to provider: If selecting music to play over speakers, press start.)
2. Begin to march in place to the rhythm.
3. Focus on the following:
    - Feel the sensations on the bottoms of your feet as they hit the floor.
    - Sense the pressure pushing through the joints of your ankles and legs.
    - Listen to the sound of the music.
4. Once complete, take a gentle breath through your nose, and blow the air out of your mouth.

IN-SESSION ACTIVITY

BODY MAPPING POETRY

Age Range: Adolescents and adults

Objective: To release internal stressors and express how trauma manifests internally

Directions: In this activity, the client will create a poem by developing a personal awareness of their body's function and needs. This activity is intended to be personal and allow for self-reflection, so although you can offer support and guidance, you should follow the lead of your client. If the client desires, they may invite you to view their poem at the end of the exercise, but it is their choice whether or not they want to share. To start, provide them with a sheet of paper and a writing utensil. You can offer to transcribe for them if they desire.

Provider Script:

Step 1: Focus on your body. Do you notice any pain, discomfort, or tightness? To simplify the activity, you can also select one region of your body toward which to draw your attention. Here are some suggested regions you might want to focus on:

- Feet and ankles
- Legs and knees
- Pelvis and middle section (belly region)
- Back and chest (heart)
- Arms, wrists, and hands
- Shoulders and neck
- Face, top of the head, and back of the head

Once you have selected a part of your body that you'd like to focus on, complete the following statement to describe what you feel in that part of your body:

In my ______________________________, I feel ______________________________.

Please write your responses on the piece of paper provided. If you are comfortable with continuing, select another region of your body and repeat this step until you are ready to move on.

Step 2: Next, think about what images come to mind as you think about these feelings in your body. List as many pictures that come to mind. This could be a random image or a word that dashes into your mind. Please write your responses on the piece of paper provided.

Step 3: Now ask yourself what it is that you *desire* to feel in your body. How will you know that you are experiencing this feeling? Where will you feel it in your body? For example, perhaps you desire to feel at peace, and you will know that you are feeling peace when your back is relaxed, your feet are no longer tense, and your heart beats in a controlled rhythmic pattern. Think about these desired feelings, and list as many pictures that come to mind. This could be a random image or a word that dashes into your mind. Please write your responses on the piece of paper provided.

Step 4: Finally, create a poem that reflects the awareness you have gained from your body. To do so, review the words you wrote down. Use them to begin writing your poem in the space provided here. Use your creativity to move beyond this suggested outline, and do not place pressure on yourself to write a perfect poem. It does not have to rhyme, and you do not have to use everything you wrote during the first three steps. The purpose is to provide an outlet for what your body is experiencing and to conceptualize it into words. At the end of the poem, develop a positive affirmation by filling in the blank to the statement "I am ______________."

(Note to provider: You can provide the following template for the client to write down their poem.)

____

____

____

____

____

____

____

____

____

____

I am ____________________________________

____

____.

Grounding Activities: Breathwork

When the sympathetic nervous system is activated, we experience changes in our body that prepare our body to respond to the threat at hand. Our pupils dilate, our muscles tense, our heart races, and our breathing quickens. Individuals with a trauma history often remain in this heightened nervous system state even after the threat has long passed, and when they feel triggered, they may take quick and short breaths. This quickened breathing only serves to further exacerbate their autonomic reactions, and they may find themselves experiencing panic attacks or exhibiting defensive reflexes as a result. By engaging in deep breathing activities, clients can activate their parasympathetic nervous system to counteract this activation and return their body to a state of homeostasis.

Breathing is an unconscious process that is directly controlled by an area in the brainstem called the medullary respiratory center, which is responsible for arousal and unconscious bodily functions (Figure 8). External factors, such as stress and exercise, modify the medullary respiratory center's output. However, we can also exhibit conscious control of our breathing by recruiting higher-order brain structures. The breathing exercises that we offer in this section will allow your client to gain practice in finding more regulated breathing that facilitates a calm and alert nervous system.

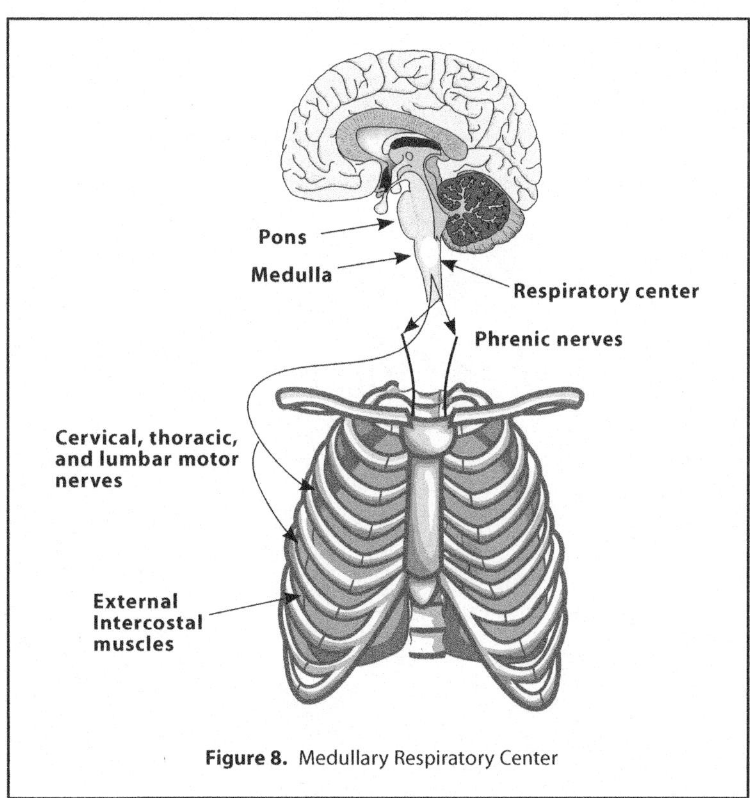

Figure 8. Medullary Respiratory Center

When introducing breathwork to clients, there are a few important aspects to keep in mind. First and foremost, be aware that individuals with a trauma history may be triggered by the breathing exercises presented here and may experience increased anxiety as a result. Present breathwork slowly by checking in to assess the client's experience and see how they are reacting. This may not be a place to start for everyone. In addition, clients with trauma often hold tension in their muscles that may make it difficult to engage in deep breathing. Therefore, consider practicing gentle stretching and mindfulness activities prior to beginning breathwork, as this may help better prepare clients.

Choose a comfortable position and location to perform the breathwork. The supine position is usually optimal, as it allows for movement of the diaphragm. However, some clients may find sitting or lying prone on their stomach more comfortable than supine on their back. Allow the client to choose what works best for them to develop a sense of trust and autonomy. As clients begin the exercises, they should focus on diaphragmatic breathing by pushing out their abdominal area on the inhale and flattening it during the exhale. They should also breathe in through the nose and out through the mouth, as this assists in filtering air and controlling carbon dioxide intake. If necessary, you can use counting cues or an external aid to help clients focus on their breaths. Breathwork should be rhythmic when possible.

IN-SESSION ACTIVITY

DIAPHRAGMATIC BREATHING

Age Range: All

Objective: To decrease sympathetic nervous system activation, decrease stress hormones, and allow for calm and focused attention

Directions: Invite clients to lie on their back, or invite them to choose a position of comfort. Explain that you will be practicing diaphragmatic breathing, and instruct them to place one hand on their belly area and another on their heart. Ask them to take a deep breath through their nose while feeling their belly rise and fill with air. On the exhale, they should allow the air to gently leave their mouth, allowing the belly area to flatten. To help clients follow this rhythmic breathing pattern, you can use reminder cues, such as "smell the roses, blow out the candles." When introducing this activity to children, you can attempt these same instructions, depending on their developmental level. Otherwise, use a visual aid, such as a toy or stuffed animal, to assist in the exercise. For example, have the child lie on their back, place the item on their belly, and allow the item to rise with the in-breath and gently fall with the out-breath.

IN-SESSION ACTIVITY

ALTERNATE DIAPHRAGMATIC BREATHING

Age Range: All

Objective: To decrease the sympathetic nervous system response, increase focus and attention, and enhance parasympathetic nervous system activity

Directions: Have clients sit on a therapy or physio ball, with their feet placed firmly on the ground. Ask them to gently roll their hips forward so their back is resting on the ball. Then instruct clients to stretch their arms above their head while taking a deep breath in through the nose. As they return to a seated position, ask them to exhale slowly out of their mouth. When doing this activity with young children, safely position the child on the ball either by having them squat in front of it or by placing them on top of it supine. Gently roll them back and forth, and encourage them to do sit-ups to produce exhalation.

Note: Those with back or spinal conditions should avoid this activity.

IN-SESSION ACTIVITY

HILLS AND VALLEYS

Age Range: All

Objective: To decrease the sympathetic nervous system response, increase focus and attention, and enhance parasympathetic nervous system activity

Directions: Use the following script while demonstrating the activity to the client.

Provider Script: Place your finger on the star to begin tracing the path. At the star, take a deep inhale through your nose, and hold it for three to five seconds. Follow along the path by tracing your finger up the hill, while exhaling out of your mouth. Once you reach the bottom of the hill, inhale again as you trace your finger forward through the valley. Continue following the path until you reach the next hill, and exhale as you climb. (Note to provider: Repeat as needed.)

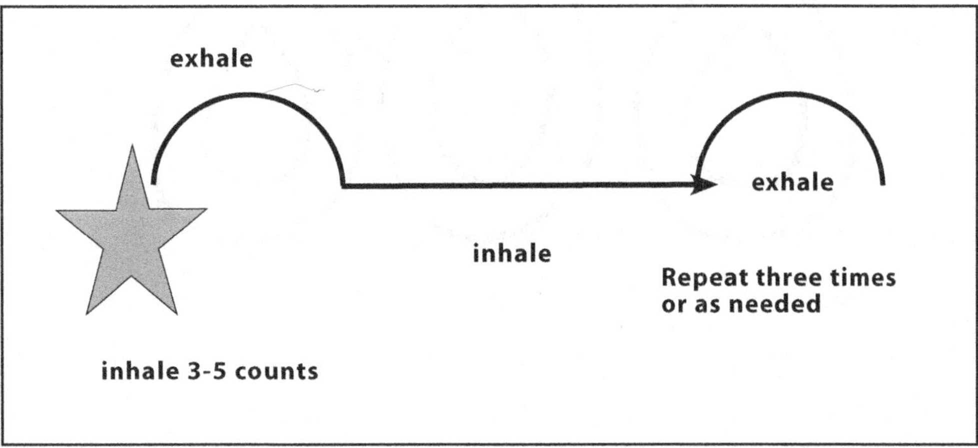

IN-SESSION ACTIVITY

BENDS AND TURNS

Age Range: All

Objective: To decrease the sympathetic nervous system response, increase focus and attention, and enhance parasympathetic nervous system activity

Directions: Use the following script while demonstrating the activity to the client.

Provider Script: Place your finger on the star to begin tracing the path. At the star, take a deep inhale through the nose, and hold it for three to five seconds. As you exhale, follow along the path, blowing slowly out of your mouth. At the stop sign, take a deep inhale in your nose again and relax. (Note to provider: Repeat as needed. You can print these images to use as needed in various environments, including while on the go!)

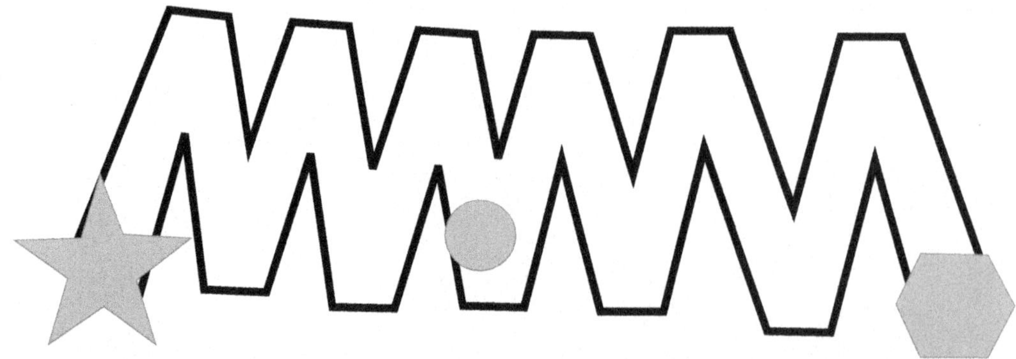

IN-SESSION ACTIVITY

LABYRINTH BREATHING

Age Range: All

Objective: To decrease the sympathetic nervous system response, increase focus and attention, and enhance parasympathetic nervous system activity

Directions: Use the following script while demonstrating the activity to the client.

Provider Script: In this activity, you will use your finger to trace the path of a labyrinth while coordinating with your breath. Place your finger on the starting star to begin. At the starting star, take a deep inhale through your nose while tracing your finger toward the stop sign. Once you reach the stop sign, exhale slowly out of your mouth until you reach the next star on the path. At the star, take another deep inhale until you reach the following stop sign. Continue this pattern of inhaling at the stars and exhaling at the stop signs until you reach the last stop sign on the path. (Note to provider: Repeat as needed. Two labyrinth templates are provided for you on the next pages. You can print these cards to use as needed in various environments, including while on the go!)

LABYRINTH BREATHING TEMPLATE

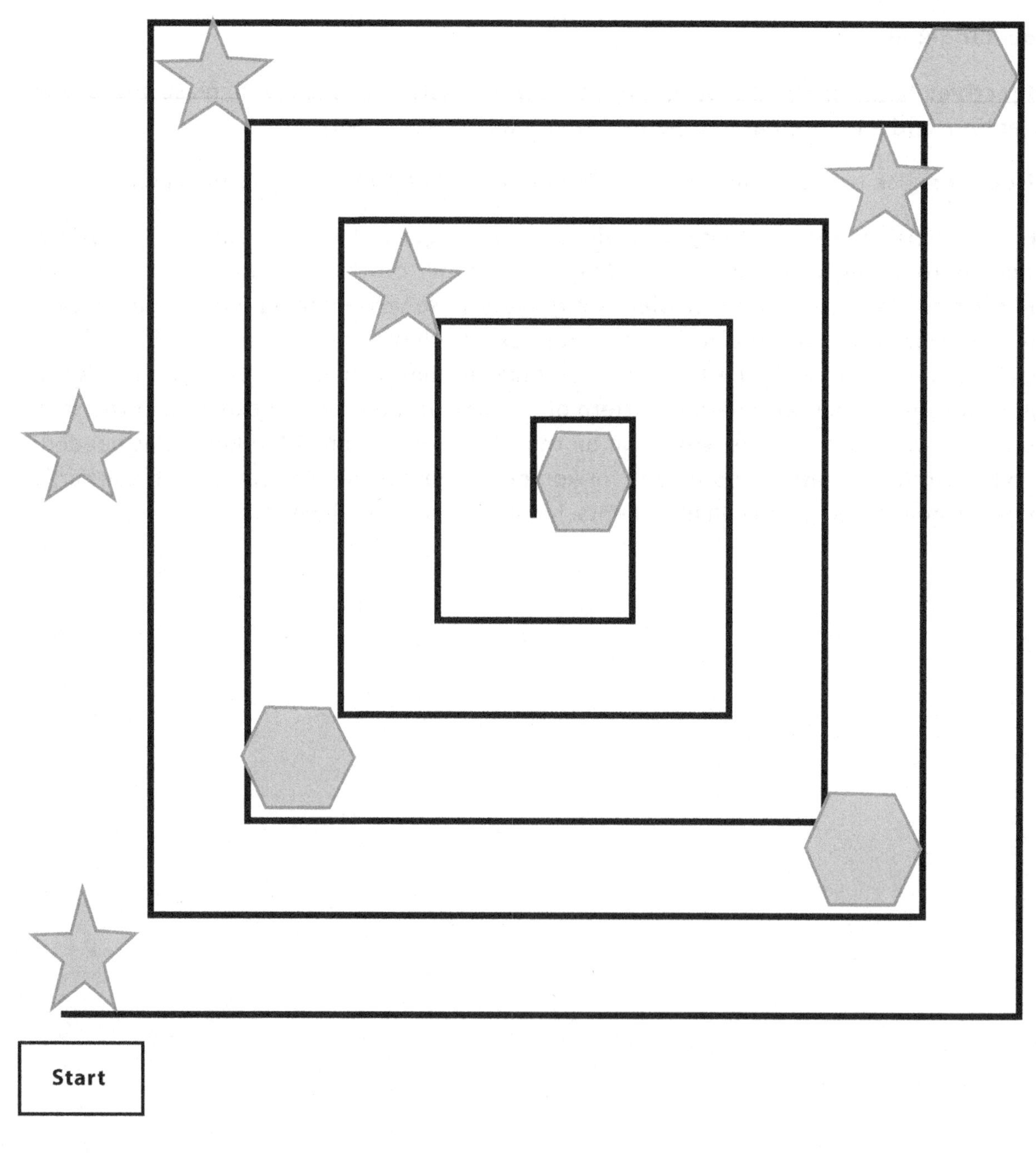

LABYRINTH BREATHING TEMPLATE

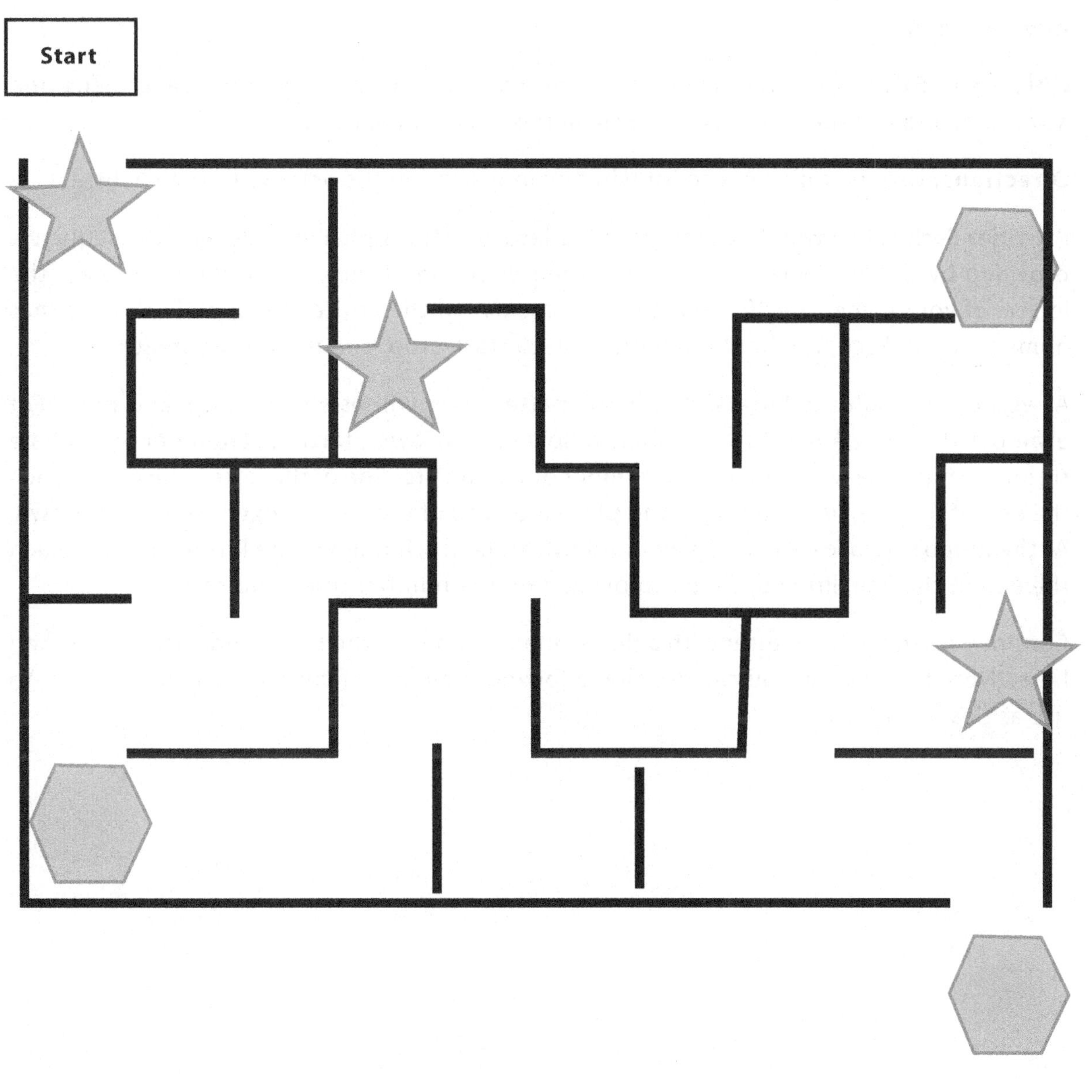

IN-SESSION ACTIVITY

LETTER BREATHING

Age Range: All

Objective: To decrease the sympathetic nervous system response, increase focus and attention, and enhance parasympathetic nervous system activity

Directions: Use the following script while demonstrating the activity to the client.

Provider Script: Use your finger to trace the letters of the alphabet, following the sequence provided by the numbered arrows and in the direction of the arrows. You may select the letters of your name, specific words (such as *relax*), or the entire alphabet. Each letter has numbers on it. Each number is an indication to start, stop, and relax your breath.

As you go through the letters, that is the pattern you will use: start, stop, and relax. For example, the letter A has three numbers followed by arrows. Starting at number one, inhale through your nose while tracing your finger down the first line of the letter. Once you reach the end of the line, lift your finger and place it on top of the letter, next to the number two. At the number two, exhale out of your mouth while tracing down the line. Once you reach the end of the line, lift your finger to place it on the number three and relax.

Continue on to the next letter with a deep inhale, following the breathing pattern outlined here. (Note to provider: You can use the following template or cut out individual letters to use as desired.)

LETTER BREATHING TEMPLATE

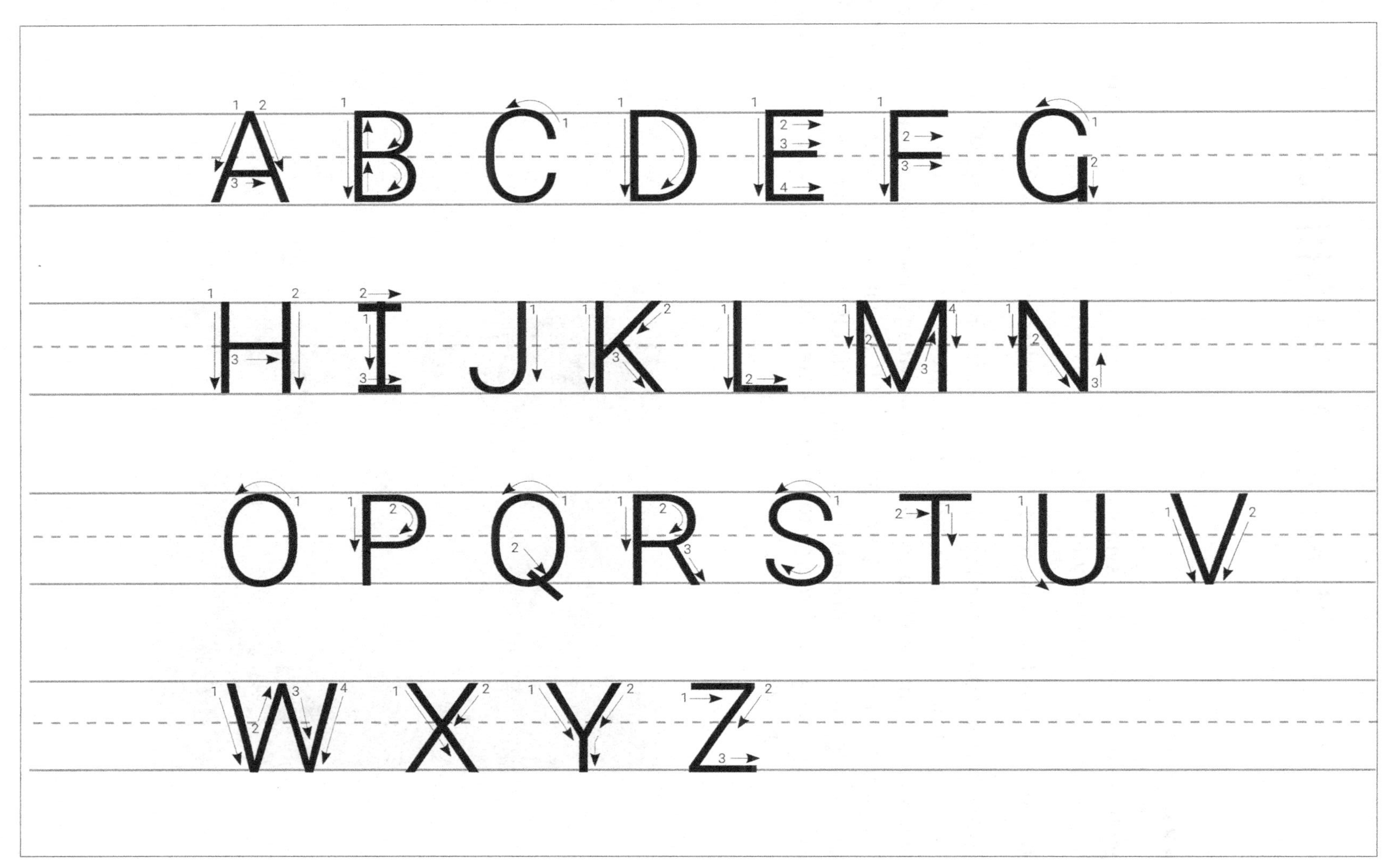

IN-SESSION ACTIVITY

TRUMPET BREATHING

Age Range: All

Objective: To decrease the sympathetic nervous system response, increase focus and attention, and enhance parasympathetic nervous system activity

Directions: Use the following script while demonstrating the activity to the client.

Provider Script: Inhale through your nose, and then place the tip of your thumb in your mouth, similar to the image provided here. After inhaling, fill your cheeks with air, not allowing any of your breath to escape. Count between three to five seconds, exhale through the mouth, and repeat. After you complete this activity a few times, discuss how it felt before, during, and after the activity. Remind yourself to use this trumpet technique if you feel upset or have a lot of energy to let out. A great way to start your day is by practicing this in the morning.

IN-SESSION ACTIVITY

TUNNEL RACE

Age Range: Children

Objective: To decrease the sympathetic nervous system response, increase focus and attention, and enhance parasympathetic nervous system activity

Items Needed:

- Cotton balls
- 2–5 cardboard paper towel or toilet paper rolls
- Straws
- Tape
- Scissors

Directions: You can choose to complete the following activity with the client or in preparation for your session. Use cardboard rolls to create a tunnel by adhering them together with tape into a desired shape. If you want, you can use scissors to cut angles for corners. If you're having the client work with another person or race against a peer, make two structures. When you're done creating your tunnel, place it on a flat surface.

Provider Script: Use the straw to blow the cotton ball through the tunnel until it gets to the end. Whoever gets to the end first wins! Or try to beat your personal best time! (Note to provider: If needed, you can tape together multiple straws to allow air to reach deep within the tunnel.)

IN-SESSION ACTIVITY

BOX RACE

Age Range: Children

Objective: To decrease the sympathetic nervous system response, increase focus and attention, and enhance parasympathetic nervous system activity

Items Needed:

- Cotton balls
- Small cardboard box (e.g., shoebox)
- 5–10 straws
- Scissors
- Glue or tape

Directions: You can choose to complete the following activity with the client or in preparation for your session. Take the straws and cut them into various sizes. Use glue or tape to adhere them to the inside of the box into whatever pattern you desire.

Provider Script: Choose a starting point where you can place a cotton ball, and use a straw to blow the cotton ball along the path to the other side of the box. See how long it takes to get to the end. You can take this home to practice after our session. If you want, we can make two boxes so you can race someone!

IN-SESSION ACTIVITY

WALL RUN

Age Range: Children

Objective: To decrease the sympathetic nervous system response, increase focus and attention, and enhance parasympathetic nervous system activity

Items Needed:

- Cotton balls
- 2–5 cardboard paper towel or toilet paper rolls
- Straws
- Painter's tape
- Scissors

Directions: You can choose to perform the following activity with the client or in preparation for your session. Take the cardboard rolls and cut them in half lengthwise. Then use painter's tape to adhere the rolls to the wall, placing them in staggering tiers.

Provider Script: Take a cotton ball and place it on the top tier, and then use a straw to blow it from the top level until it reaches the end. Try to beat your personal best time by prolonging your exhale! Let me show you how!

CLIENT ACTIVITY

FIRE-BREATHING DRAGON

Age Range: Children

Objective: To decrease the sympathetic nervous system response, increase focus and attention, and enhance parasympathetic nervous system activity

Items Needed:

- Plastic or paper cup, construction paper, or cardboard toilet paper roll
- Tissue paper or party streamers
- Glue or tape
- Scissors
- Craft pom-poms (optional)
- Googly eyes (optional)

Directions: (Adult to assist as needed) To start, you will need a tube to make the body of the dragon. This can be a plastic or paper cup with the bottom cut off, construction paper rolled together with tape or glue, or a cardboard toilet paper roll. Select whatever color paper you desire. You can use paint for additional fun. Next, cut tissue paper into strips, or select a few pieces of party streamers, and adhere them inside one end of the tube. Decorate the top of the tube with eyes by adhering pom-poms with optional googly eyes. Place your mouth on the end of tube without tissue paper or streamers, take a long deep breath, and blow!

CLIENT ACTIVITY

HOMEMADE KAZOO*

Age Range: Children

Objective: To decrease the sympathetic nervous system response, increase focus and attention, and enhance parasympathetic nervous system activity

Items Needed:

- Pen or pencil
- Cardboard paper towel or toilet paper roll
- Wax paper
- Rubber band
- Scissors

Directions: (Adult to assist as needed) Use a pen or pencil to poke holes in a straight line along the top end of the cardboard tube. Cut out a small square of wax paper just big enough to cover one end of the tube, and use the rubber band to secure the wax paper in place. To play the kazoo, put your mouth on the open end of the tube, and blow into it while making a humming sound. Try to see if you can change the sound of the notes that the kazoo makes by covering different holes with your fingers.

* Adapted from *Self-Regulation and Mindfulness* (Gibbs, 2017b)

Practitioner Check-Ins and Daily Schedules

Practitioner check-ins and daily schedules can also support the use of grounding activities. Within your session, or throughout the day depending on the setting in which you work, be intentional about checking in with your client. For example, if you work in a school setting, establish a routine wherein various team members consult with the child to bring attention to the child's personal needs. For example, team members might check in to see if the child needs a break or if it's okay to proceed, or they can check in to see if the child needs to talk about feelings based on any nonverbal signals they may have witnessed.

When scheduling check-ins, look for opportunities in the client's current schedule. In order for this to be a successful practice, you should intentionally identify times within an established routine. Table 5 provides some examples of daily schedules for different age ranges, which involve various check-in points throughout the day. The ACTION Creating Growth tools presented at the end of this chapter can also assist with checking in.

Time of Day	Early Intervention Schedule	Daycare/School Schedule	Adult/Older Adult Schedule
Morning	Caregiver takes a quiet moment before engaging with the child. Caregiver provides the infant with a massage. Caregiver checks in with support teams, such as a friend, family member, or early intervention provider/case manager (at least once per week).	Caregiver checks in to gauge the child's needs. Child performs stretching, massage, and breathwork with the caregiver. Quiet moment to start the school day, such as covering eyes and being still.	Take a quiet moment, either sitting on the floor or in comfortable position, to perform grounding activities. Perform self-massage. Check in with support teams, such as a friend, family member, or counselor.
Lunch	Take the opportunity to engage during mealtime. Notice the child's reaction to the food presented. Acknowledge and describe their reaction (e.g., "Was that yummy?").	Have a mindful snack (before or after lunch if not within the same room). Teacher or staff member to check in and see what the child needs to move toward goals.	Take a moment to perform mindful eating at the start of a meal.
Afternoon	Take a mindful walk together and perform sensorimotor activities, such as yoga, swinging, and tactile play (e.g., sandbox activities).	Take a mindful walk, perform stretching or yoga, and practice breathwork activities before returning to work or scheduled activities.	Take a mindful walk or perform body scanning, stretching, and breathwork.
Evening	Check in and debrief from the day with support teams, such as a friend, family member, or counselor. Perform aromatherapy for calming and a caregiver-provided massage before bed.	Debrief from the day and check in with a caregiver-initiated discussion. Perform breathwork, aromatherapy for calming, a caregiver-provided massage, and stretching before bed.	Debrief from the day with support teams, such as a friend, family member, or counselor. Share area of growth toward personal goals. Perform breathwork, aromatherapy for calming, and stretching before bed.

Table 5. Sample Check-In Schedules Across Age Groups

In addition, you can use the following worksheet to track the use of grounding exercises throughout the day. It is particularly helpful for teachers or parents to use with children and adolescents so they can record their reactions to the activities and share them with their provider. Be sure to review the directions to ensure the caregiver has a solid understanding of the intent of the worksheet.

CLIENT WORKSHEET

ACTION DAILY GROUNDING PRACTICES

Age Range: Children and adolescents

Objective: To organize the use of grounding exercises throughout the day and document reactions to the exercises

Directions: Use the following chart to record the child's use of grounding practices throughout the day. You can choose to replace the exercise listed with other grounding practices. It is important to record the child's reaction to the exercise to ensure the selected activity does not trigger distressing symptoms, such as anxiety. The observation notes can also highlight continued areas of need (e.g., a need to increase the frequency of daily check-ins).

Take the Following Breaks Each Day	AM (Identify Time/Period)	PM (Identify Time/Period)	Observation Notes
Breathwork Take breaks every 3–5 minutes to blow out the energy (can use feathers, tissues, pinwheels, etc.).			
Brain Freeze Use a bell, chime, or gentle drumbeat to indicate that it is time to freeze; Turn down lights and have the children stop their activity and get into a comfortable position with their eyes closed for 1–3 minutes.			
Check-Ins Perform check-ins throughout the day or session by performing grounding activities for 3–5 minutes.			
Stretch and Exercise Take 3–5 minutes to stretch the upper and lower body muscles. Perform progressive relaxation or yoga poses (or other physical activities).			
Exercises of Choice:			

THE SENSORY CONNECTION

Now let us delve deeper into the connection between our emotions and the physical reactions in our body. According to the James-Lange theory of emotions, our emotions arise in response to physiological changes we experience in our body (Borg et al., 2013). For example, if you are walking alone at night and hear footsteps quickly approaching behind you, your heart may start to race, and you may begin to tremble. The James-Lange theory maintains that it is the physical sensation of your heart pounding and your body trembling that makes you realize you are afraid. The manner in which we interpret our physiological arousal determines our emotional experience. That is, emotions occur in response to internal body sensations.

Sensory stimuli can occur in various forms, such as visual (sight), olfactory (smell), auditory (sound), gustatory (taste), tactile (touch), proprioceptive (body awareness in space), vestibular (sense of balance and coordinated eye movement), interoceptive (internal sensations), nociceptive (perception of pain), thermal reception (detection of temperature), or pruritic (itch). When experiencing any emotion, such as fear, the unconscious brain processes the sensations through the various sensory systems. Therefore, to best understand the emotional responses of someone dealing with acute or chronic stress, or exposure to significant trauma, you must first understand the physical presentation of trauma.

When individuals have experienced acute stress or trauma, the memories associated with the traumatic or stressful event are often encoded as sensory memories, which reflect the physical sensations that the individual experienced at the time of the traumatic event. It is for this reason that certain textures, sounds, or other sensory stimuli can elicit an intense emotional memory of the trauma. For example, a woman who was sexually assaulted by a man wearing a strong cologne may now have an unconscious aversion to the smell of men's cologne. The smell may immediately elicit a sensory memory of the trauma and mentally transport her back to the time of the assault.

These sensory memories are often experienced as intense fragments rather than fully developed memories. In these situations, the amygdala responds unconsciously via our senses. That is because the sensory areas of our brain are connected to our limbic system, which is the region of the brain involved in the experience of fear. In this respect, the sensory brain provides a gateway from the unconscious brain to the conscious neocortex. Therefore, it is not uncommon for individuals who have been exposed to trauma to experience sensory dysfunction, including hypersensitivity, atypical processing, increased pain, dermatological irritation, hypoventilation, frequent yawning, dry mouth, dry eyes, and increased perspiration (Gutpa, Jarosz, & Gupta, 2017; Mueller-Pfeiffer et. al, 2013; Wallwork et al. 2017; Yochman & Pat-Horenczyk, 2019).

In extreme cases, the sensory dysfunction that accompanies trauma can lead to the development of a comorbid sensory processing disorder (SPD). Specific subtypes of SPD include sensory modulation disorder, sensory discrimination disorder, and sensory-based motor disorder (Miller, Anzalone, Lane, Cermak, & Osten, 2007). Although SPD is not recognized in the latest edition of the DSM, practitioners continue to recognize the impact of sensory processing dysfunction, as individuals with SPD present with dysfunction in a variety of areas, including sensory modulation, discrimination, and sensorimotor activity. In particular, they may:

- Display challenges in responding to incoming sensory stimuli and adapting to the demands of the sensory stimulation presented

- Exhibit inappropriate emotional responses, inappropriate social behaviors, and an inability to functionally attend to a task
- Present with challenges in sensory modulation, which may lead to the appearance of defensiveness or under-arousal or to the seeking of sensory stimulation
- Overreact to sensory input secondary to taking in sensory information too quickly or for an extended time frame
- Exhibit hyperactive or inattentive symptoms
- Have difficulty with sensory discrimination (i.e., interpreting the "where" and "what" in regard to sensory stimuli)
- Avoid certain activities and prefer routine and predictable activities
- Need motivation and encouragement to attend to activities, especially gross motor play
- Crave sensory input
- Exhibit uncoordinated motor patterns, poor body mechanics, and "clumsy" motor skills (Gibbs, 2017b)

For individuals with PTSD, this sensory dysfunction appears to have a unique pathology that is absent from other disorders involving hypersensitivity to threat, such as generalized anxiety disorder (Clancy, Ding, Bernat, Schmidt, & Li, 2017). These findings support a need to include sensory-based interventions to assist in sensory processing and integration for those with PTSD. In addition, being able to recognize the comorbidity between PTSD and SPD is crucial given that misinterpretation of symptomology can result in misdiagnosis. For example, someone displaying hyperarousal or craving behaviors may receive an inaccurate diagnosis of ADHD, and this misdiagnosis can then lead to unsuccessful treatment approaches.

To ensure accurate diagnosis, you should prioritize the use of standardized assessment tools in any evaluation process. The following tools can assist you in initiating a screening of sensory dysfunction in your client while using an ACTION-from-Trauma approach. These tools can provide guidance for proceeding with a more formal assessment process. Of note, these tools should not be used in isolation of the evaluation process. They should serve as a guide to make connections between a client's sensory systems and symptoms associated with trauma, and they should be used in conjunction with other standardized tools.

PROVIDER WORKSHEET

ACTION SENSORY BODY SCAN

Client Name: ______________________________

Date of Birth: ______________________________

Date: ______________________________

Check all that apply (as reported or observed)

- ○ Atypical auditory processing
- ○ Auditory distortions
- ○ Sensitivity to sound

- ○ Atypical vestibular processing
- ○ Sensitivity to movement
- ○ Seeking of gross motor activity

- ○ Increased nociception (pain)/ pruritus (itch) sensitivity
- ○ Hypersensitivity to pain
- ○ Nociceptive reflexes (eye blink, flexion, flexor withdraw)

- ○ Atypical thermoreception
- ○ Seeking of cold temperatures

- ○ Atypical proprioceptive processing
- ○ Seeking of proprioceptive input
- ○ Clumsiness

- ○ Atypical visual processing
- ○ Dry eye syndrome
- ○ Sensitivity to light

- ○ Gustatory sensitivity to certain food textures
- ○ Dry mouth

- ○ Olfactory sensitivity to unpleasant odors

- ○ Atypical tactile processing
- ○ Tactile sensitivity
- ○ Seeking of tactile input
- ○ Frequent perspiration
- ○ Skin picking disorders

- ○ Atypical interoception processing
- ○ Seeking or avoiding (urination, bowel movements, gross motor movement, eating, drinking)
- ○ Frequent yawning
- ○ Poor discrimination between bodily functions (e.g., late detection of the need to go use the bathroom)

ADMINISTRATION INSTRUCTIONS

ACTION SELF-REGULATION SELF-ASSESSMENT

Age Range: Adolescents and adults

Objective: To help identify the client's typical threshold tolerance and arousal levels, as well as stimuli supporting or impeding their function

Items Needed:

- A pencil and paper (optional)
- List of provided questions

Directions: Ask the client to fill out the Self-Regulation Self-Assessment, and use their answers to select appropriate target activities. Follow up with the client by discussing how certain environments and sensory stimuli can help us get through our day or make it challenging. Explore how the client can use that knowledge. Lastly, use the information to select daily activities to support their preferences.

Scoring: Only questions 1 through 3 receive a score. Give 5 points for each item the client endorses, with the exception of the last item ("None of the above apply"), which receives a score of 1. Please note that this is not a standardized tool. It is intended to provide you with some insight into the client's ability to self-regulate. It will also assist in how you interact with them and set goals. Use the following guidelines to interpret your client's scores:

- **16–85 (High):** The client may have significant challenges with self-regulation. Review the remaining questions to gain better insight and discuss with the client. Goals should emphasize areas of concern as defined by the client, as well as areas related to sensory processing and emotion regulation.
- **4–15 (Moderate):** The client may have moderate areas to address regarding self-regulation. Review the remaining questions to gain better insight and discuss with the client. Goals should address areas of concern as defined by the client, as well as areas related to sensory processing and emotion regulation. The clinician can consider incorporation of cognitive-based goals.
- **3 (Low):** While the client may not express any areas of concern, be sure to review the remaining questions to gain better insight and discuss with the client. Goal development should address areas of concern as defined by the client.

CLIENT WORKSHEET

ACTION SELF-REGULATION SELF-ASSESSMENT*

This activity can assist you in determining where your energy is focused, what causes you stress, and how you adapt your arousal and react to such experiences. To follow, we will make goals to address any areas of concern. Complete each of the following statements, and select the answer(s) that applies to your personal experiences.

1. I would best describe myself as: (circle all that apply)

    a. Enjoying a lot of activity (e.g., movement, running, jumping)

    b. Avoiding physical activity

    c. A thrill-seeker (e.g., enjoy climbing)

    d. Disliking loud or irritating sounds (sometimes this may be other people talking)

    e. Disliking certain lighting, such as the lights at school

    f. Preferring to wear only one type of clothing (e.g., sweatpants)

    g. None of the above apply

2. I would describe my daily eating as: (circle all that apply)

    a. Sometimes I have difficulty knowing when I am hungry until the last minute.

    b. I am always hungry and/or thirsty.

    c. I only like certain foods and am somewhat picky.

    d. None of the above apply

3. In social environments, like work or school, I: (circle all that apply)

    a. Often have to use the bathroom and have to rush to get there in time

    b. Do not like using the bathroom (Explain: ______________________________)

    c. Often feel my heart racing

*Adapted from *Self-Regulation and Mindfulness* (Gibbs, 2017b)

d. Often feel myself getting anxious and will breathe quickly or heavily

e. Prefer to be alone

f. Do not like a lot of movement and prefer to stay in one spot

g. Have challenges working with others or in a group

h. Often get into debates or arguments with others

i. None of the above apply

4. I am a daydreamer (e.g., drifting off in class).

_______Yes _______No

5. What bothers me the most while around others is:

____

____

6. What bothers me the most while in public is:

____

____

7. What makes me feel better when I am upset, sad, or irritated is:

____

____

IN-SESSION ACTIVITY

INFORMAL SENSORY STRESS INVENTORY: HOW FULL ARE YOUR CUPS?*

Age Range: Adolescents and adults

Objective: To help identify the client's sensory preferences and stimuli supporting or impeding their function

Directions: Obtain the necessary items listed here, and then use the provider script and provider instructions that follow to complete the activity.

Items Needed:

- 7–10 disposable cups
- Marker
- Water
- Food coloring (optional)
- 1 gallon-size pitcher (or alternative container)

Provider Script: Sometimes we must address the feelings and emotions hiding in our emotional brain to make sense of our reactions. Assume that this pitcher of water symbolizes you. We often have to spread ourselves to assist others, tolerate social environments, and simply navigate our day. Symbolically, we start with a full pitcher that depletes throughout the day. Yet we cannot allow ourselves to be completely depleted. There still needs to be something left for us. This activity will help you determine where your energy is focused and how much energy you use on a daily basis. Following the activity, we will make goals to address the areas that cause you stress and hyperarousal.

Provider Instructions for the Client: To start the activity, be sure you have a tabletop or flat surface available. Use a marker to draw three lines on each cup and write the words *okay*, *a lot*, or *too much* under each line.

*Adapted from *Self-Regulation and Mindfulness* (Gibbs, 2017b)

Next, ask the client to use the words *okay*, *a lot*, or *too much* to fill in the blank for each statement. You can also select your own questions and modify them as needed. Once the client answers each item, fill up a cup to the corresponding line for each response. Some cups may remain empty if the client does not identify that as an area of concern.

Thinking about your workplace (or school or home):

1. Describe the noise level: ___________________
2. Describe the lighting: ___________________
3. Describe the seating or chairs: ___________________
4. Describe the smells: ___________________
5. Describe your interaction time with others: ___________________
6. What do you like about the setting? ___________________
7. What do you dislike about the setting? ___________________

Discuss the results to identify ACTION goals that can address each area of concern. Are there any empty cups? Be sure to discuss those as well. Now that the client experienced the exercise, request for them to label additional cups. What other questions (daily experiences) do they think should have been included? Where would they fill those cups to?

At the end of the session, how much water remains in the pitcher? Are their cups too full, and is the pitcher too empty? How much energy do they expend throughout the day on sensory and social stressors? Can they make a connection with the underlying trauma and the triggers they experience in the environment? What are the signs that they may be triggered or reaching their threshold (tolerance level)? What objects or events in their environment can better support them?

PROVIDER WORKSHEET

ACTION SENSORY-SEEKING OR SENSORY-AVOIDING SCREENING

Age Range: All

Objective: To help identify the client's typical sensory preferences of seeking or avoiding behaviors to identify activities to support their needs

Directions: Use the checklist below to identify sensory preferences in the areas of vestibular, proprioception, tactile, gustatory, auditory, visual, olfactory, and thermoreception. You can interview the client or caregiver, or complete the checklist based off of observation across sessions.

Client Name: ______________________ Date of Birth: ____________

Date: ____________

	Notes (e.g., no specific preference)	Sensory-Seeking Preferences	Sensory-Avoiding Preferences
Movement, Touch, and Pressure		Intense physical activity, climbing, rough activities, deep pressure, various textures	Slow, calm, or predictable movements; grounded activities; gentle pressure; specific textures
Food		Intense, spicy, or sour flavors; crunchy textures	Mild or bland flavors, soft textures
Music		Intense, upbeat, or unpredictable sounds	Predictable, calm, or soothing sounds
Sight		Visual stimulation, such as video games or fast-paced movies	Dim light and calming visual stimulation
Smell		Intense, strong smells or unusual smells	Mild smells that do not result in noxious reactions
Temperature		Cold, intense, and alerting temperatures	Warm, comforting temperatures

Based on these findings, what activities would you recommend to support the client's needs?

CONTEXTUAL SENSORY INVESTIGATION

The human body receives multiple forms of sensory stimulation throughout the day. We must integrate these sensations in order to make sense of and use them. That is how we function and connect to the world. Therefore, along with identifying potential cues that can trigger an emotional response, assessment and intervention also require that you analyze the various contexts in the environment that can trigger or support the client. A contextual approach to examining the storage of traumatic memory must be as dynamic as the human nervous system itself. The environment must not solely be comfortable, but it must also support emotional safety. When possible, the therapeutic environment should consist of items that provide a home-like feel. It should be clean and devoid of clutter, and you should limit the use of smells and aromas, or use them conservatively. To support emotional safety, you also need to ensure the areas surrounding the therapeutic environment, such as parking lots, are well-lit.

Use the following Contextual Sensory Investigation Tool to consider the changes you can make (if feasible) to the various settings that the client frequents—including the home, school, private practice office, foster care and respite care settings, inpatient settings, and work environments—to promote safety and contextual sensory integration.

PROVIDER HANDOUT

ACTION CONTEXTUAL SENSORY INVESTIGATION

Scan the environment, starting with the floor and then moving to the perimeter, ceiling, and finally the space within the room. What does the client prefer? What do they need to perform at their optimal level? It may not be what you desire. They might require noise to focus and attend, or they might need visual stimulation or movement to have a prolonged conversation. What changes can you make in accordance with these preferences? Consider the following from their perspective by asking guiding questions or observing their reactions.

- Is the artificial lighting too bright? Can you use natural light or a floor lamp?
- Are there decorative items on the ceiling that may be a distraction or irritant?

- What electronics are in the space and in use?
- Are the screens producing high levels of blue light?
- What is the volume level in the space? Is it preferable?

- What decorations are on the walls? Are they visually distracting or stimulating?
- Does the room feel closed-in and lack ventilation?
- What other individuals are in the space? Do they provide support or distraction?

- Does the room feel comfortable?
- Does the positioning of the seats allow them to feel safe (e.g., facing the foor versus having their back to the door; sitting to see the location of others)?
- Are there a lot of objects of furniture?
- Does it feel too sterile?
- What smells are in the space?
- Are the smells comforting, or could they cause distress (e.g., perfume/cologne, natural odors, air fresheners)?

- What type of flooring is in the room?
- Does it produce an echo or loud noise when walking or moving chairs?
- When doing floor-based activities, does the flooring produce discomfort or irritation?

Although the previous handout can help you organize certain settings in a way that promotes contextual integration and emotional safety, this can be more difficult to accomplish when clients are living in unsafe and impoverished neighborhoods. It is certainly easy to assess the environment within a structured setting, such as a school, but some individuals unfortunately live in areas that are unsafe and lack resources to appropriately support health and well-being. The social determinants of living in such impoverished environments are clear, with trauma certainly topping the list of potential risks. The lived experiences are ongoing and persistent for individuals living in these environments. With that in mind, what can professionals do to support the impact of trauma as it continues? How does one find safety in the midst of a storm? The following are some suggested strategies you can apply and recommend:

- ☐ Do not make assumptions. Determine the client's or caregiver's perspective of their living environment. Trauma is a subjective experience.
- ☐ Children in unsafe neighborhoods are an at-risk group who most likely have indications of trauma. Therefore, make efforts to educate *everyone* who plays a role in the child's life, including parents, teachers, administrators, medical providers, extended family, and so on. Work with these individuals to address verbal and nonverbal strategies they can use to avoid triggers and support growth.
- ☐ Employ ongoing self-regulation strategies to prevent acute stress from turning into long-term trauma.
- ☐ Keep in mind that re-traumatization may occur when individuals receive disciplinary actions that remove them from secure settings (e.g., school or work). In addition, the use of physical restraints or other parental disciplinary actions (e.g., yelling, physical discipline, removal of activities supporting arousal) can result in re-traumatization for children.
- ☐ Address the home and school environments to identify safe spaces. For adults, it could be a room or large closet where they can feel protected and calm. Take care that the space the client selects is indeed safe and well-ventilated. For children, use large bins or boxes to create sensory bins filled with rice, beans, or balls. You can also offer a large beanbag chair that they can safely sit on, or you can cover a table with a large sheet of fabric to make a tent under which children can sit.

ACTION CREATING GROWTH TOOLS

There must be provisions to establish a safe and protective context and environment. Practitioners must work with clients and caregivers to set boundaries and expectations. Those with trauma should have a way to communicate their needs, to be able to cease activities that trigger them and cause them discomfort, and to feel in control to support resilience. The following are tools for creating growth. They target the clients and the caregivers of young children and older adults. Remember that clients, including very young and older populations, require that you work with their families or support systems. While clients are the focus, these tools may also be implemented with those providing care for your client.

PROVIDER WORKSHEET

ACTION GROWTH PLAN

Age Range: All

Objective: To develop an ACTION plan toward creating growth

Directions: Work with the client or caregiver to highlight areas of strength, support systems, opportunities, and needs. Interview the client using the questions from each of the sections below. Include ACTION goals that you can implement on the ACTION Growth Chart that follows.

What personal skills and abilities do you (or the person you are caring for) have? What external supports do you (or the person you are caring for) have? Actions to grow this area:	Who can assist (e.g., family, interdisciplinary team members, educators)? Actions to support growth in this area:
What do you (or the person you are caring for) desire when it comes to self-care (e.g., sleep, diet, emotion regulation, socialization, school, employment, spirituality)? Actions to grow this area:	Who can assist (e.g., family, interdisciplinary team members, educators)? Actions to support growth in this area:

ACTION step notes:

____

____

____

Date to be initiated: ____________________ Date to revisit: ____________________

CLIENT WORKSHEET

ACTION GROWTH CHART

Age Range: Children

Objective: To highlight gains and progress toward growth

Directions: Based on the child's Growth Plan, list their ACTION goals on this sheet or on another document. Reflect on the progress the child has made toward these goals in a given time frame, such as during one class or therapy session, daily, or monthly. Write in the action the child performed that moved them toward their goal in each gardening box, moving from left to right. Adults can complete this worksheet on behalf of the child, but the child should be involved as much as possible. For younger children, you also need to consider caregiver goals. Use this chart to check in whenever you see opportunities for growth throughout the day. This activity is not meant to focus on any negative events or failures. Highlight even small gains!

ACTION goals for growth:

1. ______________________________
2. ______________________________
3. ______________________________
4. ______________________________
5. ______________________________

First Action	Second Action	Third Action	Fourth Action	Fifth Action

CLIENT WORKSHEET

ACTION GROWTH CHART

Age Range: Adolescents and adults

Objective: To highlight gains and progress toward personal growth

Directions: Based on your Growth Plan, list your ACTION goals on this sheet or on another document. Reflect on the progress you have made toward these goals in a given time frame, such as daily, monthly, or bi-monthly. In each box, write in the action you performed that moved you toward your goal (moving from the bottom up), or simply place the ACTION goal number in the box. This activity is not meant to focus on any negative events or failures. Highlight even small gains!

ACTION goals for growth:

1. ____________________
2. ____________________
3. ____________________
4. ____________________
5. ____________________

Fifth Action
Fourth Action
Third Action
Second Action
First Action

CLIENT WORKSHEET

ACTION "I NEED" DAILY TOOL

Age Range: Children

Objective: To develop a method to communicate needs to support the child's progress toward growth

Directions: When children are working toward goals, you can use this tool to keep track of what tasks need to be done, what the child needs to support their growth, and what reward they can receive once the task is complete. In the "I need" box, place images of actual items that are known to support the child (e.g., a self-regulation and mindfulness break, food or water, sensory stimulation). In the "To do" box, place images of daily tasks the child needs to complete, such as eating, doing schoolwork, or sleeping. Lastly, in the "I want" box, place an image of an activity or item the child will earn once they complete each required task.

I need:	To do:	When I am done, I want:

CLIENT WORKSHEET

QUALITY OF LIFE ANALYSIS TOOL

Age Range: Adolescents and adults

Objective: To track daily or weekly areas to identify needs for balance for improved quality of life

Items Needed: Colored pencils, crayons, or different-colored ink pens

Directions: Developing weekly goals can assist you in improving your quality of life and increasing satisfaction toward life goals. This worksheet allows you to record your small gains as you work toward long-term goals. To start, develop long-term goals—one month, six months, or one year from now—in each of the areas listed in the following wheel. Write down your goals on the list provided. Then choose a color that symbolizes success and growth, and color in each section of the wheel to indicate if you believe you've achieved success or growth toward the goals you listed for each of those areas. Consider coloring in 50 percent for goals that are in progress. At the end of each day or week, try your best to take 10 minutes to reflect on your participation in the areas identified within the wheel. You can adjust those areas if desired.

Weekly Goals:

Work: ______________________________

____

____

Leisure: ______________________________

____

____

Rest and sleep: ______________________________

____

____

Physical, emotional, and mental health: ______________________________

____

____

Self-care: ______________________________

____

____

Caring for others: ______________________________

____

____

Social participation: ______________________________

____

____

CASE SCENARIO*

Review the following case study. After, we will demonstrate how we applied some of the ACTION approaches discussed in this chapter.

Name: Clare
Setting: Community-based
Age: 55

When Clare was born, her mother, Mary, had a challenging delivery. They questioned if Clare had cerebral palsy when she failed to meet her developmental milestones. Clare was 3 years old when she began to walk. She also displayed repeated behaviors, such as rocking and biting her lip and fingers. Her speech was loud, and she had challenges with receptive language. Once she began school, she had challenges both academically and socially. She presented with significant defensive reactions and aggression due to verbal attacks from her peers and continued discipline from her teachers. Some of the negative peer interactions resulted from her hyperactivity, which made them uncomfortable. However, she also faced racism, being one of the few students of color at her school. Mary found herself having to go to the school frequently throughout the week on Clare's behalf.

Luckily, Clare was able to get through her schooling and obtained a job after high school, though she had difficulty maintaining work and was often unemployed. In addition, she had challenges maintaining relationships—as her personality went from happy and cheerful to defensive and argumentative in a narrow window of time—and she had several romantic partners before finding her husband. While she loved being around her family and friends, she had a history of getting into physical altercations with her loved ones. She would also leave when confronted about her behaviors. Nonetheless, Mary and her other family members were very supportive of Clare.

Clare also reported having frequent back and joint pain, which impeded her ability to function on the job. As a result, she often visited the doctor for pain management intervention. Eventually, she had surgery on both her shoulders and wrists and was told it was due to repetitive stress on her joints. Despite everything, Clare became a mother to a son named Sam. Like Clare, Sam had difficulty at school and with his peers. The school frequently called Clare to attend meetings in which Mary accompanied her as the grandmother. Both Clare and Mary would sit for hours, appearing numb, listening to the team proposing plans for Sam, often suggesting disciplinary action, including removal from his current school. This even resulted in Sam being sent to an inpatient psychiatric program for children. Sam would later share stories about being placed in a quiet room and hating the inpatient program. The cycle seemed to continue.

After speaking with Clare and Mary, I learned more about their family history. Mary lived with a chronic illness and was frequently hospitalized while Clare was growing up. As a child, Clare found it challenging not knowing if her mother would survive and return home or not. For Mary, dealing with the burden of her illness, experiencing violent racism in her town, being a mother to Clare, and then caring for her grandkids as another parental figure started to weigh on her. She presented with "battle fatigue." Their reactions were that of going through the motions and just getting through each day.

The following pages contain a completed ACTION Growth Plan and Growth Chart for Clare, who we focused on for this analysis. As you review Clare's plan, take into account that Clare is attending occupational therapy and physical therapy services following one of her shoulder surgeries. She has consistently attended sessions but does display moments of frustration and aggression. Her symptoms of pain continue in other joint areas.

* Case study by Varleisha Gibbs, PhD, OTD, OTR/L

CASE SCENARIO: CLARE

ACTION GROWTH PLAN

Age Range: All

Objective: To develop an ACTION plan toward creating growth

Directions: Work with the client or caregiver to highlight areas of strength, support systems, opportunities, and needs. Include ACTION goals that you can implement on the ACTION Growth Chart that follows.

What personal skills and abilities do you (or the person you are caring for) have? *Enjoys socialization, self-advocates (i.e., voices her opinion when unhappy), respects health care providers* What external supports do you (or the person you are caring for) have? *Strong family support, close community, social services/school-based team for Sam* Actions to grow this area: *Address communication skills to increase socialization with family, friends, and social services/school team. Develop a Communications Needs Plan. Use language from the Communication Plan at least once daily.*	Who can assist (e.g., family, interdisciplinary team members, educators)? *Son's school social worker, Clare's family and friends* Actions to support growth in this area: *We must identify a case manager with employment services to also assist with other available resources. With Clare's permission, follow up with the referring medical provider to discuss plan of care and possible correlation of joint pain to stress, body mechanics, and fatigue.*
What do you (or the person you are caring for) desire when it comes to self-care (e.g., sleep, diet, emotion regulation, socializing, school, employment, spirituality)? *Clare desires decreased pain! She enjoys attending services at her church. But sometimes she is too tired to attend due to not sleeping secondary to her pain.* Actions to grow this area: *Use body mapping to investigate areas of tension. Utilize breathwork to decrease stress and anxiety. Address sleeping positioning to avoid muscle tension.*	Who can assist (e.g., family, interdisciplinary team members, educators)? *Mary and other family members can assist and may benefit from some of the activities. Physical therapy and counseling services are recommended to address areas of concern as expressed by Clare.* Actions to support growth in this area: *Complete sensory inventory and screening to determine sensory needs, and explore sensory-based activities in sessions to follow. Provide Clare referrals based off of her insurance coverage. Check in with her via telephone a few days after to see if she requires support to initiate the appointments.*

ACTION step notes: *Neuroeducation is an important next step for Clare. The occupational therapist (OT) will check in with Clare at least one time a week via phone between sessions and will follow up with case management. We will complete sensory screenings and inventories, including a contextual sensory investigation.*

CASE SCENARIO: CLARE

ACTION GROWTH CHART

Age Range: Adolescents and adults

Objective: To highlight gains and progress toward personal growth

Directions: Based on your Growth Plan, list ACTION goals on this sheet or on a supplementary document. Reflect on the progress you have made toward these goals in a given time frame, such as daily, monthly, or bi-monthly. In each box, write in the action you performed that moved you toward your goal (moving from the bottom up), or simply place the ACTION goal number in the box. This activity is not meant to focus on any negative occurrences or perceived failures. Highlight even small gains!

ACTION goals for growth:

1. *Use Communication Plan at least 1x daily ("I need" statements, "I feel" statements, and self-expression when upset).*
2. *Utilize breathwork and body mapping 1-2xs daily.*

Fifth Action
Fourth Action
Third Action
Second Action *Goal #2: Performed diaphragmatic breathing in the morning*
First Action *Goal #1: Expressed concern to teacher about how a comment made her feel regarding Sam's performance*

CHAPTER 3

TEACH NEUROEDUCATION

Cells make up our bodies. Our nervous system in particular consists of billions of cells called neurons. The neurons form neural pathways that connect the body to the brain and to other structures of the central nervous system. The neurons that fire together wire together, meaning that neurons that communicate frequently with one another develop stronger interconnections (Hebb, 1949). This process reflects the basic premise of neuroplasticity in that neurons can change and adapt themselves in response to our experiences. This process, however, occurs in a very organized manner that requires activation of a presynaptic neuron to then stimulate a postsynaptic neuron. The firing is not necessarily simultaneous but more sequential, and it results from the *repeated* stimulation of a presynaptic neuron on a postsynaptic neuron (Hebb, 1949).

Accordingly, our experiences shape our neurological makeup, and this process occurs despite how we define or perceive our experiences. Certainly, it would be great for our brains and nervous systems if we could grow and be shaped based only on the occurrences that support us and allow us to be most productive. Unfortunately, experiences that interfere with our quality of life can also shape who we are neurologically. When it comes to stress and trauma, experiences involving acute stress can transition into posttraumatic stress when the neurons associated with that experience grow or exhibit metabolic changes, resulting in structural alterations to the pathways between them.

In this chapter, we aim to review the neurophysiological changes resulting from exposure to stress and trauma and present strategies for neuroeducation through the following sections:

- ☐ Stress and Physical Health
- ☐ Anxiety versus Fear
- ☐ Memory
- ☐ Perceptual and Recognition Memory
- ☐ Fear Conditioning
- ☐ Bio Signs
- ☐ The Brain-Gut Connection to Trauma
- ☐ Trauma and Secondary Conditions
- ☐ Case Scenario

STRESS AND PHYSICAL HEALTH

If our emotions provide the bedrock for trauma, then we must examine them first. How do our experiences help shape the pathways connected to these emotions? And when there are alterations in such pathways, what structural changes occur in our brain? Let us start by examining our emotional brain center, known as the limbic system. The limbic system controls basic functions, such as our emotional reactions and affective experiences (like fear and pleasure), and is implicated in the formation of memories. To this end, it is vital for our emotional processes. The structures of the limbic system include the amygdala, hippocampus, hypothalamus, thalamus, mammillary bodies, cingulate gyrus, olfactory system, parahippocampal gyrus, orbital frontal cortex, nucleus accumbens, and fornix. It should be noted that the specific structures constituting the limbic system continue to be controversial, as experts are not in complete agreement.

The structures that form the limbic system are often considered more primitive parts of the brain that serve as a "watchdog" in ensuring our protection and survival. When things do not go as expected, the limbic system sends out an alert to our body that activates our autonomic nervous system. This alert is automatic and instantly activates our fight-or-flight response. For this reason, some people identify the limbic system as our "survival" brain. In contrast, our more "rational" brain consists of structures that make up the neocortex, which are newer in terms of our evolutionary development. The neocortex is more involved in logic and control, and it provides a foundation for our imagination and conscious thoughts. While the rational brain is crucial to our daily functioning, it requires time to process our experiences and is slow in comparison to the automatic inner workings of the limbic system.

So how does the limbic system work to serve as our "watchdog"? It does so by detecting threats and unexpected events. In the presence of such events, a neurochemical reaction occurs that results in the release of stress hormones into the body. The release of these stress hormones, in turn, leads to elevations in blood sugar levels and the storage of fat in areas of the body such as the abdomen. Epinephrine and norepinephrine trigger an adrenaline rush characterized by a burst of energy. This quick, yet systematic, reaction initiates when the amygdala acknowledges that there is a "threat" present. The amygdala communicates with the hypothalamus, resulting in the release of corticotropin-releasing hormone (CRH), which then initiates the release of adrenocorticotropic hormone (ATCH) by the pituitary gland. Ultimately, this process causes the adrenal glands, located at the top of the kidneys, to produce cortisol. The hypothalamic-pituitary-adrenal (HPA) axis assists in the eventual return to baseline. The specific chemicals and hormones released during the fight-or-flight response are as follows:

- ☐ **Catecholamines (epinephrine, norepinephrine):** Released by the adrenal glands, triggering the fight-or-flight reaction
- ☐ **Corticosteroids (glucocorticoids, cortisol):** Involved in the stress response and are also involved in controlling our energy, metabolism, inflammation, and immunity responses
- ☐ **Oxytocin:** Assists in a return to baseline by reducing cortisol levels and blood pressure (enhancing feelings of pleasure), which promotes the healing and recovery process but can inhibit the consolidation of memories
- ☐ **Opioids:** Dampen the effects of stressful or traumatic events by decreasing the pain response but can also compromise the consolidation of memories

Given the physical effects of stress on the body, there are several long-term implications of a prolonged or chronic stress response. First, given that stress results in elevations in cortisol (which is the hormone involved in maintaining and regulating metabolism), chronic stress and anxiety can interfere with metabolic functioning. Additionally, because the fight-or-flight process heightens one's senses—for example, sharpening one's visual, auditory, and tactile sensory systems—extended exposure to heightened levels of epinephrine may lead to hypersensitivity to sensory stimuli. Furthermore, norepinephrine causes narrowing of the blood vessels, in turn increasing blood pressure, which can affect physical health over time. These physical effects are further complicated by the fact that stress suppresses the immune system as a means of preserving energy, and it increases the body's inflammatory response (Pelt, 2011). For certain racial groups whose history is riddled with traumatic events, such as Black Americans, the physical effects of trauma are especially significant to consider.

The following is a list of secondary conditions that may occur following repeated and prolonged trauma that impacts a person's physical and mental health and well-being:

- ☐ Cardiac disease
- ☐ Hypertension
- ☐ Stroke
- ☐ Type 2 diabetes
- ☐ Ulcers
- ☐ Obesity
- ☐ Chronic fatigue syndrome
- ☐ Chronic pain
- ☐ Alcoholism and other forms of addiction
- ☐ Poor self-care
- ☐ Comorbid psychiatric conditions, such as depression and anxiety disorders

ANXIETY VERSUS FEAR

Those suffering from traumatic experiences often have high levels of fear and anxiety, and although these two emotional experiences are related, they are distinct. Fear is an emotional response that occurs in reaction to tangible events, objects, or experiences in our lives that pose some threat or danger. In contrast, anxiety arises in anticipation of some future perceived threat that is unknown or more diffuse in nature. This is not to say that anxiety is bad or shameful. In fact, anxiety can serve us by highlighting the things that are of importance to us. At the same time, it can also prevent us from accomplishing our desires when it paralyzes us from taking action.

Despite the differences between fear and anxiety, they both involve similar physiological changes associated with the stress response. Even the imagined dangers associated with anxiety become tangible through physiological changes in the body. After the perceived or real danger has passed, most people can return to emotional baseline. However, when there are challenges in recovery, this can lead to ASD and possibly even PTSD. To further explore the neurochemical reactions of trauma, we must start with the HPA axis.

During stress, the release of CRH triggers the pituitary gland to release stress hormones, which consequently activates the adrenal gland to release cortisol and then works in a feedback loop. In order to move out of acute stress, individuals must return to a state of homeostasis, which is achieved when cortisol exhibits a negative feedback effect on the pituitary gland, inhibiting further release of stress hormones. Although this occurs in normal conditions, it is more difficult for individuals with a history of trauma and chronic stress. In fact, cortisol levels are often ironically lower in those with PTSD (Yehuda et al., 2016), which may make them more susceptible to the long-term effects of trauma. Given that cortisol is a marker of stress, it may seem counterintuitive that PTSD would be associated with lower baseline levels of cortisol. However, the lower levels of this hormone may actually explain why these individuals struggle to find recovery. They do not have high enough levels of cortisol to contain the feedback loop triggered by the HPA axis, resulting in continued activation of the stress response.

When individuals are in this constant stress loop, they are unable to properly store, encode, and retrieve traumatic memories. It becomes unprocessed emotional chaos. In fact, the temporal lobe—which houses the amygdala and hippocampus, both of which are responsible for the formation of emotional memories—decreases in volume in response to trauma. When trauma and stress are prolonged, research reveals that these structural changes even extend to include decreased total brain volume as well (Hedges & Woon, 2010; Krugers, Lucassen, Karst, & Joëls, 2010; Schoenfeld, McCausland, Morris, Padmanaban, & Cameron, 2017; Shonkoff et al., 2012). Not surprisingly, these changes in neurological makeup and structural alterations can interfere with learning and academic performance.

In order to provide clients and caregivers, including educators, with education regarding the development of trauma and the neurochemistry of the stress response, you can review the following handout. This handout contains key points and facts that you can develop into a script or use as an informational factsheet to share. We also provide a subsequent handout for children that presents this information in a more simplified manner.

CLIENT HANDOUT (ADULTS)

LEARNING ABOUT TRAUMA

- ☐ There are many life challenges that can result in traumatic experiences. Trauma is not your fault!
  - For example, there is evidence that trauma can be passed between generations. What your parents and grandparents experienced could affect you now.
  - Sometimes, society and cultural differences can lead to trauma too. For example, witnessing racial attacks and violent riots are traumatic experiences for some individuals. Even within an organization or work environment, we can have traumatic experiences, such as workplace bullying.
- ☐ The more trauma someone is exposed to, the more likely they are to have complex trauma.
- ☐ When you experience traumatic and stressful events, it can cause physical dysfunction. These physical effects are real and not imagined! Some examples of the physical effects of trauma include:
  - Difficultly sleeping
  - Gut issues, such as diarrhea and constipation
  - Heart conditions and high blood pressure
  - Lung problems, such as respiratory infections
  - Neurological problems, such as numbness or pain
  - Issues with the kidneys and urinary system
  - Skin issues, such as rashes
  - Strokes
  - Type 2 diabetes and high blood sugar
  - Ulcers
  - Weight gain and obesity
  - Chronic fatigue syndrome
  - Chronic pain
  - Alcoholism
  - Poor self-care
- ☐ Trauma can affect your memory and your ability to regulate your emotions. You may find it difficult to control your anger or calm down after getting upset.
- ☐ Even though trauma is associated with many challenges, you came *before* the trauma. That means you have areas of strength that you can draw on to enhance beyond the trauma!

CLIENT HANDOUT (CHILDREN)

LEARNING ABOUT YOUR BRAIN

There is a part of our brain that is really smart and playful, kind of like a small dog.

Sometimes, things happen that make that part of our brain angry, mad, sad, or afraid. It has trouble listening, playing, or learning. We do not feel like ourselves. That little dog starts to get really loud and active.

That part of your brain tries to get happy and will run around, bark, or jump—whatever it takes to get happy! It loves feeling good!

Like having a small dog as a pet, you have control. Not only can you train that part of your brain to feel good, but *you* can feel good too! You have a leash and other training tools we will share.

MEMORY

When the body senses a threat and goes into survival mode, the brain structures involved in this process now switch modes and focus on protecting the individual. For example, the hippocampus virtually changes roles—from a storer of memory to a protector—as it seeks to determine similarities in prior experiences. It analyzes the sensory stimuli to determine if the present event aligns with stored emotions that once posed a threat. In doing so, it identifies whether there is a need to respond in a similar fashion to how it did with previous stressful or threatening experiences.

Similarly, when there is a perceived threat, the amygdala bypasses the cortical circuits involved in higher-order functioning, allowing it to react without awareness through a direct pathway triggered by stress, fear, or a novel event. As a result, there is frontal lobe degradation and shutdown in the presence of severe stress and fear, and cognitive flexibility is impaired. Once the amygdala receives the signal of possible impending danger, it communicates with the hippocampus, which typically works to encode memory into experiences in context and sequence. When the hippocampus cannot pull from past memories or recognize the present experience, memories are not stored long term.

In addition, the flood of stress hormones released into the body further prevent memories from being consolidated. In particular, excessive amounts of cortisol interfere with the storage of long-term memory while enhancing short-term emotional memories that involve more sensory details associated with the event rather than specific details. It is for this reason that trauma is often associated with fragmented sensory memories of the event as opposed to explicit memories that are verbal in nature. The painful and fearful aspects remain easily accessible as the brain attempts to make sense of the trauma. As the body releases opioids and oxytocin in an attempt to comfort and return the body to baseline, individuals are not afforded the opportunity to make sense of the traumatic details. Instead, they continue to revisit the event through flashbacks and nightmares. Meanwhile, crucial details remain blocked and hidden as the brain works to protect the person from further harm (Maren, 2014). Individuals may struggle to recall the details of the event or even feel pain.

When the brain cannot properly file these memories, they become "stuck" in the brain's limbic system. In turn, these memories remain active and can be easily triggered by external stimuli that we interpret through our senses. When these memories become triggered, the prefrontal cortex—which plays a major role in executive functioning and our ability to respond appropriately to our environment—starts to shut down and is unable to process what is happening fast enough. As the body is exposed to prolonged levels of stress hormones, the hippocampus decreases in volume and the amygdala increases in volume (Krugers et al., 2010) (Figure 9). The brain, body, and sensory systems become overwhelmed in the presence of prolonged stress.

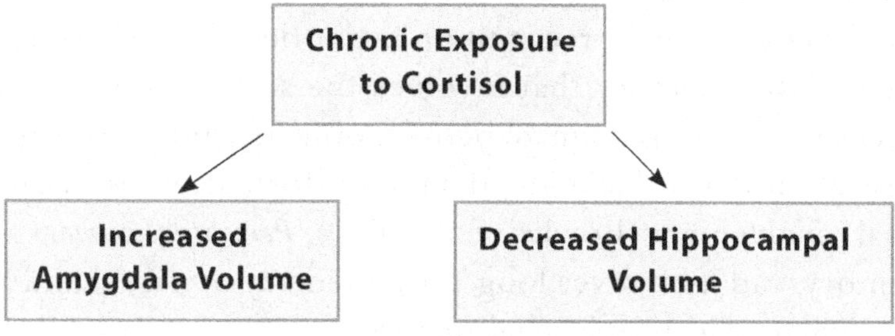

Figure 9. Changes in Amygdala and Hippocampal Volume as a Result of Increased and Chronic Exposure to High Levels of Cortisol

PERCEPTUAL AND RECOGNITION MEMORY

Trauma memories are not your typical memories. It is for this reason that we store trauma in a complicated sensorial way. *Engrams*, which are units of cognition within the brain, provide us with a more quantifiable view of memory storage. In particular, Ryan and colleagues (2015) postulate that engram cells are located throughout the cortex as opposed to existing simply within one area. More complex experiences require engrams in various locations to store these multifaceted sensorial occurrences. While there are specific areas of the brain correlated to very explicit forms of memory, most memories are stored in complex biophysical and biochemical means throughout the brain. Traumatic memories in particular are stored within various engrams in the sensory brain structures.

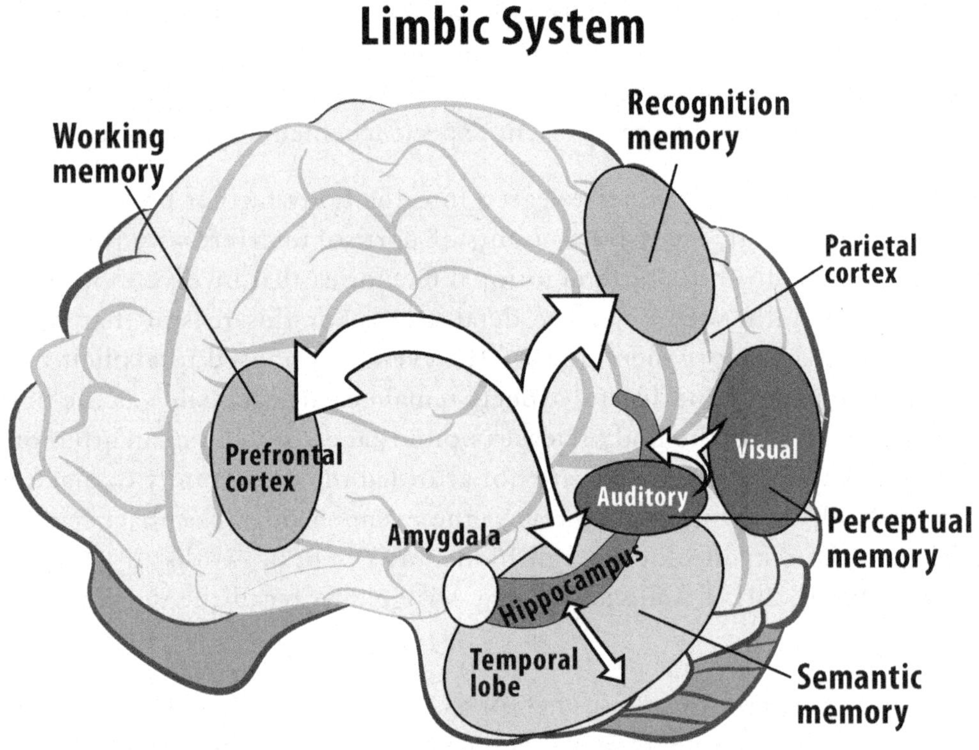

Figure 10. The Sensory Aspects of the Brain Are Involved in the Storage of Perceptual and Recognition Memories

The parietal, occipital, temporal, and insular lobes allow for the processing of sensations and present a connection to our body schema. These structures communicate with the unconscious brain to try to make sense of the incoming information. Fear conditioning has a strong connection with these cortical areas, which results in recognition memories and perceptual memories. *Recognition memory* is a form of declarative memory that involves the ability to match stored memories with similarities in experiences so we can recognize people, objects, and events as familiar. Recognition memory differs from recall in that it lacks the detailed information of recall memory, and it may not require hippocampal involvement (Bowles et al., 2010). *Perceptual memory* also lacks the detail of recall and semantic memory, and it involves long-term memory of visual and auditory information, such as memory of particular voices and facial features.

While the specific memory processes involved in traumatic experiences are controversial, this knowledge leads us to consider that recognition and perceptual memories supersede episodic and semantic memories. Given that trauma can also result in hyperactivity in the lateral and posterior parts of the brain, trauma can impact working memory as well, which is required for day-to-day tasks. With decreased activation of the anterior portions of the brain, individuals with a trauma history can be easily triggered by sensory stimuli and contextual factors—all the while lacking explicit details of traumatic events.

In the next section, we present a handout to help clients understand the role of memory in the trauma response and fear conditioning, followed by various tools and activities that are intended to improve memory and help clients navigate challenges they may be experiencing in completing daily tasks. We also provide visualization techniques and methods to structure the day.

CLIENT HANDOUT (ADULTS)

THE NEUROCHEMISTRY OF TRAUMA

- ☐ The parts of our brain that are in charge of memory, speaking, listening, and learning are the same parts of our brain that control our response to fear and stress. We call it the emotional brain.
- ☐ When we are afraid or stressed, our emotional brain triggers a release of chemicals in our body that prepares us to respond to the threat.
    - When the emotional brain responds to a perceived threat in this manner, it goes into protective mode. In this protective mode, the emotional brain is overly focused on our survival and does *not* do a good job when it comes to encoding specific details of the event into our memory.
- ☐ While we may remember a traumatic event right after it happens, the stress of the event can cause us to forget specific details over time.
    - Instead, we remember trauma through our senses—through specific sounds, sights, smells, textures, or places that remind us of the trauma.
    - When there is some sort of sensory input in our environment that reminds us of the trauma—like a certain sound or smell—our body reacts to the experience as if the trauma was still occurring.
    - These body reactions drive our emotional responses, like fear.
- ☐ But we can learn how to slow down and notice our sensory body responses, and in doing so, we can learn to respond to triggers instead of reacting to them.
- ☐ Although trauma can cause the brain to not develop as it should, our brains change and grow with each experience. That means we can make *new* experiences to allow growth.
- ☐ Then we come up with ways to make our bodies feel better, and our minds will start to grow!

IN-SESSION WORKSHEET

ACTIVITIES OF DAILY LIVING: MEMORY ACTIVITIES

Age Range: All

Objective: To improve working memory, assist in planning to prepare for necessary tasks, and decrease daily stress

Directions: Identify an activity of importance that may be causing the client challenges. For example, perhaps they are struggling to arrive to work on time or to maintain appointments, which is leading to additional dysfunction and stress. Discuss the needed steps to complete that particular activity, and write down each step in sequential order. As a follow-up activity, write the steps out of order and have your client place them in the correct sequence. Here is a sample memory activity for getting to their therapy appointments on time, followed by blank spaces for you to use with your client.

Sample Activity: Getting to Therapy Appointments on Time

- ☐ Locate house and/or car keys
- ☐ Dress yourself (and others you care for, such as children or older parents)
- ☐ Prepare food and eat (and feed others if applicable)
- ☐ Awaken at least one hour before departure time
- ☐ Comb hair
- ☐ Brush teeth
- ☐ Ensure you have proper transportation, including enough gasoline for the car
- ☐ Identify how much time is required for travel, taking into account traffic or wait time for public transportation
- ☐ Communicate with necessary parties—such as your partner, childcare providers, and home health aides—regarding your departure time
- ☐ Plan to leave the home at least 15 minutes earlier than required to reach your destination

Ask your client to use the space here to write out the steps they need to take to complete an activity.

☐ Step 1: ____________________

☐ Step 2: ____________________

☐ Step 3: ____________________

☐ Step 4: ____________________

☐ Step 5: ____________________

☐ Step 6: ____________________

☐ Step 7: ____________________

☐ Step 8: ____________________

☐ Step 9: ____________________

☐ Step 10: ____________________

IN-SESSION ACTIVITY

MEMORY STRATEGIES

Age Range: All

Objective: To improve overall memory, assist in participation in daily activities, and decrease daily stress

Directions: The following 10 activities can assist with enhancing memory. We provide specific examples for each activity, which you can expand upon and tailor to your client's specific intervention needs, or you can suggest self-directed activities for your client.

1. Memory Cards
2. Chunking (Categorization)
3. Rehearsal/Role-Play
4. Visualization
5. Mnemonics
6. Mindful Activities
7. Structure Everyday Routines
8. Association
9. Contextual Organization
10. Think Out Loud

Memory Cards

Place a row (or more) of playing cards on the table. Allow the client to study the cards for a few minutes, and then take the cards away. Wait a few minutes, and ask the client to replicate the card order from memory.

You can modify this activity with young children by asking the child to place two to three simple images in order of what comes next. For example, you can provide three images that demonstrate the steps involved in blowing bubbles and ask the client to order them sequentially. You can also play a memory game by hiding objects in the environment and asking the child to recall their location.

Chunking

In this activity, clients will enhance their ability for short-term recall by "chunking" related pieces of information together. Ask clients to study the shopping list in the left-hand column and to come up with four categories that describe the items listed. Then ask them to make another "chunked" list of the items within each appropriate category, as shown in the right-hand column here. Instruct clients to study the chunked list for three to five minutes. Remove the list, and ask them to recite the shopping list from memory as best they can.

List	Chunked List
Hamburger rolls Cereal Ice cream Potato chips Apples Grapes Rice Potatoes Soup Loaf of bread	**Bakery** Hamburger rolls Loaf of bread **Frozen Food** Ice cream **Produce** Apples Grapes Potatoes **Prepared Food** Cereal Potato chips Rice Soup

Rehearsal/Role-Play

Identify a daily activity that is an obstacle for your client, such as cooking dinner for the family or helping the children with their homework. For children, this activity could involve coming home from school and completing their required routine (e.g., homework, chores) before bedtime. Discuss the various steps needed to complete each task, and write them down as you both verbalize your thoughts. You can use the Activities of Daily Living worksheet to help you organize the activity into steps. Make sure to assist the client in identifying any missed steps. Once you are finished, review the steps and allow the client to determine if anything appears inaccurate or needs revisions. Next, invite the client to participate in a role-play activity where you pretend to act out each step of the activity. Prompt the client if they appear to miss a step. Be sure to take notes so you can reflect on areas of success and address any missed steps that you need to continue to work on.

Visualization

Similar to the Rehearsal/Role-Play activity, identify a daily activity that causes difficulty for your client. Have them write down the steps required for the task. Then ask the client to close their eyes if they are comfortable doing so, or they can simply sit quietly. Next, have the client visualize themselves performing each step that the activity requires. Ask them to verbalize each step. As they share the steps, take a moment to ask what they are feeling. At the end, inquire whether they were successful at fully completing the task. Lastly, ask them to reflect on their visualized performance and to identify any areas in which they think they require improvement.

Mnemonics

This activity provides a method for storing, encoding, and recalling information, experiences, or tasks (such as to-do lists). Make a list of concepts or tasks that the client needs to complete, like the example provided here. Take the first letter of each task to make a mnemonic, such as WARS:

Wash laundry

Answer emails

Request extension on paper

Study for exam

Mindful Activities

Mindfulness practices have been shown to increase the volume and density of the hippocampus, which is the area of the brain associated with memory. Therefore, one way to improve overall memory is to ask clients to incorporate mindfulness into their daily routine by having them focus their full attention on the task at hand. To start, ask clients to focus on monotasking (as opposed to multitasking) by selecting one activity to perform at a time. The activity should be slow and, if possible, rhythmic. The following are some examples of mindful activities that clients can try:

- ☐ Walk slowly with bare feet on a grassy lawn or sand, while focusing their attention on their surroundings and breathing
- ☐ Cook a meal and focus solely on the preparation
- ☐ Allot time to speak with someone, such as a friend, child, or parent, and listen to them without any distraction
- ☐ Eat a meal while chewing slowly, focusing on the taste, smell, and texture of each bite
- ☐ Breathe slowly while sitting or lying down in a relaxed position, and focus on their breath
- ☐ Sit and mindfully pet their pet
- ☐ Practice grounding activities (see chapter 2)

Structure Everyday Routines

One way to help clients remember the tasks they need to complete is to have them create a structured schedule of their daily routines and to set reminders for each task. Doing so can increase focus and attention, and it can also decrease stress. Compensatory strategies, such as writing down appointments and setting reminders, can alleviate anxiety related to disorganization and problems with running late or missing appointments.

Here are some examples of strategies:

- ☐ Use a journal to write down daily tasks that need to be completed, starting in the morning when stress hormones are low.
- ☐ Place sticky notes on the bathroom mirror with tasks to complete, remove them as the day goes on or at the end of the day, and replace the sticky notes for the next day.
- ☐ Use a visual schedule that contains pictures to depict the tasks within your routine.
- ☐ Utilize a smart phone or email system to set reminders and alerts.

Association

Associative memory is the ability to learn and remember the relationship between unrelated concepts or items, such as the name of a person we just met. To assist with memory storage and recall, clients can connect new information with already established information. For example, they can sing the components of new information to the rhythm of a song they know well. They can also perform associative memory tasks to recall the names of people, places, or objects. The following is a simple example to illustrate the use of a face-name associative memory task:

> *You want to remember the name of someone you just met. To do so, you associate their name with one of their features or with something they wore. For example, Julie had on beautiful jewelry. She reminds you of a childhood friend who had the same name.*

Contextual Organization

Clients can decrease stress and improve efficiency by having the environment set up and organized for each activity they need to complete. Help the client choose a specified location where they will perform each task, and then ask them to write down the commonly used materials they need to complete each task. Then assist them in identifying ways to keep these materials nearby. For example, if a parent needs to assist their child with homework, or a child needs to perform their own homework, they can have all the necessary items (e.g., pen, paper, highlighter, calculator) in a drawer near their desk or within specific containers. The containers can be inexpensive, such as shoeboxes. That way, they can avoid having to search for the items when they are needed.

Similarly, contextual organization can support successful completion of morning self-care tasks. For example, clients can identify what clothing they will wear the night before and place the needed items for the morning in convenient locations for quick access (e.g., hanging on the closet door). They can also utilize a similar method for other needed items for the morning (e.g., locating their keys and wallet and placing them on a tray). In the kitchen, they can continue using such organizational methods. For example, clients can consider putting items on the counter as visual reminders and plan meals ahead by meal prepping. In addition, they can place shopping lists, recipes, and reminders on corkboards or sticky notes on the wall nearby.

Think Out Loud

Research has found that we can improve memory and facilitate learning when we say words out loud to ourselves compared to saying them in our head (MacLeod, Gopie, Hourihan, Neary, & Ozubko, 2010). Therefore, the next time clients need to organize their thoughts and actions, have them consider the following questions, and ask them to answer each question out loud to determine the most appropriate course of action:

- ☐ What do I want to do?
- ☐ Who needs to be involved?
- ☐ What do I need to successfully complete this task?
- ☐ When does it need to be completed?
- ☐ How often does it need to be completed?
- ☐ Where do I need to be to complete the task?
- ☐ Why do I need to do this task?
- ☐ How can I improve at doing this task?
- ☐ How long will it take?

FEAR CONDITIONING

When examining how traumatic memories are stored, it is important to consider the role of classical conditioning. In classical conditioning, a previously neutral stimulus (conditioned stimulus) is paired with an unconditioned stimulus that naturally elicits a reflexive (or unconditioned) response (Pavlov, 1927). For example, in Pavlov's classic experiment with dogs, he repeatedly presented a bell (conditioned stimulus) and then provided the dogs with food (unconditioned stimulus), which naturally resulted in an increase in salivation (unconditioned response). After several repeated pairings, the dogs began to salivate in response the bell tone alone in the absence of any food presentation. This new response to the bell reflects a conditioned response. While most clinicians are very familiar with classical conditioning, we often fail to discuss the *defense reflex* that may also emerge.

The defense reflex (or defense response) is a protective reflex that occurs in the presence of an unexpected or threatening stimulus. It is accompanied by a sudden change in motor and neurophysiology that can trigger a defense cascade, which is five-step reaction that occurs on a continuum in response to perceived threats (Kozlowska, Walker, McLean, & Carrive, 2015). The first step in the cascade involves a state of high *arousal*, in which the body mobilizes for action in response to the identified trigger. This is subsequently followed by the *fight-or-flight response* as the body activates the resources necessary to deal with the threat head-on or escape from it. At the third step, the body may enter a state of *freeze*, which halts the fight-or-flight response while still allowing the body to remain on high alert.

If the threat is too overwhelming—and fighting or escaping is not possible—then the body shuts down and enters into a state of *tonic or collapsed immobility* as somewhat of a last resort for self-preservation. In this state, the person experiences paralysis in movement and speech, and loss of muscle tone may occur as well, resulting in collapsing and fainting. Once the threat has passed, individuals may enter into the fifth stage of the cascade—*quiescent immobility*—which is an adaptive reaction intended to allow the body to recover and heal from the trauma. Although quiescence is initially an adaptative response, it can become maladaptive if it continues to persist beyond the time needed for healing (Kozlowska et al., 2015). The end result could be chronic fatigue and pain syndromes.

The defense cascade can become conditioned when an individual's autonomic nervous system and sensorimotor responses become part of the individual's habitual response pattern (Figure 11). Their brain becomes wired to respond to sensory stimuli and contextual factors like it did at the time that the threat occurred (Kozlowska et al., 2015). The fear response becomes conditioned, and undesired memories regarding the trauma surface in the presence of similar sensory stimuli (Pavlov, 1927).

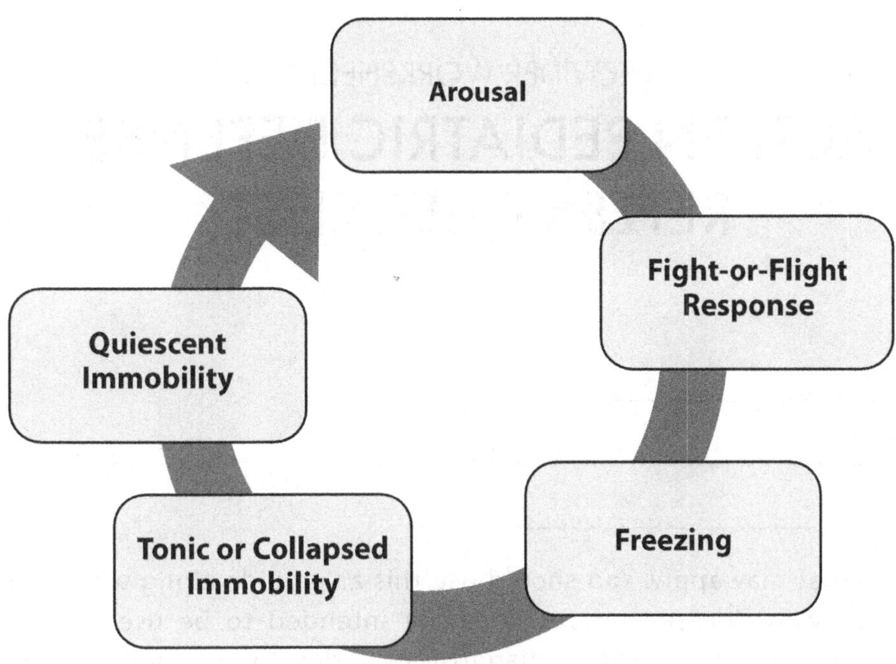

Figure 11. Fear Conditioning and the Defense Cascade

When fear conditioning occurs, individuals can present with *physical trauma* even in the absence of a true threat because they perceive the need to protect themselves. They may have a reduced reflex threshold secondary to pain and exhibit enhanced nociceptive reflexes (e.g., blinking, enhanced limb withdrawal reflex). They may also exhibit exaggerated startle responses, physical aggression, and elopement or escape behaviors. Children in particular may manifest these behaviors by scratching, biting, or rolling on the ground while kicking and screaming. They may also run away from home (Darwin, 1872/2009; Wallwork, Grabherr, O'Connell, Catley, & Moseley, 2017).

To assist in screening for defense reflexes, utilize the following defense checklists. The first checklist is intended for children and adolescents under 18 years of age, while the latter is for adults. When conducting these screenings, please note that the presence of defense reflexes does not necessarily indicate a correlation to trauma. Other factors may be the cause, such as other diagnoses, phobias, or recent physical injury or procedures.

PROVIDER WORKSHEET

ACTION PEDIATRIC DEFENSE REFLEX CHECKLIST

Client Name: ______________________________

Date of Birth: ______________________________

Date: ______________________________

Check all boxes that may apply. You should use this as a guide along with standardized assessment and evaluation procedures. It is not intended to be used in isolation of standardized instruments to determine diagnosis or to develop treatment plans.

Part 1:

☐ Complains about pain or discomfort, or displays hypersensitivity to:

- ☐ Smell
- ☐ Visual input (e.g., lights)
- ☐ Touch
- ☐ Sound
- ☐ Taste
- ☐ Gross motor movement
- ☐ Using the bathroom

☐ Such complaints or observations occur (circle): Sometimes / Occasionally / Often

☐ Notes: ____

Part 2:

☐ Presents with sensory-seeking behaviors through the following forms of input:

- ☐ Smell
- ☐ Vision
- ☐ Touch
- ☐ Sound
- ☐ Taste
- ☐ Gross motor movement

☐ Such behaviors occur (circle): Sometimes / Occasionally / Often

☐ Notes: ____

Part 3:

☐ Presents with nociceptive reflexes (eye blinking, trunk flexion, limb withdrawal reflex):

- ☐ Physical aggression, such as scratching and biting
- ☐ Eloping or escaping behaviors (e.g., sitting with head and hands covered)
- ☐ Pulling away
- ☐ Rolling on the ground while kicking and screaming
- ☐ Heightened startle responses
- ☐ Hyperarousal
- ☐ Rage

☐ Such behaviors occur (circle): Sometimes / Occasionally / Often

☐ Notes: ____

Summary and Key Findings:

____

____

____

____

____

____

PROVIDER WORKSHEET

ACTION ADULT DEFENSE REFLEX CHECKLIST

Client Name: ______________________________

Date of Birth: ______________________________

Date: ______________________________

Check all boxes that may apply. You should use this as a guide along with standardized assessment and evaluation procedures. It is not intended to be used in isolation of standardized instruments to determine diagnosis or to develop treatment plans.

Part 1:

- ☐ Complains about pain, or discomfort, or displays hypersensitivity to:
  - ☐ Smell
  - ☐ Visual input (e.g., lights)
  - ☐ Touch
  - ☐ Sound
  - ☐ Taste
  - ☐ Gross motor movement
  - ☐ Using the bathroom
- ☐ Such complaints or observations occur (circle): Sometimes / Occasionally / Often
- ☐ Notes: ____

Part 2:

- ☐ Presents with sensory-seeking behaviors through the following forms of input:
  - ☐ Smell
  - ☐ Vision
  - ☐ Touch
  - ☐ Sound
  - ☐ Taste
  - ☐ Gross motor movement

☐ Such behaviors occur (circle): Sometimes / Occasionally / Often

☐ Notes: ___

Part 3:

☐ Presents with nociceptive reflexes (eye blinking, trunk flexion, limb withdrawal reflex):

- ☐ Eloping or escaping behaviors (e.g., sitting with head and hands covered, ending session prematurely)
- ☐ Aggression
- ☐ Heightened startle responses
- ☐ Speaking loudly
- ☐ Hyperarousal
- ☐ Rage

☐ Such behaviors occur (circle): Sometimes / Occasionally / Often

☐ Notes: ___

Summary and Key Findings:

___

___

___

___

___

___

BIO SIGNS

Given that trauma is often stored in fragmented sensory memories that are easily triggered by external stimuli, it is important to teach clients how to tune into their body signals (or "bio signs") so they can recognize when they are becoming triggered. This involves learning to notice changes in heart rate, respiration, and skin appearance. When clients learn how to detect these changes in their body, they have the ability to perform self-regulation techniques to help them respond instead of reacting.

Before working with clients to develop awareness of their body signals, it is crucial that you acknowledge the client's tolerance for experiencing touch, remaining seated, and participating in tabletop activities. The client should have the tolerance to sit still or lie down for at least 15 to 30 seconds. They must also tolerate minimal touch for short intervals of time. Also make sure to identify effective methods of communication and signals that clients can use if they become uncomfortable.

In addition, obtain a baseline measure of the client's breathing and heart rate while they are sitting down. Avoid recording this information immediately following activities of high arousal. If possible, use a timer and heart rate device to gather the needed information. There are several inexpensive sports watches available that measure heart rate and pulse. If you are using a timer, obtain the pulse rate on the client's wrist or neck for a 60-second period (or for 30 seconds and multiply by two). To detect their respiratory rate, count the number of times the client's chest rises and falls during the same 60-second time frame. Obtaining a baseline measure of skin appearance and feel is more qualitative, but it is still an important biomarker. To do so, ask clients to turn their hands with their palms facing up. Gently stroke their palm to detect its temperature and moisture. Use descriptors to categorize its appearance and feel, such as cold, clammy, warm, hot, or sweaty (Gibbs, 2017b).

Once you have obtained these baseline measures, you should measure the client's physiological responses before and after selected activities, such as breathwork and sensorimotor work. This information may provide you with additional information regarding their reaction to certain techniques. You can use the following chart to monitor pre- and post-differences in heart rate, respiration, and skin temperature. Be sure to guide the client as you measure these recordings. If you are providing trauma-specific interventions, you can use this chart to record their physiological responses before and after discussions regarding their trauma history or when conducting exposure therapy. In the next section, we also provide several additional tools and activities clients can use to develop greater body awareness.

PROVIDER WORKSHEET

ACTION BIO SIGNS CHART

Client Name: ______________________________

Date of Birth: ______________________________

Directions: Use this chart to detect physiological responses to stimulation to the body. Monitor pre- and post-differences in the client's heart rate, respiration, and skin temperature following an activity or sensory stimulation.

Date	Pre-Breathing Rate (per 60 seconds)	Post-Breathing Rate (per 60 seconds)	Pre-Heart Rate (per 60 seconds)	Post-Heart Rate (per 60 seconds)	Pre-Skin Appearance and Feel	Post-Skin Appearance and Feel

IN-SESSION ACTIVITY

ACTION BIO SIGNS SELF-MONITORING

Age Range: Adolescents and adults

Objective: To develop greater body awareness

Directions: Use the following script to teach your client how to self-monitor bio signs.

Provider Script: Certain emotions can increase your arousal and cause you to feel overwhelmed or out of control. It is similar to having the volume on the radio turned all the way up. When the radio is too loud, you cannot focus on anything else because the sound is too distracting. In contrast, when you feel tired or sluggish, it is like having the volume on the radio turned down, perhaps playing some light, soft, and slow music. If the volume on the radio is too low, though, you will not be able to hear it. For most of our activities, we need our volume to be somewhere in the middle.

In this activity, we will practice detecting your body's volume so you can gain greater body awareness. Begin by describing the temperature of your hands. Are they dry, clammy, or sweaty? Next, place one hand on your heart and the other on your belly. As you breathe in and out, describe your breathing and heart rate. Would you describe it as fast (loud), slow (quiet), or in the middle? Now take a deep breath, and see how your heart rate and breathing rate change. Does your skin temperature change? What happens to your body responses when you think about something that makes you angry or frustrated?

After you complete this activity, try to begin using language to describe your body sensations—such as "It feels too loud" or "I feel really quiet"—and see if you can get yourself somewhere in the middle where you desire.

CLIENT ACTIVITY

THE SELF-REGULATION AND MINDFULNESS (SAM) BOX*

Age Range: Children

Objective: To provide a tool for children to acknowledge their arousal levels—low (quiet), just right (middle), or high (loud)—and how it supports or impedes daily function

Items Needed:

- A small cardboard box, shoebox, or tissue box (or a pencil case with a zipper)
- Glue
- Brass brad or pushpin
- Paint (optional)
- Construction paper or cardstock (or any other durable material that can be cut into an arrow shape and attached to the box)
- "Feelings" images, such as printed pictures of different facial expressions or emojis
- Markers or crayons

Directions: (Adult to assist as needed)

If using a cardboard box:

1. Take the box and decorate it with construction paper or paint.
2. Draw a circle on the top center of the box to make the "volume gauge."
3. Draw an upside-down "Y" in the circle to divide it into three even sections.
4. Starting at the bottom section and going clockwise, color and label each section: Quiet, Middle, and Loud. Use different colors for each section.
5. Cut an arrow out of construction paper or cardstock.
6. Poke a hole in the top center of the box, and use the brad or pushpin to adhere the arrow to the box.

---

* Adapted from *Self-Regulation and Mindfulness* (Gibbs, 2017b)

7. Cut out images that represent different feeling states reflecting quiet, middle, and loud levels of arousal. You can also use emoji symbols, draw your own images, or use photos of the child. Place these images around the dial near the corresponding arousal level (quiet, middle, or loud).
8. Identify sensory items that can help the child self-regulate when their arousal is loud or quiet, such as fidgets, a device that plays music, coloring pages, mandalas, exercise cards, pinwheels, and bubbles.
9. Use the inside of the SAM box to store these preferred sensory items. The goal is for children to be in the middle level during functional activities.

If using a pencil case with a zipper closure:

1. Take a small, round piece of cardstock or other durable material and poke a hole in the center.
2. Follow previous steps 3 and 4 to make a volume gauge small enough to fit on a keychain ring.
3. Push a mini metal paper fastener through the center and bend it to serve as the "arrow."
4. Take a keychain ring, place it through the gauge on the zipper, and adhere it to the pencil case attaching the cardstock.
5. Store preferred sensory items inside the pencil case, as indicated in the previous section.

IN-SESSION ACTIVITY

BODY SCANNING FOR TRIGGERS AND REPETITIVE MOVEMENTS

Age Range: All

Objective: To help identify clients' triggers and physical trauma presentations

Directions: Trauma sometimes leads to repetitive movements and sensorimotor dysfunction. Our bodies take over, and we go into autopilot. In this activity, the practitioner and the client (depending on developmental level) will scan the body for evidence of these movements.

Part 1: Practitioner Observation

Ask the client to have a seat. Take note of any repetitive movements that the client makes, such as eye twitching, squinting, writhing movements of the hand, mouth movements, rocking, or tapping. Observe their posture, looking for slouching and flexed positions. Do they present with self-soothing behaviors?

Part 2: Adolescent and Adult Self-Observation

Provider Script: To start, acknowledge any repetitive movements you may be making, such as eye twitching, squinting, hand writhing, mouth movements, rocking, or tapping.

Sit in a calm, relaxed position as you continue analyzing your body. As you tune into your body, focus on your breathing and heart rate. Try to take slow, deep breaths. Now widen the focus of your attention to your whole body, and detect any tension, pain, coldness, numbness, or warmth. Starting from your feet, work your way to the top of your head. Suggested body regions to focus on are:

- ☐ Feet and ankles
- ☐ Legs and knees
- ☐ Pelvis and middle section (belly region)
- ☐ Back and chest (heart)
- ☐ Arms, wrists, and hands
- ☐ Shoulders and neck
- ☐ Face, top of the head, and back of the head

(Note to provider: Document and discuss the findings. Address areas of concern with stretching, exercise, and sensory-based interventions.)

IN-SESSION ACTIVITY

MY BODY*

Age Range: Children

Objective: To teach children about their body, sensory system, and connection to the brain

Items Needed:

- Paper
- Crayons, pencils, or paint
- Provided body template

Directions: Review the song *Head, Shoulders, Knees, and Toes*. Talk about the role that each of these parts plays for our bodies. For example, share how all of our parts are important and strong. Talk about how we do not use just one part at a time. You can provide examples, such as needing our eyes to look when listening with our ears. Next, have the child draw a self-portrait using the image on the provided printout. This can include their facial features, ears, hair, preferred clothing and footwear, and any other components they wish to include.

Once the child is done with their self-portrait, have them share and explain their picture. See what is missing, and help them fill in those items. Then talk about our inside parts, such as the heart (feel the heartbeat), lungs (take slow breaths), and stomach (discuss a full and empty tummy). Ask them to show you where those parts are by pointing to the various locations on their portrait.

Optional:

1. Discuss how our inside parts can become loud (fast heartbeat and quick breathing) or very quiet (slow heartbeat and slow breathing), causing us to feel energized or tired.
2. Have the child perform loud activities, such as running in place, followed by quiet activities, such as closing their eyes and sitting still.
3. Review that sometimes we need to be "in the middle" between loud and quiet, such as when we are at school or going to public places.

---

* Adapted from *Self-Regulation and Mindfulness* (Gibbs, 2017b)

MY BODY TEMPLATE

THE BRAIN-GUT CONNECTION TO TRAUMA

Just as disorders of trauma are complex, so is the human body. Our systems do not function in isolation but are interconnected. The vagus nerve in particular provides a bidirectional connection between the brain and the gut (Figure 12). It contains both parasympathetic and sympathetic nervous system fibers that impact gut digestion, inflammation, and nutrient absorption. Even more, the enteric nervous system allows the digestive system to have an independent, yet connected, nervous system. We actually have 100 million neurons in our gut wall. So our guts are somewhat of a second brain!

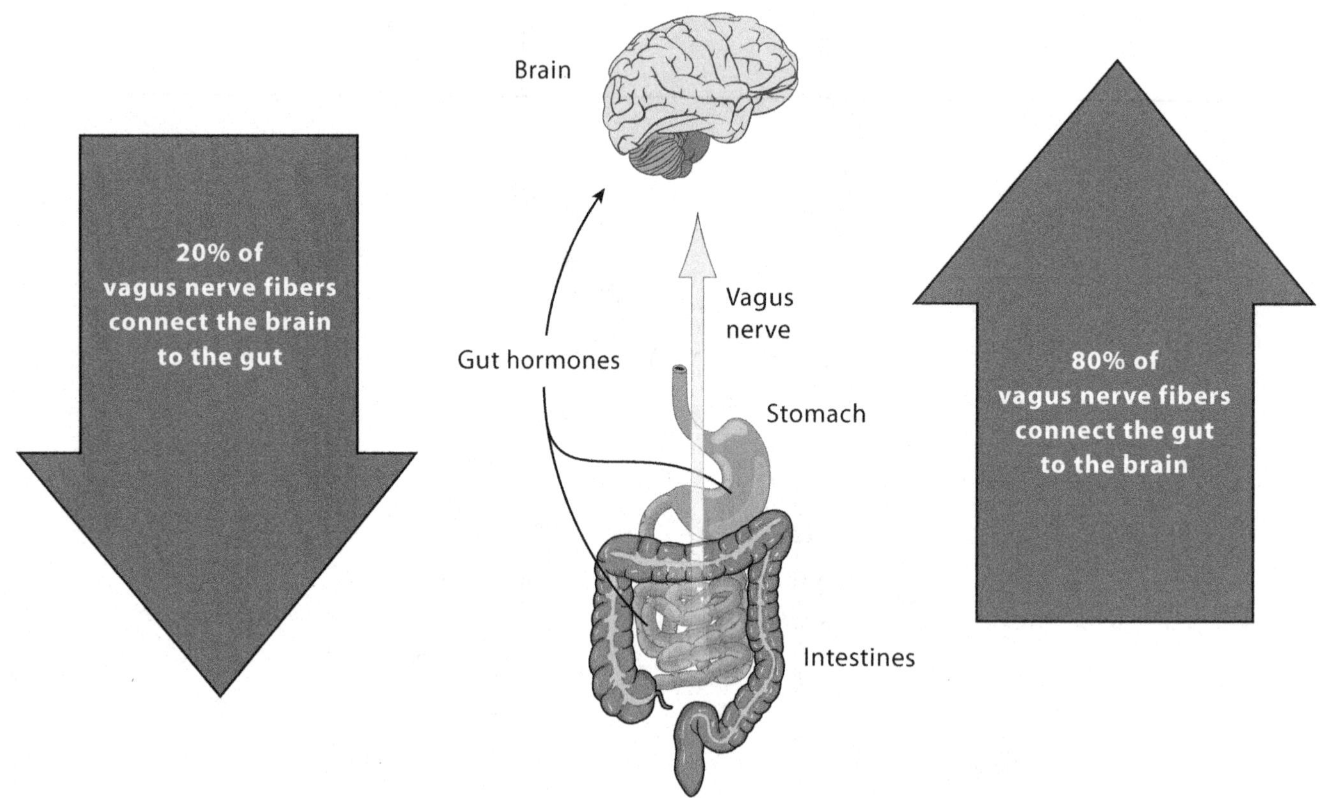

Figure 12. The Vagus Nerve Plays a Major Role in the Brain-Gut Connection

In the gut, endocrine cells produce the same molecular serotonin that the brain makes, which is the neurotransmitter that provides us with a sense of well-being. In fact, the gut produces approximately 90–95 percent of the body's serotonin and 50 percent of its dopamine (Carpenter, 2012). Therefore, neurotransmitters in the gut can affect mood and behavior. Too much or too little can have adverse effects on emotional well-being, as well as physical digestion. Research theorizes that the impact of gut function directly correlates with other diagnoses, such as anxiety and depression (Carpenter, 2012).

While neurotransmitters serve a vital role in well-being, gut bacteria (or microbes) are crucial players as well. There are 100 trillion microbes in the gut (Carpenter, 2012), and these gut bacteria play a role in the production of the neurotransmitters that influence several important functions, such as memory, emotions, and learning. Importantly, infection, illness, or even hunger and malnutrition can impact the work of these microbes, which in turn affects brain functioning (Kane, Dinh, & Ward, 2015).

Stress can also have a significant effect on the brain-gut connection. In the presence of stress, beneficial gut bacteria levels decrease, which results in increased inflammation and lower production of necessary neurotransmitters. As it directly relates to trauma, research has revealed a connection between early life adversity and alterations in gut microbes (Callaghan et al., 2020), and differences in gut microbes have been found among individuals with PTSD (Hemmings et al., 2017). As a result, some research has suggested that the intake of probiotics, as well as other methods to modulate gut bacteria, may positively impact mood disturbances and gastrointestinal dysfunction (Yang, Wei, Ju, & Chen, 2019). Additionally, research has found that early exposure to gut bacteria during crucial developmental periods in childhood can impact both physical and neuropsychiatric development (Zhuang et al., 2019).

TRAUMA AND SECONDARY CONDITIONS

When individuals are frequently triggered or exposed to chronic stress, their body is in a state of prolonged sympathetic nervous system activation, which can result in increased blood flow to the extremities and tension in the muscles. As a result, individuals with PTSD may present with physical trauma in the form of joint and muscle pain (Fishbain, Pulikal, Lewis, & Gao, 2017). The constant anxiety and fear they experience can lead to chronic and persistent body tension and pain. Even during rest, some individuals may find themselves in a protective position, such as a fetal pose, which results in pain upon awakening. Furthermore, trauma affects the production of certain hormones in the body, such as prolactin, which is a protein hormone correlated with pain sensitivity, hypothalamic modulation, immune modulation, and regulation of mood. In PTSD, prolactin levels may increase, which results in increased pain sensitivity (Fishbain et al., 2017; Oliveira et al., 2020).

The experience of significant stress or trauma can also result in sudden seizures, syncope (i.e., fainting episodes), and vision loss. In her own experience, Dr. Gibbs has witnessed clients, as well as those in her personal life, suddenly experience a significant change in their health following trauma. She has had several clients experience unexplained dizzy spells, witnessed the sudden onset of seizures, and had a family member suddenly lose sight. In all of those cases, the individuals recovered. Why did these physical symptoms occur? According to the defense cascade model, these individuals experienced a state of collapsed mobility, which then led into prolonged quiescent immobility and eventually resulted in physical immobility.

When these secondary trauma reactions occur, clients usually undergo a full medical process to investigate the root cause of their symptoms. After ruling out cardiopulmonary and neurological conditions, medical professionals may suggest a psychological explanation behind their symptoms. This can make clients feel like doctors are dismissing their lived experiences. In addition, labeling these symptoms under the umbrella of a "psychological condition" can result in feelings of shame for clients due to the stigma often associated with mental disorders.

We must do a better job of connecting the medical and psychological worlds through biopsychosocial approaches. The defense cascade reveals the possible source of these physiological conditions. For example, individuals with a history of trauma often continue to experience heightened anxiety in response to environmental triggers, resulting in the same neurochemical reactions that occurred at the time of the trauma. In the case of seizures, the structures that govern the fight-or-flight response are located within the same lobe where some seizures originate, which explains the connection between stress and epilepsy. Lack of sleep and diet may also contribute to physical stress.

When it comes to vision, stress can result in distorted and blurry vision because adrenaline puts pressure on the eyes. In addition, the intense contraction of the eye muscles can result in twitching called lid myokymia. Over the long term, these physical stressors can deteriorate the nerves required for vision (Sabel et al., 2018). There is also a connection between cortisol and vision disorders, such as diabetic retinopathy, glaucoma, optic neuropathy, and macular degeneration.

That being said, these connections between mental and physical health are speculative in nature, as the direct connection is unclear. What *is* clear is the correlation with trauma and stress. The impact of trauma has emotional, cognitive, psychological, social, and physiological implications. Therefore, we must take care to address all these various areas. If you are a provider who does not perform specific trauma-related care, or if you feel like these roles should be left for medical doctors or psychiatrists, you must consider altering your view. Every interaction with the client matters and can be impactful toward healing.

PHYSICAL AND SENSORY APPROACHES

In this section, we introduce a variety of activities that you can use with clients to decrease stress and pain within the body. In particular, these activities aim to address the connection of trauma to physical symptoms and provide relief to the body.

CLIENT ACTIVITY

STRETCH AND RELEASE

Age Range: Adolescents and adults

Objective: To decrease stress and pain within the body

Directions: This activity provides a range of different stretches that you can use to decrease stress and pain within your body. Complete these stretches when you experience stress and whenever you need to take a movement break throughout the day. To help address pain and tension that may occur from sleeping in the fetal position, try to sleep with a pillow between your legs and arms, and avoid propping up your head too high. You can also perform these stretches prior to bed.

Note: Be aware of any pain or injuries you may have. Do not perform any exercises that do not feel safe or that are contraindicated by your doctor.

Pillow Stretch

Lie on your back. Place a pillow or towel under your lower back and place your hands overhead while holding the stretch for a couple of minutes.

Towel Stretch

Take a towel and place it around your neck. Gently pull the towel forward as you push your head back for a resistive stretch.

Chair Stretch

Position a chair in front of you. Sit on the floor. Lie on your back and place your feet on the seat of chair. Use a pillow or rolled towel under your neck. Hold the stretch for a few minutes.

IN-SESSION ACTIVITY

PROGRESSIVE MUSCLE RELAXATION

Age Range: Children

Objective: To decrease stress and pain within the body

Directions: In this exercise, clients will practice tensing and relaxing various parts of their body as they work from their head down to their feet. To start, have the child get into a comfortable position, such as lying down, and place a soft stuffed toy on their belly. Ask them to take slow, deep breaths—as if they were going to smell a cupcake with a candle on top. Then have them "blow out" the candle. Do this a couple of times. Then use the following script to guide clients through the exercise, or have them complete the steps on their own.

Note: Use precautions for any injuries. Do not perform if contraindicated.

Provider Script:

- In this exercise, you will focus on squeezing and relaxing different muscles throughout your body. You will squeeze each muscle group for a couple of seconds, and then relax that muscle group. You will take a deep breath before moving to the next body part. I will tell you what you need to do at each step.
- We will start by squeezing the muscles of our face and holding these muscles tightly. Then we will let go, allowing them to relax. To start, raise your eyebrows like you are surprised. Hold them there. A bit longer. Now release. Breathe in through your nose, and slowly blow the air out of your mouth.
- Now squeeze all your face muscles like something smells really stinky and looks yucky. Squint your eyes closed and wrinkle your nose. Hold it there. A bit longer. Now release. Breathe in through your nose, and slowly blow the air out of your mouth.
- Okay, now make a really big smile, keeping your teeth together. Hold it there. A bit longer. Now release. Breathe in through your nose, and slowly blow the air out of your mouth.
- Let's stretch the muscles of your mouth. Open your mouth really wide. Hold it there. A bit longer. Now release. Breathe in through your nose, and slowly blow the air out of your mouth.
- Now pucker your lips. Hold them there. A bit longer. Now release. Breathe in through your nose, and slowly blow the air out of your mouth.

- We will now move to the muscles in your neck. Look up to the ceiling. Hold it there. A bit longer. Now release. Breathe in through your nose, and slowly blow the air out of your mouth.
- Bring your chin to your chest. Hold it there. A bit longer. Now release. Breathe in through your nose, and slowly blow the air out of your mouth.
- We will now release the muscles of your shoulders. Bring up your shoulders as if to say, "I don't know." Hold them there. A bit longer. Now release. Breathe in through your nose, and slowly blow the air out of your mouth.
- Now for your arms. Make a big muscle and flex your arms. Hold it there. A bit longer. Now release. Breathe in through your nose, and slowly blow the air out of your mouth.
- Let's focus on your hands. Make a fist with each hand. Hold it there. A bit longer. Now release. Breathe in through your nose, and slowly blow the air out of your mouth.
- Now put your hands flat and push down on your lap. Hold it there. A bit longer. Now release. Breathe in through your nose, and slowly blow the air out of your mouth.
- Next, we are going to focus on your belly muscles. Squeeze in your belly muscles by pulling in your belly button toward your spine. Hold it there. A bit longer. Now release. Breathe in through your nose, and slowly blow the air out of your mouth.
- Let's move to your legs. Lift your legs slightly off of the floor (or flex at the hip to raise your leg if you are sitting). Hold them there. A bit longer. Now release. Breathe in through your nose, and slowly blow the air out of your mouth.
- Now your feet. Point your toes up toward the ceiling. Hold it there. A bit longer. Now release. Breathe in through your nose, and slowly blow the air out of your mouth.
- Next, curl your toes under the soles of your feet. Hold it there. A bit longer. Now release. Breathe in through your nose, and slowly blow the air out of your mouth.
- Finally, let's make all of our muscles tense. Hold it. A bit longer. Now release. Breathe in through your nose, and slowly blow the air out of your mouth.

IN-SESSION ACTIVITY

PROGRESSIVE MUSCLE RELAXATION

Age Range: Adolescents and adults

Objective: To decrease stress and pain within the body

Directions: In this exercise, clients will practice tensing and relaxing various parts of their body as they work from their head down to their feet. You can use the following script to guide clients through the exercise or have them complete the steps on their own.

Note: Use precautions for any injuries. Do not perform if contraindicated.

Provider Script:

1. Choose a comfortable position, such as lying down.
2. Begin to ground yourself by taking in slow, deep breaths—in through the nose and out through the mouth.
3. In this exercise, you will focus on tensing and relaxing different muscle group throughout your body. You will tense each muscle group for a couple of seconds, then relax that muscle group. We will incorporate a slow, deep breath before moving to the next body part. I will guide you through each step.
    - We will start by focusing on the muscles of our face. Let's begin by raising your eyebrows. Hold them there. A bit longer. Now release. Breathe in through your nose, and slowly blow the air out of your mouth.
    - Now tightly squint your eyes closed and wrinkle your nose. Hold it there. A bit longer. Now release. Breathe in through your nose, and slowly blow the air out of your mouth.
    - Let's continue. Raise your cheeks by smiling and clenching your teeth. Hold them there. A bit longer. Now release. Breathe in through your nose, and slowly blow the air out of your mouth.
    - We will now move to the muscles of your mouth. Open your mouth wide. Hold it there. A bit longer. Now release. Breathe in through your nose, and slowly blow the air out of your mouth.
    - Now pucker your lips. Hold them there. A bit longer. Now release. Breathe in through your nose, and slowly blow the air out of your mouth.

- Moving to the muscles of your neck, tilt your head back, arching your back while lying on your back. Hold it there. A bit longer. Now release. Breathe in through your nose, and slowly blow the air out of your mouth.
- Now tuck your chin toward your chest. Hold it there. A bit longer. Now release. Breathe in through your nose, and slowly blow the air out of your mouth.
- Moving to your shoulder muscles, shrug your shoulders toward your ears. Hold them there. A bit longer. Now release. Breathe in through your nose, and slowly blow the air out of your mouth.
- Now for your arms. Flex your biceps by moving your forearms toward your upper arms. Hold them there. A bit longer. Now release. Breathe in through your nose, and slowly blow the air out of your mouth.
- Now make a fist with each hand. Hold it there. A bit longer. Now release. Breathe in through your nose, and slowly blow the air out of your mouth.
- Place your hands flat on the floor or your lap, and gently push down while applying pressure. Hold it there. A bit longer. Now release. Breathe in through your nose, and slowly blow the air out of your mouth.
- Moving to your abdomen muscles, squeeze in your belly muscles by pulling your belly button toward your spine. Hold it there. A bit longer. Now release. Breathe in through your nose, and slowly blow the air out of your mouth.
- Let's move to your lower body. Lift your legs slightly off of the floor (or flex at the hip to raise your leg if you are sitting). Hold them there. A bit longer. Now release. Breathe in through your nose, and slowly blow the air out of your mouth.
- Now point your toes up toward the ceiling. Hold them there. A bit longer. Now release. Breathe in through your nose, and slowly blow the air out of your mouth.
- Push the heels of your feet against the floor. Hold it there. A bit longer. Now release. Breathe in through your nose, and slowly blow the air out of your mouth.
- Next, curl your toes under the soles of your feet. Hold them there. A bit longer. Now release. Breathe in through your nose, and slowly blow the air out of your mouth.
- Finally, let's make all of our muscles tense. Hold it. A bit longer. Now release. Breathe in through your nose, and slowly blow the air out of your mouth.

IN-SESSION ACTIVITY

ILIOPSOAS STRETCHES

Age Range: All

Objective: To decrease stress and anxiety, reduce sympathetic nervous system activity, and address secondary symptoms of trauma related to anxiety and stress

Directions: The iliopsoas muscle, which comprises the iliacus and psoas, has a connection to the diaphragm. The psoas muscle is known as the "fight-or-flight muscle" because it is triggered when the sympathetic nervous system activates this defensive response. However, when someone is in a prolonged fight-or-flight state—due to significant stress or prolonged anxiety related to trauma—the iliopsoas muscle can become tight, resulting in flexed posture and abdominal extension. Stretching this muscle group can greatly calm the sympathetic nervous system and decrease secondary symptoms of stress. This activity provides a variety of iliopsoas stretches that clients can perform to release any tension from this muscle group. Use the following script while demonstrating these stretches to the client.

Note: Be aware of necessary precautions secondary to any physical injuries or conditions.

Provider Script:

Lunges

- ☐ Get into a half-kneeling position with one knee forward and one knee on the floor.
- ☐ Ensure that the forward knee does not move over the toes.
- ☐ Gently press your front hip forward to stretch the hip and pelvic area.
- ☐ Hold 30–60 seconds and repeat with the opposite leg forward.

Squat

- ☐ While standing on a flat surface, separate your feet so they are slightly greater than hip-width part.
- ☐ Turn your heels toward each other so your toes are facing outward at 11 o'clock and 1 o'clock.
- ☐ Safely bend your knees and squat toward the floor slowly, keeping your knees in alignment with your toes.

- ☐ Use a chair or wall to stabilize yourself as needed.
- ☐ Hold the squat for 30–60 seconds or as tolerated, then return to a standing position.

Bridges

- ☐ Lie on the floor or a flat surface with your back in a supine position.
- ☐ Place your arms down by your side.
- ☐ Bend your knees and place your feet firmly on the floor.
- ☐ Lift your hips up toward the ceiling and hold for 30–60 seconds.

Supine Hip

- ☐ Lie on the floor or a flat surface with your back in a supine position.
- ☐ Stretch your legs out in front of you.
- ☐ Bend one knee, pulling it toward your body with your arms, and hug it to your chest.
- ☐ Maintain the other leg firmly on the flat surface.
- ☐ Hold for 30–60 seconds and repeat on the other leg.

IN-SESSION ACTIVITY

FACIAL AND EAR MASSAGE

Age Range: All

Objective: To decrease stress and anxiety, reduce sympathetic nervous system activity, and address secondary symptoms of trauma related to anxiety and stress

Directions: We know that certain input, such as massage to the face and acupressure points, can decrease stress and the sympathetic nervous system response (Lee, Park, & Kim, 2011). In addition, the external ear has connections to the vagus nerve, which allow access to the parasympathetic nervous system and can promote rest and digestion. The following activity provides specific directions for facial and ear massage. Although this activity is intended for all age ranges, young children may require imposed input.

Instruct the client to use two to three fingers to massage each of the areas illustrated here (or choose the specific areas you desire). Have them gently apply pressure and move their fingers in a circular fashion for at least five seconds in each location. This massage can be used daily to prevent stress responses and increase self-regulation.

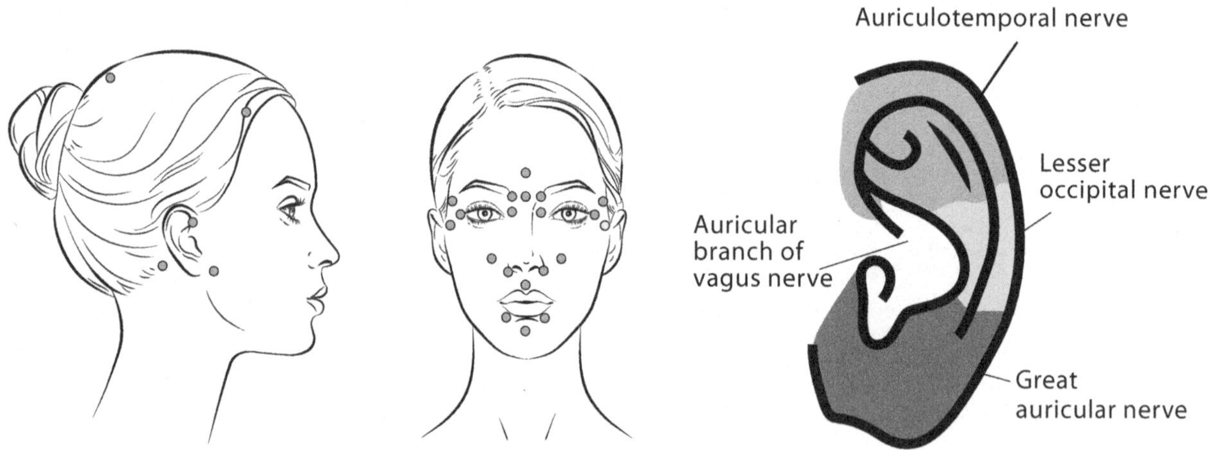

IN-SESSION ACTIVITY

INVERSION EXERCISES

Age Range: All

Objective: To decrease stress and anxiety, reduce sympathetic nervous system activity, and address secondary symptoms of trauma related to anxiety and stress

Directions: Placing the body into an inverted position involves placing one's head toward the floor. Inversion can help with blood flow, enhance the immune system, decrease fight-or-flight reactions, decrease muscle tension, and improve sleep. It activates the vagus nerve, which increases parasympathetic nervous system activity and triggers rest and digestion. The following are 10 inversion activities you can use with clients. Although these activities are intended for all age ranges, young children may require imposed positioning. Be sure to avoid activities that may exacerbate any existing injuries or that are contraindicated due to secondary conditions.

1. **Safely rolling on an exercise ball on the belly or back**
   - Stabilize the ball with your hands (or if working with a small child, sit on the floor and position the ball between your legs). Ask the client to lie over the ball, either on their belly or back. For small children, safely place them on the ball in the desired position. Provide gentle movement of the ball back and forth in a rocking motion.
2. **Inverted pull-ins on an exercise ball**
   - Stabilize the ball with your hands (or if working with a small child, sit on the floor and position the ball between your legs). Have the client lie over the exercise ball on their belly. If needed, provide support by placing your hands around their core. Be sure to have the client's permission before proceeding. Have them walk their hands out away from the ball to place their body into a forearm plank (i.e., their neck and trunk should be in alignment in a straight horizontal position, while their lower legs should remain on the ball). Have the client bend their knees (so the ball slowly rolls toward their toes) while they move their hips toward the ceiling and their head toward the floor. With their body inverted, hold for a few seconds, then allow the client to return to the plank position. Select the amount of repetitions you would like to have the client perform.
3. **Downward-facing dog yoga pose**
   - Ask the client to get down on all fours into the quadruped position. Then have them tuck their toes under as they lift their hips toward the ceiling and place their head toward the floor. Allow them to remain in this position while bearing weight

through their arms. Select the amount of time you would like for them to maintain the position.

4. **Tripod yoga pose**
   - Ask the client to get into a high-kneel position. Then have them bend at the hips, placing the top of their head on the floor. Have them place their palms flat on the floor, with their fingers facing forward toward their face. Their wrists should be bent at a 90-degree angle, and their upper arms should be parallel to the floor. Ask them to straighten their knees, allowing their hips to move toward the ceiling while they bear weight through their upper body. With permission from the client, you can provide stability by placing your hands on the outside of their hips. Select the amount of time you would like for them to maintain the position.

5. **Legs-up-the-wall pose**
   - Locate a clear and safe area near a wall. Ask the client to sit down on the floor facing the wall. Then have them lie on their back, raise their legs and feet, and place their legs gently against the wall. Select the amount of time you would like for them to maintain the position.

6. **Standing forward fold**
   - Have the client stand in an upright position. Then ask them to bend at the hips as they bring their chest toward their thighs. Their head should be pointed toward the floor. They may place their hands on the floor or on their shins, or they may grab their ankles. Select the amount of time you would like for them to maintain the position.

7. **Placing items on the floor for retrieval, such as at the desk**
   - Use a box, storage container, or supply bag to place needed items under a desk or table in preparation for an activity. For example, if you are performing arts and crafts, place the supplies in a bin under the client's chair. Have them remain seated while they bend over to retrieve the items. They may reposition their legs or hold onto the tabletop surface to stabilize themselves and to avoid loss of balance. Clients can incorporate this exercise into their daily activities.

8. **Wheelbarrow walking**
   - Have the client get down on all fours into the quadruped position. Ask them to keep their palms flat on the floor. Standing behind them, grab one of their legs at a time, and hold up their lower body while they bear weight through their arms. Then ask them to walk their hands forward as they move across the floor with you moving with them as you hold their legs.

9. **Wall handstands**
   - Locate a clear and safe area near a wall. Place a small pillow in front of the wall, and ask the client to kneel on the floor facing the wall. Then have them place their palms

flat on the floor and the top of their head onto the pillow. With permission, you can assist them in getting into a handstand position by guiding their legs toward the ceiling and eventually against the wall. They should be in an upside-down position. Select the amount of time you would like for them to maintain the position.

10. Inversion tables and trapeze swings

- If you work in a clinic with an inversion table (e.g., a physical therapy or chiropractic facility), you can have the client lie safely on the table to go into an inverted position. Be sure to follow safety precautions, and be aware of any contraindications. If you are in a pediatric sensory integration clinic and have access to a trapeze swing, explore having the child sit on top of the swing while you support them. Then have them lock their legs on the swing by bending their knees around the bar. While they hold onto the side of the swing ropes, have them bend backward into an inverted position with their head toward the floor. Ensure their safety by providing any necessary support. Select the amount of time you would like for them to maintain the position while swinging them in a desired motion.

IN-SESSION ACTIVITY

SENSORIMOTOR WORK: SELF-IMPOSED INPUT

Age Range: All

Objective: To decrease stress and anxiety, reduce sympathetic nervous system activity, and address secondary symptoms of trauma related to hypersensitivity to sensory stimuli and hyperarousal

Directions: We know that certain input, such as imposed sensory stimulation, can improve interaction with the environment and engagement with others. The following provides self-imposed techniques you can review with clients.

Shiatsu Self-Massage

While sitting down, instruct the client to use their thumbs to provide pressure to the soles of the feet, moving in a circular manner. Then have them use their thumbs to provide a pressure massage to each toe on their feet. Instruct them to apply pressure and to massage the webbed spaces of their hands. Next, have them apply pressure to their palms, using their thumb and working down to the wrist area, continuing with gentle pressure. Then have them use their opposite hand to pull the other hand backward to stretch the wrist area. Lastly, invite them to massage their scalp using their fingertips. (Note to provider: If performing self-massage on the feet, ensure the client is comfortable with removing their shoes.)

Back and Lower Body Massage

Apply deep pressure input to the muscles of the extremities and back using a massager, tennis ball, or small bolster. You can also roll an exercise ball over the body with gentle pressure.

Aromatherapy Lotion Massage

In session, ask permission to use lotion when performing a massage, or have the client (or caregiver) apply the lotion themselves for a self-massage.

IN-SESSION ACTIVITY

SENSORIMOTOR WORK: PARENT-CHILD MASSAGE

Age Range: All

Objective: To decrease stress and anxiety, reduce sympathetic nervous system activity, and address secondary symptoms of trauma related to hypersensitivity to sensory stimuli and hyperarousal

Directions: Stress hormones can increase heart and respiratory rate, enhance hypervigilance and focus, and suppress immunity and the digestive system. Overactivation of stress hormones can also decrease activation in the prefrontal cortex. Thus, it is crucial to find ways to release these hormones from the body to enhance executive functioning. Providing deep pressure input to the body is one way to release stress hormones and relax the body through the release of calming neurochemicals.

Caregivers can use the following steps to provide a massage to children of all ages, depending on their individual needs. For adolescents, consider other activities that allow for self-imposed input. Demonstrate the following steps while instructing the caregiver on how to provide a parent-child massage:

1. Starting with the child's face, use your thumbs to gently massage the lips and surrounding muscles of the face.
2. Gently massage the child's scalp using your fingertips.
3. Massage the child's external ears using slow, circular movements.
4. Next, massage the child's extremities. Starting with the lower body, use your whole hand to gently pull the child's hips toward their feet. Then pull their shoulder toward their hands when massing the upper body. Gently roll their arms and legs between your open palms. Hold the child's calves and bring their knees toward their chest, holding for a few seconds.
5. Perform a belly massage using the side of your hand closest to the pinky finger and moving in a water paddle motion (one hand follows immediately after the other).
6. Finally, use your hand to gently provide pressure to the belly. From left to right, spell out the inverted letters I, L, U as indicated here (McClure, 2017).

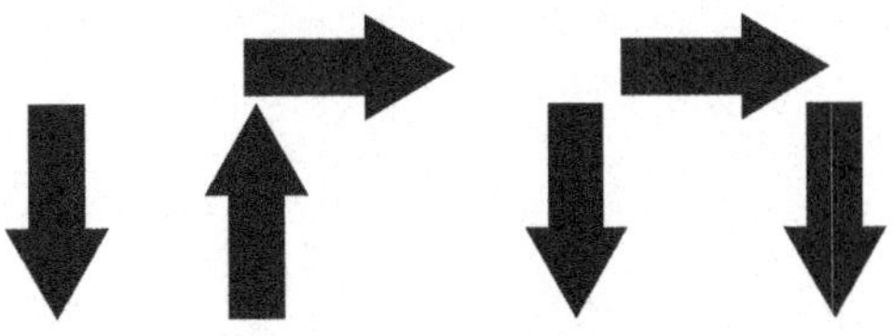

IN-SESSION ACTIVITY

SENSORIMOTOR WORK: MULTISENSORY APPROACHES

Age Range: All

Objective: To decrease stress and anxiety, reduce sympathetic nervous system activity, and address secondary symptoms of trauma related to hypersensitivity to sensory stimuli and hyperarousal

Directions: Our interaction with the world requires that we integrate various senses at one time. As part of treatment interventions, stimulating more than one sensory area at a time can improve our ability to interact with the environment and engage with others. Long term, clients may reveal decreased hypervigilance, increased attention to tasks, and improved self-regulation. Consider using the following sensory-based techniques with your clients:

- ☐ Rhythmically swinging with music
- ☐ Using a metronome during exercise (e.g., jumping jacks, jumping in place, push-ups).
- ☐ Visually scanning for objects in a tactile bin while exploring textures (e.g., placing objects in a bin of dry, uncooked rice)
- ☐ Bouncing on a ball while reciting the alphabet, states, or names of sport teams, or while reading letters on a Snellen chart.

IN-SESSION ACTIVITY

SENSORIMOTOR WORK: THERMORECEPTIVE ACTIVITIES

Age Range: All

Objective: To tap into the parasympathetic nervous system via thermoreceptors and adjust arousal levels to support the demands of required tasks

Directions: Thermoreceptors, which are located on the skin, allow us to detect variation in temperatures within our environment. Not only can the use of ice and heat provide relief from pain, but it can also tap into the parasympathetic nervous system, allowing for adjustments to our arousal level. Cold temperatures stimulate the vagus nerve, which has the strongest innervation to the parasympathetic nervous system. Moreover, warm temperatures allow for a sense of safety and security. The manner in which an individual reacts to cold and warm temperatures depends on their sensory needs. The following guidelines provide you with some considerations when implementing thermoreceptive activities with clients:

- ☐ **Hypervigilant and anxious clients:** Explore the use of (safe) warm temperatures, such as a warm heating pad available for use during work or school, a heated blanket, or a heated massager. You can perform this prior to the client having to do work or in preparation for other session activities. Set a timer to indicate an end time. This can also assist in relaxing the body before bedtime. Be sure to periodically check the skin for excessive redness to ensure the temperature is not too hot. Check in with the client to ensure they are comfortable and not experiencing any pain as a result of the temperature.

- ☐ **Hyperactive and seeking-sensory clients:** Explore the use of cold temperatures, which can involve eating ice chips, hiding objects within ice cubes and holding the cubes until melted, freezing finger paint in ice cube trays to use for artwork, and freezing disposable water bottles for deep pressure massage. Have the client perform such activities before having to do work or in preparation for other session activities. Avoid injury to the skin and teeth by checking that the client is not experiencing pain or discomfort. Ensure activities are age appropriate and prioritize safety.

PROVIDER HANDOUT

AROMATHERAPY GUIDELINES*

Age Range: All

Objective: To tap into the parasympathetic nervous system via the olfactory system and adjust arousal levels to support the demands of required tasks

Directions: Aromatherapy, with the use of essential oils, can assist in addressing arousal and emotions. This handout provides general guidelines that providers should consider when using aromatherapy with clients, as well as a list of essential oils (though this is not a comprehensive list). Aromatherapy practitioners have the expertise to assist in appropriate guidelines and application.

Note: Be sure to assess for allergies, sensitivities (e.g., nausea), preferences, and chronic diseases, such as seizure disorders. Ensure that the treatment area is properly ventilated. Allow a minimum of five minutes to breathe fresh air between aromatherapy sessions.

Essential Oil	Potential Uses
Sweet orange	Improves mood, increases alertness, and assists with digestion
Lemon	Improves mood and digestive issues
Sandalwood	Has a calming effect and increases focus
Bergamot	Reduces stress and improves dermatological conditions
Rose	Decreases anxiety and enhances mood
Lavender	Decreases stress and has a calming effect
Chamomile	Improves mood and enhances positive emotions
Peppermint	Increases energy levels and improves nausea
Ginger root	Improves appetite and boosts immunity
Mandarin	Decreases anxiety and improves dermatological conditions
Ylang-ylang	Decreases nausea and improves dermatological conditions
Tea tree	Boosts immunity and improves dermatological conditions
Jasmine	Improves mood

*Adapted from http://tisserandinstitute.org/wp-content/uploads/2019/02/Clinical-Aromatherapy-Generic-Policy-2019.pdf

Utilize a device in which you can place the essential oils for diffusion. Ingestion or skin application is not recommended without proper training. The following are some devices for diffusion:

- **Active diffusion:** Actively diffuses the essential oil through the air with the use of an electrical device
- **Passive diffusion:** Uses warmth to diffuse essential oils, such as the use of a ceramic heated stone diffuser
- **Carrier diffusion:** Involves placing the essential oil within a container (e.g., a cup), using a cloth on which to place the oil, or making a satchel in which to carry the oil (e.g., placing dry rice infused with essential oil into a small chiffon bag)

IN-SESSION ACTIVITY

VISUAL STRATEGIES

Age Range: All

Objective: To tap into the nervous system via the autonomic nerves connected to the visual system

Directions: Our visual system connects to the neurological structures involved in arousal, as the nerves for eye movement originate in the brainstem and travel to the areas involved in the inhibition and facilitation of our arousal levels. Vision also has a strong role in our emotional reactions, as sensory input facilitates the reticular activating system, thus impacting arousal. By providing clients with visual stimuli and input to the structures of the visual system, you can alter their arousal level and improve their ability to respond to stimuli in the environment. Incorporating continued calming and organizing input through the visual sensory system can improve arousal, attention, emotion regulation, and overall functioning over time. Prior to starting, be sure to ask the client's permission before introducing these activities, and recognize any triggers so you can avoid activities that may result in re-traumatization. Young children may also require imposed positioning.

- ☐ Start with gentle eyelid massages. Have the client close their eyes, and gently use two or three fingers to massage their eyelids by moving them in a circular pattern three to five times in one direction, and then repeat in the other direction. Repeat this three times on both eyes.
- ☐ Next, perform butterfly breathing. Have the client take their thumbs and place them gently in each ear, with their palms facing forward and their fingers pointing upward. Have them then wrap their fingers toward the front of their face to cover the eyes. Have them take a deep breath in the nose, hold it for five seconds, and then blow out of the mouth.
- ☐ If they are unable to perform butterfly breathing, consider simply hiding the eyes. Have them cover the eyes for a period of time to destress and recharge. This is especially useful with young children to prevent overstimulation or to help them calm down when they are becoming overwhelmed.
- ☐ Next, perform a room-scanning activity, such as an I Spy game, by identifying objects in the environment. Without sharing what the object is, state to the client, "I spy something ______," and then fill in the blank with characteristics that describe the object (e.g., saying you spy something blue to describe a blue ink pen on the desk). Have them scan the room to locate the object, taking a guess at what it could be. If they are not correct with their selection, repeat by sharing another characteristic of the object. In place of an I Spy game, you can also simply have the client scan the room, select an object, and describe the object in detail.

CLIENT ACTIVITY

EYE YOGA*

Age Range: All

Objective: To tap into the nervous system via the autonomic nerves connected to the visual system

Directions: Consider including eye yoga as part of your visual-based activities to enhance focus, increase attention, and regulate arousal. First review the following instructions, then give it a try.

Place your arms straight out in front of you at nose level.

Then tuck your fingers into your palm and raise your thumbs up (i.e., thumbs-up position).

Focus your attention on the thumbs.

Avoiding head movement, use your eyes to follow your thumbs as they move slowly in the following directions:

(1) up and down,

(2) left to right,

(3) bringing thumbs toward the nose and pushing thumbs away from the nose, and

(4) in a circular motion. You can repeat each of these movements or simply do one of each. Incorporate yoga music if desired.

* Adapted from *Self-Regulation and Mindfulness* (Gibbs, 2017b)

IN-SESSION ACTIVITY

AUDITORY STRATEGIES

Age Range: All

Objective: To tap into the autonomic nervous system via the nerves connected to the auditory system

Directions: The use of music before or during a task is one way to change arousal and decrease stress. When using auditory activities, consider whether the client's arousal level is high, low, or in the middle. For example, if clients are avoidant, hypervigilant, or overresponsive to sensory input, use music with predictable rhythms, such as drumming. In contrast, if clients are seeking sensory input, use upbeat, high-tempo music to meet their needs. Additionally, attempt to assess the client's music preference. This involves the selection of the genre of music. Finally, consider the client's threshold for music. That is, consider how much can they tolerate before desiring to end the activity. The following are examples of auditory activities to explore:

- ☐ Listening to music through headphones
- ☐ Playing games requiring the client to respond to verbal directions (e.g., playing Simon Says or line dancing to a song with directions, such as the "Cupid Shuffle")
- ☐ Listening to a story read aloud, then answering questions corresponding to the details
- ☐ Playing auditory bingo (see next page)

IN-SESSION ACTIVITY

AUDITORY BINGO

Age Range: Children

Objective: To tap into the autonomic nervous system via the nerves connected to the auditory system

Directions: This activity will help clients to focus and attend to sounds in their environment to enhance their auditory discrimination skills. Before introducing the activity to clients, take some time to locate sounds online, such as through social media sites, and record any sounds that correspond with the images on the bingo card provided here. Then play these sounds in session with your client, and have them locate the images that correspond with the sounds on their bingo card. You can also develop the bingo boards on your own.

IN-SESSION ACTIVITY

AUDITORY BINGO

Age Range: Adolescents and adults

Objective: To tap into the autonomic nervous system via the nerves connected to the auditory system

Directions: Before introducing the activity to clients, take some time to locate sounds online, such as through social media sites, and record any sounds that correspond with the words on the bingo card provided here. Then play the sounds in session with your client, and have them locate the words that correspond with the sounds on their bingo card. You can also develop the bingo boards on your own.

Stream	Writing	Mixing
Walking	Television	Weeping
Sweeping	Burning Flame	Shoveling

CASE SCENARIO*

Review the following case study. Then use the worksheet to analyze some of the ACTION approaches discussed in this chapter.

Name: Nadine
Setting: Inpatient Psychiatric Hospital
Age: 15

I encountered Nadine at my clinical affiliation at an inpatient psychiatric facility. During her intake, we reviewed various reports describing a myriad of physical, emotional, and sexual abuse. The documents almost led me to tears. Yet my tears had to take a backseat as I sat as a young student in a room full of psychiatrists, fellows, and nurses. The team soon invited Nadine in to meet with her and perform further evaluation. I did not recognize it then, but the entire event was traumatic for myself and involved a reexperience of trauma for Nadine.

With each question, the answers became more graphic in nature. Nadine described the sexual encounters she had experienced with an adult cousin as if she were writing a novel. She shared his smell and the sexual sensations she experienced at the time. When asked if she knew what happened to her was wrong, she shrugged her shoulders and stated, "I don't know." Nadine maintained a smile the entire interview. It seemed like she put on an act that she had performed on a multitude of occasions. Along with her smile was the voice of a younger child. Her voice reminded me of an innocent 5-year-old girl. It baffled me how she could appear so pure yet speak of such horror.

I began working with Nadine in individual and group sessions, and she began to look forward to our encounters. As the weeks passed, I realized the coping mechanisms she had previously revealed had transformed into psychosis and hallucinations. Nadine expressed that nighttime was her least favorite part of day. She would experience night terrors and dreams that I would later discover were flashbacks of torturous acts imposed by her caregivers during her younger years. From what I could gather, her abuse ranged from her toddler years to the present. One of her abusers now resided in prison for his acts against her.

One day, I arrived to work with Nadine to discover she was placed in the quiet room. As I approached the padded, locked box in which she was placed, one of the nurses pulled me aside. Apparently, Nadine had presented with dangerous behavior and become very physical and aggressive toward the staff. They feared she would harm herself and others, so she was placed in the quiet room. Unfortunately, this became a trend and not an isolated event for Nadine. To further complicate this situation, I would soon be ending my clinical affiliation and leaving my role at the facility. When I shared this with Nadine, she once again expressed the experience of loss. In the voice of a very young child, she said, "Everyone good always leaves!" Along with the ache that this statement placed in my heart, I also left with the fear that Nadine would soon age out of that facility. Where would she go? And under whose care? I thought about her eventually becoming homeless and experiencing self-imposed abuse to survive.

---

*Case study by Varleisha Gibbs, PhD, OTD, OTR/L

PROVIDER WORKSHEET

CASE ANALYSIS

In this chapter, we have reviewed the neurophysiological changes that result from exposure to stress and trauma. After reading through Nadine's case, see if you are able to connect her trauma to her functioning. Use the following worksheet to analyze the case.

Task #1: Describe Nadine's trauma. Use the Five Dimensions of Trauma Model when developing your description, and consider the different categories of trauma that describe her experience (expected versus unexpected, isolated versus pervasive, etc.).

____

____

____

____

Task #2: What are some precautions you must take into account when selecting activities? What physical or sensory activities would you recommend? Why? What challenges would you suspect or anticipate for Nadine as she eventually enters into the world?

____

____

____

____

Task #3: What are the next steps? Based on the ACTION-from-Trauma approach activities presented in this chapter, what would you recommend?

____

____

____

____

PART TWO

ION

CHAPTER 4

INTERGENERATIONAL FACTORS

While a diagnosis of PTSD requires that individuals directly experience trauma, or that they learn of a traumatic event that occurred to a loved one, it fails to acknowledge a crucial aspect of trauma: that trauma can be transferred between family members and generations. Known as *intergenerational trauma*, this type of trauma affects generations of a specific group of people and does not require directly experiencing a traumatic event. The hearing of stories, learned behaviors, and subsequent rules that emerge all feed into the well-being of generations that follow. Indeed, there are stories within our history riddled with trauma. Survivors carry that trauma not only in their minds but in their bodies. The cells in their body hold onto the trauma and serve as a history book to be shared with offspring. In this chapter, we aim to review the impact of intergenerational and vicarious trauma through the following sections:

- ☐ Introduction
- ☐ Prevention and Early Intervention
- ☐ Primitive Reflexes
- ☐ Understanding the Self: Connection to Intergenerational Trauma
- ☐ Genogram
- ☐ Inner Child Work
- ☐ Case Scenario

INTRODUCTION

One of the first studies to highlight the concept of intergenerational trauma analyzed the grandchildren of Holocaust survivors and found that such individuals presented with signs of trauma, such as less-than-adequate coping skills (Rakoff, Sigal, & Epstein, 1966). Since then, hundreds of studies continue to investigate what was first deemed "survivor syndrome." For example, the presence of intergenerational trauma has been found among descendants of enslaved Africans, Native Americans, refugees, and victims of genocides. For individuals who are a part of such lineages, the impact of individualized traumatic events—in addition to the historical generational experiences of their ancestors—further compounds the complexity of trauma. Societal and cultural factors, such as oppression and lack of access to basic necessities, can add to the layer of intergenerational trauma as well.

Beyond historical and cultural factors, there are underlying neurological connections that also explain the experience of intergenerational trauma. In particular, epigenetics provides a deeper explanation for what we see emerge from our ancestral connections. While many assume that DNA is fixed, there is an aspect of it that is malleable. Alterations in our genes can occur as a result of our experiences, particularly those that are impactful. The process by which such experiences can alter our gene expression is called methylation. Research has found high rates of methylation among individuals who survived the Holocaust and their offspring (Kellerman, 2013; Yehuda et al., 2016), demonstrating that exposure to severe stress leads to changes in gene expression beyond vicarious trauma.

The events of 9/11 further support the existence of intergenerational trauma, with studies finding that those who were pregnant at the time had children who exhibited biomarkers associated with increased susceptibility to PTSD, such as low salivary cortisol levels (Yehuda et al., 2005). Ironically, at the time of this writing, our society is experiencing a global pandemic caused by COVID-19. Again, we are faced with an event that will create a catastrophic and traumatic aftermath. This societal tragedy threatens the development and resilience of unborn infants and young children being parented by individuals experiencing this trauma, as the descendants of trauma are vulnerable to inheriting the emotional, psychological, and physical adverse effects of trauma. Hence, it is vital we target those at risk and highlight the impact of their ancestral history. Exploring these familial connections can provide some solace and potential answers to the personal difficulties they may be experiencing.

PREVENTION AND EARLY INTERVENTION

For those who are at the beginning stages of life, early intervention services can curtail the effect of intergenerational trauma that could later emerge and impact an individual's quality of life. Therefore, taking an ACTION-from-Trauma approach also involves providing intervention to newborns, infants, and toddlers who may be at risk for experiencing future trauma. Let us explore methods to address the needs of those in early childhood who are exposed to trauma in utero or during infancy and the toddler years.

During the infant years, over one million neuronal connections are established every second (Center on the Developing Child, n.d.). The early years set the stage and tone for what is to follow. While not all trauma is preventable, we can certainly address the effects of intergenerational trauma through early intervention services that consider the relationship between the child and the adults involved in their life. Our neurological reactions are dependent on our environment and on the individuals with whom we engage. In her book *Self-Regulation and Mindfulness*, Dr. Gibbs coined the term *reciprocal regulation* to describe the significance of this interaction between two or more individuals (Figure 13). Neurologically, reciprocal regulation reflects the process by which our mirror neurons become activated when we interact with someone else, which then triggers an autonomic reaction based on that interaction. Not only do we detect and perceive the feelings and emotions of someone in our presence, but we also begin to regulate or dysregulate based on that encounter.

Therefore, practitioners need to address the individuals who are involved in a child's life to achieve the most optimal outcome in decreasing or preventing future trauma. Children imitate the adults around them—from how loudly they speak to the facial expressions they make. They model how adults exhibit and respond to experiences with frustration, joy, happiness, or empathy. In order to cease the cycle of trauma, it is thus necessary to teach caregivers how to regulate themselves so they can provide a model from which children can learn to self-regulate.

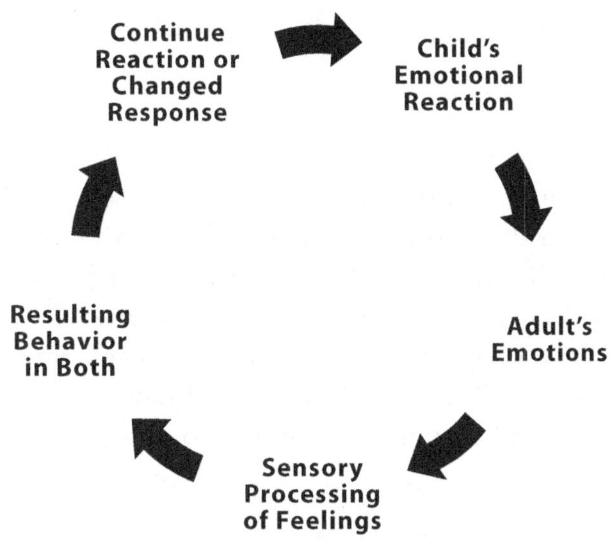

Figure 13. Reciprocal Regulation (Gibbs, 2017b)

Thus, from the start of life, it is critical for caregivers to engage with the infant as much as possible. Even when children are unable to develop an initial bond with a primary attachment figure, such as babies who enter into the foster care system or who go through the adoption process, there are strategies to enhance the bonding process with their adult caregivers (e.g., their foster or adoptive parents). These strategies enhance the caregiver-child bond and facilitate mental health outcomes for the child and caregiver alike, whether these strategies are used in the face of traumatic experiences or as preventative measures (Clark & Kingsley, 2020):

- ☐ Provide skin-to-skin contact during the first days and months of life.
- ☐ Perform a caregiver-provided massage, which has been shown to not only calm the infant but to decrease parental stress and anxiety. Addressing reciprocal regulation prior to such techniques is vital.
- ☐ Participate in shared experiences, such as reading to the child.
- ☐ Ensure consistent play with the child at least once daily.
- ☐ Feed the child based on their needs rather than doing so at scheduled mealtimes.

In addition, practitioners should consider providing coaching to caregivers, teachers, and daycare providers regarding how to interact with children in a way that facilitates brain development. Here are some strategies to consider:

- ☐ Recognize and acknowledge the start of an interaction.
- ☐ Make eye contact during the interaction.
- ☐ Listen to the child and allow them to lead during play-based activities.

- ☐ Share the child's attention and focus.
- ☐ Be sure to return the focus by engaging and responding to the child.
- ☐ Assist the child with labeling and naming objects in the environment, as well as those used during the interaction.
- ☐ Establish an ending to the interaction with words and gestures, such as signing "all done."

PRIMITIVE REFLEXES

Early childhood preventative interventions must not only involve parental interaction. We must also utilize activities focused on the body, as doing so allows us to address how intergenerational trauma might manifest physically. In particular, the presence of primitive reflexes, or motoric actions, in children may provide a red flag for future emotional and behavioral challenges. Primitive reflexes typically subside in the early childhood years, but when there is a lack of appropriate integration, these reflexes persist. This may lead to dysfunction, including poor coordination, emotion regulation challenges, and difficulty attending to and performing tasks (Konicarova & Bob, 2013).

Primitive reflexes are most observable during the beginning stages of life (see Table 6). These reflexes are most necessary for motoric development and engagement with the environment during the early years. Additionally, such involuntary reflexes help to transition a newborn through the birthing canal and assist with feeding. As the baby gains the ability to move and attend to a caregiver, bonding and attachment occur. Eventually, primitive reflexes become less observable as they integrate and work with the motoric system to establish a more coordinated sensorimotor system. Consequently, they may re-emerge in times of stress and trauma. This is due to their association with brainstem level functioning.

Given that the presence of primitive reflex patterns is a strong predictor of future functioning, the halting of these developmental milestones can impact successful interaction with the environment (Deiss et al., 2019). Trauma is one particular risk factor that can lead to developmental delays among children, with evidence demonstrating a correlation with motor dysfunction and challenges with self-regulation. This includes poor emotion regulation, sensory processing, and executive functioning. We further expand upon the areas of dysfunction in Table 7.

Depending on the scope of your practice, you should consider including the activation and evidence of such reflexes in your evaluation and intervention processes, and reflect on the general need to include gross motor activities within sessions to address trauma. The following three tables provide guidelines for such analysis by highlighting some of the various primitive reflexes, their function, and examples of dysfunction if primitive reflexes are retained. However, this is not a comprehensive list. Depending on your clinical reasoning and the scope of your practice, you may need to refer clients to another professional to support the treatment you perform. Table 8 describes methods to activate the primitive reflexes. These exercises can be incorporated in a treatment plan to assist in the integration of the reflexes through exposure.

Primitive Reflex	Function
Asymmetrical Tonic Neck (ATNR) Appears 18 weeks in utero, disappears around 6 months	Extension of one side of the body and flexion of the other to assist in the birthing process and later with reaching, eye-hand coordination, and airway passage clearance
Symmetrical Tonic Neck (STNR) Appears 4–6 months, disappears around 8–12 months	Assists in preparation for crawling; when the child is on hands and knees, a flexed head results in legs extending; when the head is extended, the opposite occurs, with arms extending and legs flexing
Moro Appears in utero, disappears around 6 months	Occurs during the first breath of life; continues as a startle reflex in response to an unexpected stimulus or threat; the involuntary response is protective, as the infant is unable to distinguish threats; extension of the body (fall reaction), followed by full flexion (protective position), occurs spontaneously
Spinal Galant Appears 20 weeks in utero, disappears around 9 months	Activates when either side of the spine of an infant is stroked; neck extension, hip rotation, and body flexion occur; assists with hip movement and rotation, specifically in utero and during the birthing process, as well as in the development of crawling
Palmar Appears 18 weeks in utero, disappears around 6 months	Assists in sucking, as the hands contract as the baby sucks; stimulation of the palms results in flexion or a grasp reflex; activation also leads to the mouth opening and jaw movement
Rooting Appears at birth, disappears around 4–6 months	Assists with feeding; baby will respond to stimulation of the cheek by turning toward the stroked side and opening mouth
Tonic Labyrinthine Appears in utero, disappears around 4–6 months (Backward can sometimes last into the third year of life)	Assists baby through the birthing canal Forward: As head is flexed, the arms and legs curl toward the body Backward: As the head is extended, the body goes into extension
Landau Appears 3 months, disappears around 12 months	Head, legs, and spine extend when baby is held in the air horizontally in the prone (belly down) position; assists with muscle tone

Table 6. Primitive Reflexes in Children (Gibbs, 2017b)

Primitive Reflex	Dysfunction
ATNR	Poor balance; difficulty with coordinated eye movements needed for reading and writing; challenges in crossing midline of the body and separating the upper body and lower body movements
STNR	Difficulty crawling on all fours; poor balance; clumsiness; difficulty with midline activities; poor sitting position ("W" sitting)
Moro	Hypervigilant; overactive fight-or-flight reactions; sensitivity to light, sound, touch; poor emotion regulation; hyperactivity; poor attention to tasks; frequent illness due to a stressed immune system; fatigue
Spinal Galant	Difficulty maintaining a seated position; constant fidgeting; bed-wetting and bladder accidents; sensitivity to touch and certain textures (clothing); challenges in following directions and with short-term memory
Palmar	Mouth movement as the child performs cutting, writing, or coloring activities; chewing on objects, such as pencils; biting people; difficulty with grasp and speech due to tension in hands and mouth
Rooting	Sensitivity in the mouth; challenges with food textures; messy eating; poor speech articulation
Tonic Labyrinthine	Difficulty coordinating body movement and eye movement; motion sickness; poor balance and posture; poor timing and sequencing (dyspraxia)
Landau	Challenges with motor activities; high muscle tone (hypertonia) and difficulty learning; toe walking and lack of coordination; possible difficulty sitting against chair back; absence of the reflex during infant years indicates hypotonia and possible intellectual disability

Table 7. Dysfunction Resulting from Retained Primitive Reflexes

Primitive Reflex	Exercise
ATNR	• Place the child in supine on their back. Bring an object (e.g., toy) in their line of sight, placing it to their side once getting their attention. • Encourage them to reach for the object, observing for the presence of ATNR. • Alternative option (if age appropriate): Place the child on all fours in a quadruped position using a bolster if needed. • Gently turn their head to the side and hold for five seconds. • Look to see if they can maintain the position or if they fall to the side opposite of the head being turned, indicating the presence of ATNR.
STNR	• Place the child on all fours in a quadruped position. • Gently move or have the child move their head up and down and hold for five seconds in each position. • Look to see if they sit back on their legs, suggesting the presence of STNR.
Moro	• Safely move the infant by tilting them backward, allowing the head to move posteriorly. • Look for extension of the body and extremities followed by flexion toward midline.
Spinal Galant	• Position the infant on their belly in a prone position. • Gently stroke the left and right sides of their spine. • Look to see if they move their body toward the stroke.
Palmar	• Apply gentle pressure to the infant's palm by placing your finger into their hand. • Look for them to flex their fingers and squeeze your finger. Also detect movement in their mouth and/or tongue, and attempt to pull your finger toward their mouth.
Rooting	• Gently stroke the cheeks and above the upper lip of the child approximately three to five times. • Look for head movement toward the direction of the stroke and mouth opening and movement.
Tonic Labyrinthine	• Safely hold the infant suspended in a horizontal position in prone. • Gently tilt their head forward. • Look for flexion of their trunk and extremities.
Landau	• Safely hold the infant in a suspended horizontal prone position. • Gently tilt their upper body toward the floor. • Look for extension of the body.

Table 8. Exercises to Activate the Primitive Reflexes*

In addition to the exercises in Table 8, the following list provides you with simple activities you can consider in assisting with the integration of primitive reflexes. You can also find additional exercises in *Self-Regulation and Mindfulness* (Gibbs, 2017b).

- ☐ Provide daily tummy time, and avoid placing the baby on their back for prolonged periods of time while awake.
- ☐ Promote crawling by placing the baby on their belly while engaging in play or by propping them up on a bolster, allowing them to place weight through their extremities.
- ☐ Incorporate core-strengthening activities, such as placing the baby on their back and encouraging them to roll over or to sit up to retrieve a toy.
- ☐ Provide gentle rocking to encourage movement, such as placing them in your arms or using a baby swing.
- ☐ Introduce different food variations as appropriate.

*Ensure the age appropriateness of these activities before initiating with a client.

UNDERSTANDING THE SELF: CONNECTION TO INTERGENERATIONAL TRAUMA

Trauma wounds are not always obvious or blaring. When we hear the word *trauma*, we often think about huge, impactful, traumatic events that we call big "T" traumas. However, there are also smaller events, or those that we vicariously experience, that can also influence our fears, habits, reactions, and overall behavior. Known as little "t" traumas, these experiences do not always come with a clear memory. Nonetheless, when these little "t" events accumulate over time, they can produce an allostatic load that affects our personal health and well-being and that of our offspring. In fact, both big "T" and little "t" traumas are associated with physiological implications that have the potential to result in unhealthy habits and behaviors. Unaddressed, they transcend generations and can increase susceptibility to certain physical diseases and mental health conditions. However, knowledge can assist us in proactively addressing these factors. For this reason, we must investigate our clients' ancestral linage and their connection to intergenerational trauma.

Because clients unconsciously carry the burdens and baggage of their family history with them, they can unknowingly experience empathy overload in response to this intergenerational trauma. Their reactions may also mimic those of their caregivers and others around them. By identifying these shared emotions, clients can determine how they manifest. What are the triggers for these emotions? Where do clients feel and experience these emotions in their bodies? Once clients acknowledge the historical landscape of their family, they can liberate themselves from these past events. This allows them to set boundaries, implement useful coping strategies, and disconnect from situations that are not their own. To delve into this further, we will:

- Investigate family dynamics via a genogram
- Determine how familial beliefs and practices inform who clients become
- Identify how the client's inner child impacts their ability to address trauma

GENOGRAM

Similar to a family tree, a genogram is a diagram that uses symbols to draw connections between family relationships across generations. It can be useful to determine patterns of behavior and interactions with others. Symbols are typically used to describe gender, biological (and adoptive) offspring, and the qualities of familial relationships. Shared information can also include psychosocial history and medical genetics. A genogram has the potential to be a complex milieu of familial data. For our purposes, we will map out a simple genogram using the template that we have provided with the following worksheet. While this process can certainly allow for a better understanding of the client's history, clinicians must take into account the client's readiness to review their family history, as doing so can be a lot to handle and can cause distress. Please use your clinical reasoning. Before working with a client, consider completing your own genogram as well.

IN-SESSION ACTIVITY

GENOGRAM: FAMILY HEALING MAP*

Age Range: Adults

Objective: To illustrate family relationships and ancestral information related to intergenerational trauma

Directions: To start the process, become familiar with the symbols used in the genogram, which are described below.

Genogram Key:

Characteristics

Male Gender Identity	Female Gender Identity	Unknown Gender	Pregnancy (unborn)	Miscarriage/ Infant Death
□	○	◇ ?	△	△ X

Health and Mortality

Male Physical Illness	Female Physical Illness	Male Mental Illness	Female Mental Illness	Male Substance/ Alcohol Abuse	Female Substance/ Alcohol Abuse	Deceased Male	Deceased Female
□ X	○ X	□ M	○ M	□ A	○ A	■	●

Relationships

Close Relationship	Unhealthy Relationship or Divorce	Abuse/ Violence Relationship	Neglectful Relationship	Traumatic Event
=	≠	ΛΛΛΛΛ	→	+++++++

*Adapted from https://broadcast.lds.org/elearning/FHD/Community/en/Community/Cynthia%20Doxey%20Green/Tracing_Family_Traits_Using_a_Genogram/Genograms.pdf

Next Steps: Interview the client as you map out the genogram. Use the template that follows, starting at the bottom. Select the gender symbol for your client, and connect it to one of the vertical lines for "children." Place a double square or circle around the symbol to indicate them as the client. You can consider placing them in chronological order in comparison to any siblings (e.g., if they are the first child, place the client's symbol below the vertical line furthest to the left). Write their name or initials below it. Continue to add siblings if applicable. Moving to the parents, grandparents, and great-grandparents, write their names or initials next to the corresponding symbols. Next, update each symbol using the key provided for characteristics and health and mortality for the various family members.

The lines on the genogram indicate relationships. Vertical lines represent relationships with children, while horizonal lines represent spousal/partner relationships. Update the lines based on the illustrations in the relationship key provided. For close relationships between two individuals, draw a parallel line alongside the vertical or horizontal lines. For unhealthy relationships or divorce, draw a parallel line, then place a slash through it as indicated. The other relationship symbols should run parallel to the vertical or horizontal lines between those two family members. You can choose to add relationship lines across the genogram as needed (e.g., from a grandparent to a grandchild).

Have the client review the genogram with the goal of identifying themes and similarities among the family members. Then ask them share at least three generational characteristics they would use to define their family based on stories and/or personal interactions between family members. They can share values, beliefs, physical characteristics, cultural traditions, hobbies, unique circumstances (e.g., career-related factors, immigration history, etc.), and other personality traits they desire to share. Write down these generational characteristics and analyze the findings with the client, including how the client perceives these characteristics in relation to their own personal traits. How do these generational characteristics impact how they cope and experience stress and trauma? Use the Genogram Gratitude and Permission List that follows to assist them in processing their revelations.

GENOGRAM TEMPLATE

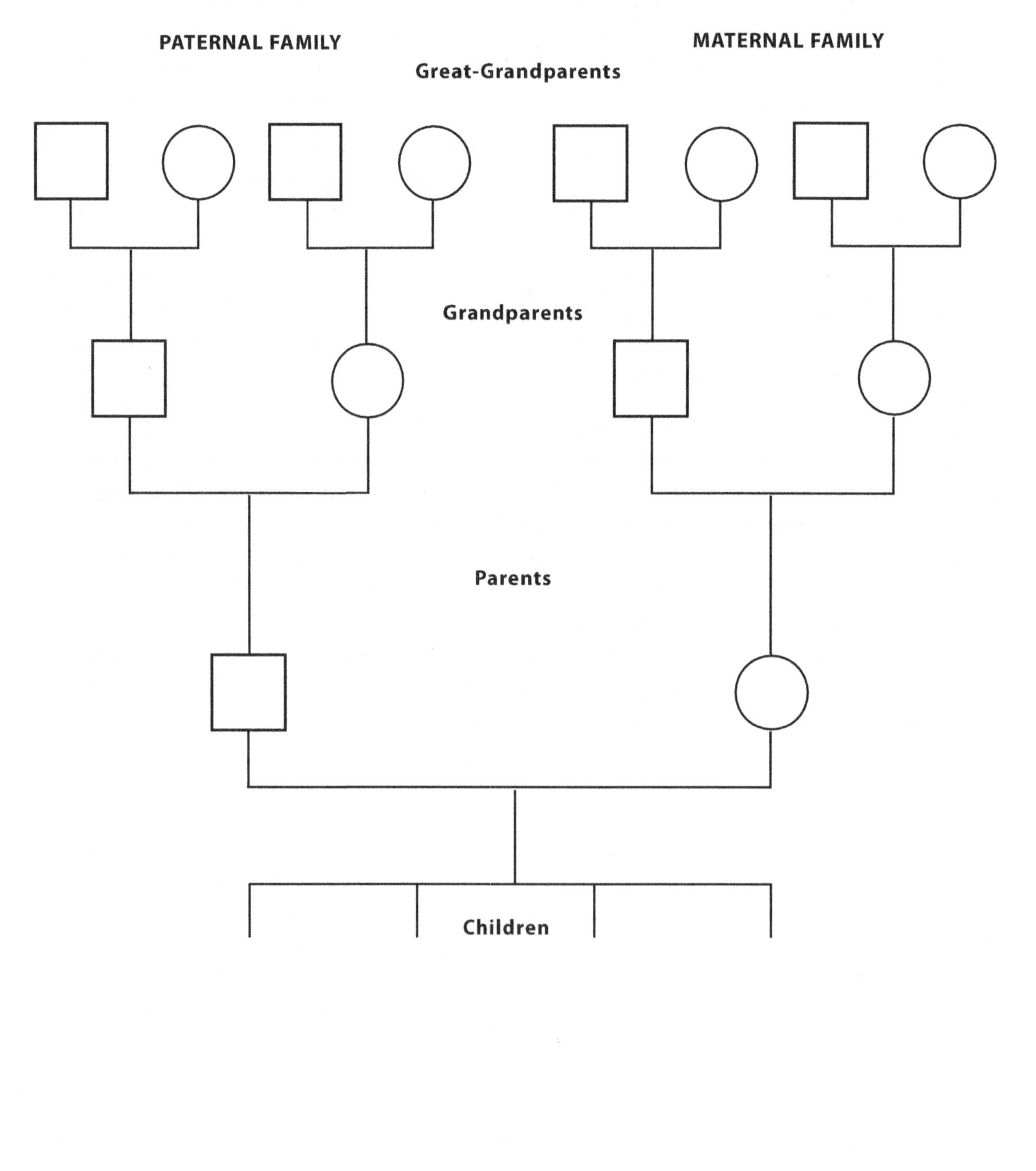

CLIENT WORKSHEET

GENOGRAM GRATITUDE AND PERMISSION LIST

Age Range: Adults

Objective: To assist in processing family relationships and ancestral information related to intergenerational trauma

Directions: After you complete your family genogram, use the chart below to list what you are grateful for and what you give yourself permission to move past with regard to your family trauma. Review the provided examples to guide you in completing your lists.

Gratitude **After reviewing my family genogram...**	**Permission** **After reviewing my family genogram...**
I am grateful for: (Examples: My spirituality, my culture, my intellect, my love for writing, my passion for dance, my sarcasm, my ability to draw, my ancestors)	I give myself permission to: (Examples: To change my mind, to leave unhealthy relationships, to say no, to be great at something, to be assertive, to share my boundaries, to be different, to ask for help)

INNER CHILD WORK

As children, we need to rely on others for our survival. Inversely, as adults, we become increasingly independent and, in turn, may no longer view trauma as a challenge or obstacle that impedes our growth. We believe we have the skills and abilities to move past those experiences that once caused fear and shame. However, addressing the needs, experiences, and beliefs of the child within can assist in a successful plan of care. To further support clients in their journey to accept and release any intergenerational trauma preventing their growth, they must address their inner child.

Children acquire more than their physical characteristics from their parents and ancestors. The family system also introduces them to rules and morals, and it provides their first exposure to judgment. When individuals deviate from these prescribed rules, they tend to develop a sense of blame or shame. Accordingly, it is important to consider how we (and our clients) form these concepts in the first place. What your parent believed is connected to their parent's belief, which is connected to their parent's belief, and so forth. These learned behaviors accompany the neurological and genetic makeup that are passed through the bloodline. Therefore, how we experience, cope with, and heal from trauma are all connected to our family.

At the same time, our personal and familial experiences alone do not explain the connection to who we are and how we reveal our intergenerational trauma. There is also a connection to the universal primitive drives and instinctual needs that we have as humans. For example, newborn babies instinctively know to seek a connection with their caregiver by crying when they require food, affection, or a diaper change. As children, we learn to balance these primitive drives with our social, familial, and cultural norms. We begin to suppress these primitive drives and innate needs, which ultimately results in the development of our inner child. This inner child causes us to judge ourselves when it appears we have broken a rule or moral code. In turn, we hold in our fear, leave behind our child activities, view our assertiveness as aggression, and conceal our stress. While we may not realize it, our inner child continues to lead the way and remains in control during adulthood. Addressing ancestral trauma calls for us to work with our inner child.

The following activity provides clients an opportunity to connect with their inner child to grow toward healing. Use this activity to guide your clients in investigating their core survival needs and desires to better understand their ability to handle and cope with trauma. Before beginning, explain your justification for performing the activity and explain how you intend to use the information. Be sure to incorporate grounding activities during and after the discussion.

CLIENT WORKSHEET

BALANCING THE ADULT AND INNER CHILD

Age Range: Adults

Objective: To connect with underlying innate physiological and emotional needs to create balance and healing from trauma

Directions: In part 1 of this worksheet, answer the questions listed to revisit to your childhood. After you have done so, use the chart in part 2 to indicate whether or not you believe your needs are currently being met by placing an X in the "yes" or "no" column. You may also place N/A in both columns if the question does not apply to you. When you are done, total up both columns to identify areas of strength and areas where you have an opportunity to address the needs in your life. Then use the last column to write a statement about a possible connection between your current state and your inner child. Lastly, in part 3, answer the synthesis questions. Follow with a grounding activity, such as any of the activities identified in chapter 2.

Part 1:

1. What activities did you love as a child?

___

___

___

2. How did you react if you were unable to do those activities?

___

___

___

3. How were you told you were supposed to act when you could not do the things you desired?

___

___

___

4. Do you still do any of those desired activities? Why or why not?

5. When you were a child, who were you expected to be or learn to be (e.g., what type of person, career, etc.)?

6. Did the expectations of your family match who you wanted to be?

7. How did you respond to disagreements or arguments?

8. Did you display behavior that was perceived as aggressive by others? Provide an example.

9. How did you handle being upset, anxious, scared, or afraid?

10. How were you told to handle those emotions?

11. What did you do to get the attention of your parents, teachers, or peers?

____

____

____

12. How did they respond to your attempts to get their attention?

____

____

____

13. Did you feel safe, loved, and accepted as a child? By whom?

____

____

____

Part 2:

	Yes	No	Connection to Inner Child
Are my basic needs met?			
My financial needs are met.			
My biological needs (e.g., food) are met.			
My housing needs are met.			
Do I feel secure?			
I feel safe in the physical environment where I live.			
I feel secure in my roles (e.g., as a parent or employee)			
I have faith in myself.			
Do I belong?			
I feel needed by others.			
I feel valued by others.			
I feel respected.			
I have positive interactions with others.			
Am I confident?			
I am confident in myself (e.g., skills and abilities).			
I am confident in those around me.			
I see opportunity for growth and healing.			

Am I helpful to others?			
I contribute to my community/society.			
I assist others in moving their goals forward.			
I desire to assist others.			
Total:			

Part 3:

1. What suppressed parts of you do you wish you could let out?

2. What did you do as a child that you wish you could do again?

3. What are you passionate about?

4. Can you turn any of your perceived "negative" or socially unacceptable qualities into useful attributes? Which of those qualities could you use to address needs that you identified as not being met in the previous chart?

5. What parts of your childhood can you now accept, and what can you release?

CASE SCENARIO*

Review the following case study. Then attempt to apply some of the ACTION approaches discussed in this chapter.

Name: Caroline
Setting: Community-Based Practice
Age: 19

I first met Caroline when she was 19 years of age. She was one of five children raised by a young single mother. Caroline's mother, Sharon, had a traumatic childhood with a history of poverty, parental neglect, and parental addiction. This included growing up with an alcoholic father who was abusive toward her mother. Sharon received public assistance to care for Caroline and her other siblings. In the past, they had experienced various evictions and stayed in homeless shelters in the interim. They eventually obtained a home through public housing. Caroline was the eldest child and cared for her siblings when her mother would work through the evenings, leaving Caroline in charge. Caroline was 8 years old when she began the role of the other primary caretaker.

In this caretaking role, Caroline would stay awake to care for her baby sister until her mother arrived home. When it came time to wake for school in the morning, both Caroline and Sharon would have difficulty rising. As a result, the children were frequently late for school or absent altogether. Eventually, Caroline decided to drop out of school and work to assist her family financially. Despite her intentions, Caroline found herself befriending a group of people from her neighborhood who introduced her to alcohol and illegal narcotics. This new group of friends gave her a sense of community and security that she had never experienced before. Caroline began spending significant amounts of time with her new friends, leaving her siblings home alone while their mother was at work.

Caroline developed a substance use disorder, which led her down a path of criminal activity to support her addiction. Secondary to unsafe behavior, she became pregnant at the age of 17. Unfortunately, Caroline did not realize she was expecting until she was five months pregnant, and she continued to utilize narcotics and alcohol throughout her pregnancy. Once she gave birth, Child Protective Services stepped in after the medical staff reported her substance use. Caroline was not able to provide the name of her newborn son's father, so Child Protective Services identified a foster family to care for the baby once he was discharged. The hospital social worker began aligning resources to identify an outpatient rehabilitation treatment program for Caroline upon discharge. Although this was not something Caroline desired, she wanted to work on getting her son back.

The social worker also reached out to the early intervention system, and a case manager developed a family plan of care, including early intervention services for the baby. They contacted my agency to begin an individualized family service plan. The plan involved Caroline attending therapy sessions at the daycare center her baby attended. I was one of the therapists who would come onsite, meet her there, and provide occupational therapy to her infant son. Other team members provided physical therapy services and additional developmental interventions as well. The intent was for Caroline to attend at least one session per week, but this proved to be a challenge as she was often absent from or extremely late to the sessions. Ultimately, it became more and more of a task for the entire team. I eventually reached out to the case manager to suggest a team meeting.

---

*Case study by Varleisha Gibbs, PhD, OTD, OTR/L

PROVIDER WORKSHEET

CASE ANALYSIS

In this chapter, we have reviewed background information on intergenerational trauma. After reading through Caroline's case, see if you are able to connect her trauma to her functioning. Use the following worksheet to analyze the case.

Task #1: Determine the risk factors for intergenerational trauma from Caroline's story. List the adverse events you acknowledged here.

____

____

____

____

Task #2: Using the space provided, practice making a genogram for Caroline based on the available information.

Task #3: What are the next steps? Based on some of the ACTION-from-Trauma approach activities in this chapter, what would you recommend for Caroline and her son?

____

____

____

____

CHAPTER 5

ORGANIZATIONS AND SYSTEMS RE-TRAUMATIZATION

The wide-ranging impacts of social trauma are felt by the collective, with consequences for those directly connected with the event, as well as indirect or vicarious repercussions for society at large. Social traumas affect the way in which we create meaning in the world. As practitioners, we increasingly operate in spaces at a time when we are both living through the wake of multiple social traumas and serving individuals who have experienced multiple dimensions of trauma. This ever-evolving dynamic requires being aware of the effects of trauma on survivors, as well as being mindful of the ways in which our lived experiences influence our perspectives and shape the environments in which we work.

In this chapter, we explore the underpinnings of social traumas and their effects. We further expound on barriers to care by discussing the impact of cultural trauma on our ability to provide optimal therapeutic outcomes and culturally competent interventions. Our ultimate aim is to explore how these traumas affect our organizational cultures and climates. We discuss the ways in which social and cultural traumas influence our organizations and systems, and we examine the potential organizational trauma that ensues in its aftermath.

Additionally, we review methods used to assess organizations in moving toward ACTION and discuss ways to create organizational cultures and climates that are inclusive for all. Finally, we provide reflective practices and techniques that practitioners can utilize to understand how we present in spaces, as well as to assist us in remaining resilient and centered in the midst of widespread turmoil. We anchor our discussion of social and cultural trauma, including how organizations and systems can result in re-traumatization, through the following sections:

- ☐ The Landscape
- ☐ Social Trauma
- ☐ Cultural Trauma
- ☐ Case Scenario
- ☐ Organizational Trauma
- ☐ Safe Spaces
- ☐ Cultural Safety
- ☐ Conflict Resolution
- ☐ Organizational Assessment
- ☐ Trauma-Informed Organizational Governance
- ☐ Case Scenario
- ☐ Self-Care Strategies for the Trauma-Informed Practitioner

THE LANDSCAPE

Social traumas are cataclysmic events that break down the basic fabric of society (Hirschberger, 2018). These include, but are not limited to, wars, natural disasters, pandemics, and genocides. Social trauma involves a definable social group, such as one's family or friends, and it encapsulates the effects of threats, disaster, deprivation, and violent conflict on a society's capacity to adapt to the world, to regulate and nourish themselves, and to develop. Most of us do not have to reflect back too far to recount a social trauma or an event that impacted society as a whole.

For many, 2020 was a year that cemented social trauma into our collective consciousness. At the time of this writing, coverage of the events influenced by the COVID-19 pandemic are front and center on every newscast, television station, and social media platform, as well as in the workplace and at the dinner table. Traumagenic events, such COVID-19, can precipitate challenges for individuals seeking intervention and recovery during times of unrest and turmoil. Though the impacts of COVID-19 are still emerging, traumatic experiences such as these are known to tax coping resources and challenge personality dynamics (Wilson, 2008).

As a society, we are collectively aware of the very real ramifications of the COVID-19 pandemic, which included shelter-in-place orders, record unemployment rates, travel bans, school closings, uncertainty, and loss of normalcy. With an estimated 24,135,690[*] reported cases of COVID-19 in the United States, adding to the 97,116,661[†] reported cases globally, and over 2,081,489 known deaths, our daily lives have dramatically changed as the world witnesses the unprecedented scale of this pandemic.

The course of this pandemic has shone light on the already vulnerable communities who struggle to access adequate resources and optimal interventions even in times of relative normalcy. It has disrupted vital food supply chains and access to critical health care for fragile communities worldwide. Each year, an estimated 243 million women ages 15–49 are subjected to intimate partner violence, with this number increasing under the conditions created by COVID-19 (United Nations Women, 2020). As this global crisis continues, resulting in continued disruptions to the health care system and food supply, maternal and child mortality is expected to increase dramatically (Roberton et al., 2020).

Moreover, the age of our 24/7 news media cycle can further disrupt, disorient, and re-traumatize individuals who have experienced social trauma, adding to an already brewing mix of dynamics. With continuing coverage of this pandemic, many are overstimulated by a constant barrage of information regarding the virulence of this virus, with ever-present updates of its spread throughout the world. As the effects of COVID-19 have begun to touch families in very intimate and personal ways, many have experienced a bombardment of updates on the health of loved ones, family members, and—in some cases—strangers who have been infected with, recovered from, or passed away from the virus.

---

[*]Centers for Disease Control and Prevention, as of January 21, 2021 (https://www.cdc.gov/coronavirus/2019-ncov/cases-updates/cases-in-us.html)

[†]Johns Hopkins University, Coronavirus Resource Center, as of January 21, 2021 (https://coronavirus.jhu.edu)

There are several long-term consequences of the continuing news coverage of social trauma. In particular, the repeated discussion of traumatic events and the proliferation of catastrophic images in times of social crisis may further traumatize already predisposed groups. It can result in the experience of secondary or vicarious trauma as individuals become emotionally over-aroused in response to repeated news coverage (Kaplan, 2008). This can disturb treatment progress and interfere with the intervention success.

For many, COVID-19 has caused lives and practices that were once foreign—such as social-distancing mandates, wearing personal protective equipment, and rising social isolation—to become familiar. Although data regarding the second- and third-order effects of these measures are emergent, we do know that loneliness and social isolation have serious impacts on mortality, with similar odds to light smoking and alcohol consumption (Xia & Li, 2018). As a health care practitioner, you may have experienced first-hand the impact of these unparalleled events in your personal life and in the lives of those you serve. As we collectively learn to adapt our behaviors, expectations, and lifestyles in response to this pandemic, many of us remain on the front lines interacting with and serving the public. This underscores the need to understand social trauma and its impacts on individuals and communities, as well as to tailor interventions that consider the cultural nuances of those we serve.

SOCIAL TRAUMA

Health care professionals provide vital expertise and intervention in response to disasters, social crises, and mass traumas. For those of us in client-facing roles, the upheaval and uncertainty caused by social traumas in particular can impact the delivery of our services and, ultimately, the success of our interventions. A large portion of those impacted are children, adolescents, and their caregivers, which underscores the need for successful interventions that promote recovery and healing (Joyce, 2020). Like other forms of structural traumas, those exposed to social trauma may also express emotion dysregulation, musculoskeletal problems, challenges with sensory perception and self-regulation, poor self-care skills, and cognitive deficits (Gorman & Hatkevich, 2016). The current and pervasive proximity of the COVID-19 pandemic has made understanding social traumas more critical for those in health care and in public service (Salas, 2020).

Social trauma can occur regardless of race, ethnicity, socioeconomic status, gender, or culture, although ethnic and racial minorities (particularly young adults) who come from low socioeconomic backgrounds are at greatest risk of traumagenic exposure (Benjet et al., 2016). Social traumas disproportionately affect historically underserved or marginalized communities, groups, and individuals. While tackling the complexities, emerging effects, and implications of the COVID-19 virus, we have found that it has also had a disproportionately devastating impact on historically disenfranchised communities, particularly Black and Latino communities.

Given that our nation has a historical past of systemically disenfranchising many communities—especially communities of color—we may not be ready, willing, or prepared to adequately provide intervention opportunities for those most affected. Although data for the COVID-19 pandemic is still emerging, early data shows an overrepresentation of Black people among hospitalized patients. In addition, while Black people make up about 13 percent of the U.S. population, they account for 27 percent of U.S. COVID-19 deaths (Kaur, 2020). Many factors contribute to these health disparities, including differences in living conditions, work circumstances, and preexisting health conditions experienced by members of ethnic and racial minorities (CDC, 2020), all of which underscore the need to explore cultural trauma and its implications on intervention.

CULTURAL TRAUMA

The potential for trauma exists among all major racial and ethnic groups in our society, yet few studies have analyzed how race and ethnicity are associated with trauma exposure and/or traumatic stress reactions. The word *trauma* implies overwhelming harm, physical injury, emotional stress, or emotional damage, and these collective experiences are often exacerbated by the proximity of generational trauma, discrimination, and historic marginalization (National Network to End Domestic Violence, n.d.).

Understanding the implications of cultural trauma, as well as its influences on the communities we serve and the interventions we create, is central to creating optimal resolutions and outcomes. Cultural trauma involves an intense loss of connection and identity that is experienced by members of a group and is permanently imprinted in the group's collective consciousness (Alexander et al., 2004). This trauma subsequently shapes the collective norms, behaviors, and mores of that culture. The trauma need not have been experienced by all in the social group, but its influence and impact are commonly accepted by those affected (Eyerman, 2019, p. 23). Examples of cultural traumas include, but are not limited to, African-American enslavement and its aftermath, the Holocaust, Native American genocide, and refugee and immigrant trauma. Though not a comprehensive account, these examples of cultural trauma provide a foundation for understanding the wide and complex experiences faced by those whom we serve.

Understanding the cultural and historical experiences and perspectives of those who seek our services is vital to producing successful treatment outcomes. It is important to understand that although the traumagenic experiences may have occurred in the distant past, the legacy of those traumagenic experiences remains for many in the collective group. Therefore, providing transformative interventions in communities that have experienced or are experiencing the effects of cultural traumas requires culturally competent environments that are safe, empowering, trustworthy, collaborative, and transparent. These environments should also facilitate personal reflection, development, and empathy.

Understanding the impacts of social and cultural trauma is critical to developing an ACTION approach and sustaining culturally competent treatment interventions. "Amidst the countless panoramas of traumas that are part of any disaster, the rendering of care must be responsive to the cultural context of suffering" (Marsella et al., 2008, p. xii). In particular, practitioners must acknowledge that trauma patterns and behaviors are repeated in a manner that impacts individuals in successive generations. Cultural traumas often exist in our family units, which affects our communities and relationships for subsequent generations. These traumas, which are a byproduct of our human experience and the experience of those who have come before us, are real and present. Cultural trauma renders an individual vulnerable to further trauma and to possible regression throughout their lifetime. An integral part of implementing effective treatment interventions and facilitating healing is understanding the impact that this cultural trauma has on clients. This means showing sensitivity to the situational and historical dimensions of the trauma, including racial, religious, socioeconomic, and political aspects.

There are many examples of practitioners facilitating interventions with good intentions, yet failing to understand the cultural, historical, and socioeconomic dimensions and context of a disaster or the complexity or nuance of the ensuing trauma, thereby subjecting clients to re-traumatization. The response to victims of Hurricane Katrina provides an example of the gross underestimation of the extent to which historic socioeconomic conditions, systemic disenfranchisement, and cultural norms can impact the provision of disaster relief and optimal interventions.

The cultural dimensions of trauma are also currently playing out in the midst of the COVID-19 pandemic. Many groups have witnessed acts of xenophobia, scapegoating, and—in some cases—physical assaults against Chinese Americans. Between January 28, 2020, and February 24, 2020, San Francisco researchers reported over 1,000 cases of xenophobia against Chinese American communities (Blanding & Solomon, 2020). These events, though not isolated, in the context of historic cultural trauma provide a foundation for the urgent requirement that we provide culturally appropriate and tailored interventions for those impacted.

In addition, racism and bias have a profound impact on the health status of children, adolescents, emerging adults, and their families (Trent, Dooley, & Dougé, 2019). In the case of Americans of African descent—who have experienced multigenerational trauma as a direct result of colonialism, enslavement, lynching, Jim Crow laws, mass incarceration, and other acts of deliberate disfranchisement and oppression—there may be a shared sense of collective memory and response around cultural trauma experiences. These experiences exacerbate disparities in health, wealth, and educational attainment and may present as maladaptive behaviors that affect emotional and behavioral development (Office of Minority Health, n.d.).

The effects of disenfranchisement are also evident in the Navajo Nation, who were hard hit by COVID-19—surpassing New York and New Jersey for the highest per capita coronavirus infection rate in the U.S. Historic disparities within the Navajo Nation have long existed, with 30 to 40 percent of residents not having access to running water, and with residents having access to few to no grocery stores (Silverman, Toropin, Sidner, & Perrot, 2020). The Navajo Nation continues to struggle with systemic challenges that are directly tied to historical disenfranchisement and the legacy of their community's experience with cultural trauma in the U.S.

When children, adolescents, and their caregivers are directly or indirectly exposed to traumagenic events such as these, it can lead to a myriad of challenges, including sadness, grief, pain, panic, confusion, despair, anxiety, and depression (Ayden, 2017). In the current era of COVID-19, these mental health challenges have been compounded by the widespread school closures that forced 90 percent of global learners (1.5 billion young people worldwide) out of school (Joyce, 2020). Schools provide important mental health resources for students, and these widespread closures resulted in students not receiving the needed care they would have otherwise received. Although we do not yet have data regarding the long-term mental health effects of COVID-19 on children and adolescents, the unprecedented scale of this health crisis underscores the importance of monitoring its effects and providing effective interventions for all affected.

CASE SCENARIO*

Review the following case study. Then attempt to apply some of the ACTION approaches discussed throughout this book.

Name: Christina
Setting: Community-Child Family Services
Age: 10

Christina is a 10-year-old, Taiwanese American girl who is currently residing in a pre-adoptive home with her younger sibling. Her biological mother was born in the U.S., while her biological father emigrated to the U.S. from Taiwan and had been living in the country on a Green Card until recently. Christina's biological mother had significant mental health issues, and her biological father struggled with substance abuse. When Christina was 5 years old, her parents separated, after which Christina's biological mother became her custodial parent, and Christina spent summers with her father's family. After one particular summer visit with her father, Christina's mother abandoned her and her younger sibling at a nearby school. Their mother simply placed the children outside of the vehicle and drove off. During this time, Christina's biological father returned to Taiwan for a few weeks to take care of family affairs. He was subsequently barred from reentering the U.S. due to multiple felony warrants and lost his Green Card status. At this point, Christina's parents relinquished parental rights for both Christina and her younger sibling, and the children were placed in a pre-adoptive foster home.

As a result of these multiple traumagenic disruptions, Christina experiences anxiety, nightmares, emotional distress, and defiance. Her defiance is currently directed at her pre-adoptive parents. When school was in session prior to the COVID-19 pandemic, I worked with Christina's teachers and support team to ensure she had support for her anxiety. She received early intervention services that included an individualized pre-adoptive family service plan and an individual development program (IDP), along with evaluations and a family history. Although Christina was a good student in school, she struggled to complete her schoolwork at home. She reported that staying at home made her feel like she was confined to a box.

As a result of the pandemic, Christina's anxiety is heightened, and she is afraid that she will catch the virus or that her friends will catch it. In addition, Christina experienced significant worries when the COVID-19 outbreak first began because she could not get in touch with her biological father. He was residing in Taiwan, which was near the epicenter of the outbreak, and she became very concerned and worried that he had fallen ill with the virus. As a result, she experienced increased anxiety, panic attacks, acts of defiance, and insomnia. She also frequently woke up screaming in the middle of the night, causing her to wake up the household. She would also often follow her adoptive parents closely around the home from room to room.

Because the COVID-19 pandemic has currently forced Christina out of school, she has not had a lot of peer-to-peer face time. She has some acquaintances from her dance class, as well as members from her father's side of the family, with whom she remains in contact via video chat. I also currently work with Christina and her family once a week on a virtual basis to provide guidance and intervention. Because COVID-19 has required families to coexist together under the same roof for months at a time, I have witnessed an increased need for practitioners to implement more interventions and to assist families and children like Christina.

*Case study by Roxanne McPherson, MSW

PROVIDER WORKSHEET

CASE ANALYSIS

In this chapter, we have reviewed background information on social and cultural trauma. After reading through Christina's case, see if you are able to connect the adverse events in her history to her current functioning. Use the following worksheet to analyze the case.

Task #1: Use the Adverse Child Experiences (ACE) Questionnaire from chapter 1 to determine Christina's ACE score. List the adverse events you acknowledged here.

____

____

____

____

____

What is her total ACE score? ____________________

Task #2: Write a reflection for Christina's case story. Did you notice any themes of trauma in her story? As a result, what challenges would you suspect or anticipate?

____

____

____

____

____

Task #3: What are the next steps? How could you address Christina's trauma to enhance the success of your services?

____

____

____

____

____

ORGANIZATIONAL TRAUMA

Trauma is not relegated to individuals, families, or communities. Organizations are ecosystems—systems built on a shared mission, vision, and values. These prescribed systems are sustained through a complex combination of organizational dynamics, norms, behaviors, ethics, and beliefs. Equally as important, these systems are predicated on the people who sustain and fuel them. Therefore, just as individuals are susceptible to trauma, the organizations in which we work are susceptible to trauma. In particular, organizations are vulnerable to the unresolved traumas of those who work and operate within its structure. Much like structural trauma, organizational trauma is emotionally and cognitively overwhelming. "It can fracture our self-protective structures, making us feel vulnerable and helpless" (Resource Sharing Project, 2016).

An organization can be traumatized as a result of sudden devastating events or be subjected to ongoing wounding (Vivian & Hormann, 2013). For example, a catastrophic event, such as the COVID-19 pandemic, can overwhelm an organization's already stressed culture and climate, devastating coping systems that normally provide a sense of control for the organization and its members. When coping systems fail, healing from these traumatic events is difficult, and sometimes impossible, causing the organization's people and culture to suffer (Table 9). In health care settings in particular, working with patients who have experienced trauma puts both clinical and non-clinical staff at risk of secondary traumatic stress (Menschner, Maul, & Center for Health Care Strategies, 2016). Indeed, many in the helping professions may have their own personal trauma histories, which may be exacerbated by working with others who have experienced trauma (Menschner et al., 2016).

Emotional Reactions	Temporary feelings of shock, fear, grief, anger, resentment, guilt, shame, helplessness, hopelessness, emotional numbness
Cognitive Reactions	Confusion, disorientation, indecisiveness, worry, shortened attention span, difficulty concentrating, memory loss, unwanted memories, self-blame
Physical Reactions	Tension, fatigue, edginess, difficulty sleeping, bodily aches or pain, starling easily, racing heartbeat, nausea, change in appetite, change in sex drive
Interpersonal Reactions	Feelings of distrust or irritability toward others; conflict, withdrawal, or isolation; feeling rejected or abandoned; being distant, judgmental, or overcontrolling of others

Table 9. Symptoms of Organizational Trauma During a Crisis (Young, Ford, Ruzek, Friedman, & Gusman, 1998)

Fundamentally, organizational trauma occurs when physical or emotional stress overwhelms the workplace. This stress can affect productivity, culture, and climate as individuals struggle with emotional exhaustion, become detached from clients or the work itself, and exhibit a reduced sense of personal accomplishment or commitment toward the workplace (Venugopal, 2016). Some of the many causes of work-related stress include long hours, unfair treatment, heavy workload, job insecurity, lack of communication and support from management, unreasonable time pressure, and conflicts with coworkers or bosses. Many organizations are facing an employee burnout crisis, with recent research finding that 23 percent of employees feel burned out at work (Wigert & Agrawal, 2018).

The following worksheet can help you assess your own susceptibility to burnout. If your score indicates that you are at high risk for burnout, it is imperative to develop a personal action plan to address your well-being. This may entail seeking professional assistance, making career and lifestyle modifications, and using tools and techniques to help you re-center (see Table 13 later in this chapter).

PROVIDER WORKSHEET

BURNOUT SUSCEPTIBILITY ASSESSMENT

Age Range: Adult

Objective: To determine susceptibility to burnout

Directions: For each statement listed here, put a check mark in the appropriate column to indicate whether you agree or disagree with each statement. Then tally the check marks for each column to determine your relative risk for and susceptibility to burnout. The column with highest number of check marks indicates your relative burnout susceptibility.

	Agree (low risk)	**Disagree (high risk)**
I am motivated and productive at work.		
I have feelings of hope and helpfulness about my position.		
I enjoy going to work.		
I contribute to my workplace and am fulfilled by my work.		
I am patient and engaged with my clients and coworkers.		
I am engaged and alert at work.		
I am currently supported in my role.		
My work life and home life are balanced and healthy.		
My work volume is balanced and manageable.		
I am in relatively good health.		
I get adequate sleep and wake up feeling refreshed and well rested.		
I feel safe and respected in my work environment.		
Total		

Organizational trauma is not part of the normal organizational life cycle. It is a disruptive occurrence or pattern outside the usual organizational experience. In environments where the organization's mission is related to assisting individuals who have experienced trauma, an organizational culture that is not reflective, responsive, and adaptive to its environment can become a source of trauma. In fact, many systems that were created to assist individuals at some of the most vulnerable times in their lives can cause harm or unintentionally re-traumatize them. This principle is applicable to both client-facing services and internal business operations.

Unresolved trauma in the workplace creates barriers to communication and innovation, and it can negatively affect productivity. Unresolved trauma draws with compound interest, ultimately creating toxic spaces full of unsettled and unhealthy conflict, which eventually compromises the integrity of the organization's mission. Across time, the organizational system "can become reactive, change-resistant, hierarchical, coercive, and punitive. Traumatized organizations may begin to exhibit symptoms of collective trauma similar to those of their clients, creating a 'trauma-organized culture'" (Bloom, 2007, p. 3).

Therefore, changing organizational practices to fit trauma-informed principles is necessary to create and sustain a healthy and safe organizational environment. Doing so ensures that we are living up to our professional ideals, standards, and obligations so we can create and sustain outcomes in alignment with our stated mission, vision, values, and goals. When an organization commits to being trauma-informed, a stakeholder committee, including individuals who have experienced trauma, should be organized to oversee the process (Menschner et al., 2016). Being trauma-informed also requires a continuous process of reflection (at the self and organizational level), assessment, and process improvement. Reflection and assessment are an essential part of the continuous feedback process, which allow organizations to acknowledge and correct systemic barriers that may impede its ability to heal, execute its mission, and facilitate its goals. When there is a healthy organizational culture and climate, it creates optimal therapeutic outcomes for clients and staff alike by promoting emotional and social well-being.

A safe, supportive, welcoming, and respectful environment is essential for optimal outcomes. Our organizations—be they private practice settings, rehabilitation centers, hospitals, schools, or corporate settings—are enhanced when they are equipped to handle clients with skill, empathy, and competency. An environment that is restorative and ACTION-focused requires foresight and purposeful planning. However, before attempting to transform, adapt, or optimize a culture or climate, we must first understand it.

SAFE SPACES

The prevalence of structural trauma in current society—specifically the social trauma stemming from the COVID-19 pandemic—is unprecedented and underscores the need for trauma-informed care and safe spaces where clients, families, staff, and others can heal, recover, and thrive. As we described in chapter 1, trauma-informed care lays the foundation for our ACTION-from-Trauma approach, and it is thus a necessary starting place for organizations and systems as well. A trauma-informed perspective is one in which program staff, agency staff, and service providers:

1. Routinely screen for trauma exposure and related symptoms
2. Use culturally appropriate evidence-based assessment and treatment
3. Make resources available to children, families, and providers on trauma exposure, impact, and treatment

4. Engage in efforts to strengthen the resilience and protective factors of children and families impacted by and vulnerable to trauma
5. Address parent and caregiver trauma and its impacts on the family system
6. Emphasize continuity of care and collaboration across systems
7. Maintain an environment of care for staff that addresses, minimizes, and treats secondary traumatic stress and that increases staff resilience (National Child Traumatic Stress Network, 2016)

In addition, ACTION-focused organizations evaluate clients and staff using trauma-informed principles, including safety, collaboration, cultural inclusivity, empowerment, and choice. It is then necessary to follow up by creating growth and teaching neuroeducation. By conducting a trauma-informed organizational self-assessment, organizations can examine their current practices and take specific steps toward ACTION (see section on Organizational Assessment). This self-assessment is a critical step in developing and sustaining an organizational climate and culture that is equipped and prepared for today's real and pervasive challenges.

Once an organization and its practitioners are knowledgeable about the prevalence and dimensions of trauma, the onus is on the organization and its leadership to sustain safe spaces that are reflective of its intentions to care for individuals with compassion, empathy, and skill. Establishing the integrity by which they create and maintain these spaces is necessary to provide optimal therapeutic outcomes and interventions for clients, families, staff, and others who have experienced trauma, including social or cultural trauma.

A safe space hinges not simply on cognitively understanding the dimensions of the lived experience but on understanding that the presentations of the experiences will be as nuanced as the individual. A culturally competent and safe organization allows providers and organizations to effectively tailor their services to meet the social, cultural, and linguistic needs of all clients. Safe spaces are empowering, collaborative, and transparent, and they garner and maintain trust.

CULTURAL SAFETY

Creating and sustaining cultural safety necessitates an organizational culture that embeds, encourages, and fosters reflective practices so the system can determine how the values of its own culture may be in conflict with another's culture or experience. Foundational in creating and sustaining culturally safe spaces is understanding the role of cultural competency, cultural inclusivity, diversity, and implicit biases in an organization's ability to deliver its standard of care. In creating safe spaces, we must ask ourselves:

1. How do we create and sustain safe spaces (for both our staff and clients)?
2. What is cultural competency and its connection to trauma dynamics?
3. How do diversity and cultural inclusivity influence trauma dynamics?
4. How do our implicit biases affect our delivery of care and intervention?
5. How does our organization handle conflict when it arises?
6. How do we as practitioners show up in spaces?

Creating safe spaces requires that organizations and practitioners make a commitment to continuing education on topics related to cultural competency, diversity and cultural inclusion, and implicit bias. They must also create space for both professional and personal reflection and development. This fosters an educated, responsive, and adaptive organizational culture.

Cultural Competency

People are not monolithic, and even if they have similar cultural, linguistic, or historical affiliations, trauma expresses itself differently across individuals. Therefore, when serving individuals from similar cultural, ethnic, religious, or linguistic backgrounds, it is critical to appreciate their many differences. This can include differences in their lived experiences, socioeconomic status, English language proficiency, and educational attainment—among many other attributes. It is particularly important to be knowledgeable about a group's cultural trauma or lived experiences when creating interventions that produce optimal outcomes. Failure to do so can result in *stereotype threat*, which involves reducing others to group stereotypes that commonly operate within the health care domain, including stereotypes regarding unhealthy lifestyles and inferior intelligence (Abdou, Fingerhut, Jackson, & Wheaton, 2016). The following paragraphs provide several considerations to create growth in our ACTION-from-Trauma approach.

Cultural competence is the integration and transformation of knowledge about individuals and groups of people into specific standards, policies, practices, and attitudes used in appropriate cultural settings to increase the quality of services, thereby producing better outcomes (National Prevention Information Network, n.d.). *Culture* refers to human behavior, such as language, thoughts, communication, actions, customs, values, and beliefs, as well as racial, ethnic, or religious backgrounds. *Competence* implies the ability to enact those esteemed behaviors, attitudes, policies, and procedures effectively (National Prevention Information Network, n.d.). When it is well executed, cultural competence facilitates effective cross-cultural communication, learning, and interventions, which produces a more agile, adaptive, and inclusive environment.

The goal of cultural competency is not simply to understand diverse cultural expressions but to harness those diverse perspectives effectively in our spaces to produce better outcomes. The prevalence of physical and structural trauma—and in particular cultural trauma—makes creating and sustaining culturally competent safe spaces imperative for the outcomes we seek.

Principles of Cultural Competence

(National Prevention Information Network, n.d.)

1. Define culture broadly.
2. Value clients' cultural beliefs.
3. Recognize complexity in language interpretation.
4. Facilitate learning between providers and communities.
5. Involve the community in defining and addressing service needs.
6. Collaborate with other agencies or organizations.
7. Professionalize staff hiring and training.
8. Institutionalize cultural competence.
9. Assess the organization or agency culture and climate.

Understanding that each client's, family's, or staff member's lived experienced is unique is the foundation of effective cultural competence. Effective cultural competence is an essential proficiency at both the individual practitioner and organizational levels (see Table 10).

Individual	Organizational
Be aware of cultural differences	Embrace diversity and inclusion
Understand your culture	Conduct a culture and climate organizational assessment
Conduct a personal self-assessment	Manage the organizational dynamics of differences
Acquire cultural competency knowledge and skills	Embed cultural knowledge within the organization
View interactions within a cultural context	Adapt to diversity
Continuous process assessment, feedback, and improvement	

Table 10. Elements of Cultural Competence*

Cultural competence is a continuum toward ACTION with the ultimate objective being cultural proficiency. As practitioners, the first step we can take is to train ourselves to increase our awareness and understanding of the presence of culture among those we serve. As we learn the unique cultural nuances and norms of our clients, it is vital that our understanding does not lead to an overreliance on cultural archetypes, which can lead to stereotyping or generalizing, the result of which may inadvertently affect health care efficacy and even prompt some patients to avoid care. Moving toward ACTION, we hold each other accountable and provide support where needed.

Diversity and Cultural Inclusivity

Diversity and inclusion have pivotal roles in creating and sustaining safe spaces for those impacted by social or cultural trauma. They build trust, establish purpose, and create understanding. Cultural competency is the framework, while diversity and inclusion are the practice. When implemented thoughtfully, diversity and inclusion initiatives can enhance collaboration, empowerment, and overall well-being, while also fostering a sense of belonging and purpose for both clients and practitioners. We understand diversity as the proverbial melting pot, where individuals across lines of differences are represented in key roles within the organization.

Diversity does not simply involve respect for physical lines of difference (e.g., race, gender, age, ability, religion, sexual orientation). It also involves attention to cognitive, relational, physical, and occupational diversity. However, diversity is moot without inclusion. To have both a diverse and inclusive team of practitioners is a practical goal in creating and maintaining safe spaces. If diversity is the proverbial melting pot, then inclusion is a gumbo. Inclusion is a tapestry made from our diverse domains. Inclusion has to do with the involvement and empowerment of others, where an individual's inherent worth and dignity are recognized, harnessed, and leveraged. Cultural inclusivity thus recognizes, appreciates, and utilizes the diversity of people of all cultural orientations.

As we have discussed, many of the well-meaning systems, practices, or principles created to assist individuals at some of the most vulnerable times in their lives can and will inadvertently cause harm or re-traumatize clients. These same systems, practices, or principles may also inadvertently damage an

---

*Adapted from Cross, Bazron, Dennis, & Issacs (1989)

organization's internal operations, such as recruitment, retention, morale, and cohesiveness. Lack of diversity and inclusion in an organization creates blind spots and ultimately impacts the organization's ability to create and sustain cultural safety for those it serves. In creating systems and environments for individuals who have experienced structural trauma, and in particular cultural trauma, it is critical to appreciate the effect that diversity and inclusion can have on healing and recovery.

Implicit Bias

Although the limbic system or "emotional brain" controls our fight-or-flight response, it also controls our automatic assumptions about what is the "other." Developed to assist humans in assessing danger, it is the center of our implicit biases. Implicit (or unconscious) biases can be understood as a "form of rapid social categorization," whereby we routinely and rapidly sort people into groups (Spectra Diversity, 2017). The implicit biases we harbor in our subconscious affect our feelings and attitudes about other people based on their characteristics, such as their race, ethnicity, age, and appearance. These associations develop over the course of our life, beginning at a very early age, and occur through exposure to direct and indirect messages about the "other." In addition to our early life experiences, the media and the news are often-cited origins of implicit biases (Staats, Capatosto, Wright, & Jackson, 2016).

Uncovering our implicit biases is a lifelong process, but it is central to building bridges across our lines of difference. The ability to see, assess, and treat those with whom we interact as individuals is fundamental to implementing authentic interventions that have lasting effects. In examining the five dimensions of trauma, we understand the underlying mechanisms and manifestations of trauma, and we also recognize the organizational climate, culture, and systemic barriers that may impede our noblest of efforts to treat it. However, if we cannot connect with those we serve on an individual level, then we will create well-meaning interventions that do not produce optimal outcomes.

What Is the Difference Between a Bias, a Prejudice, and Discrimination?

- A bias is an inclination toward one way of thinking that is often based on how you were raised. A bias lacks a neutral viewpoint (e.g., "_____ people are _____.")
- A prejudice is an opinion, prejudgment, or attitude about a group or its individual members. A prejudice can be positive, but in our usage it refers to a negative attitude that is often accompanied by ignorance, fear, or hatred. Prejudices are formed by a complex psychological process that begins with attachment to a close circle of acquaintances or an "in-group," such as a family, with prejudice then aimed at any "out-groups."
- Discrimination refers to behavior that treats people unequally because of their group memberships. Discriminatory behavior, ranging from slights to hate crimes, often begins with negative stereotypes and prejudices.

Implicit biases are persistent in that they are related to, but have distinct mental constructs from, our explicit biases. We must understand that they do not necessarily align with our declared beliefs, and they generally favor our own in-group (e.g., people of the same race, sex, religion, or spiritual faith). However, these implicit biases have been found to contribute to disparities in health care access and treatment among racial and ethnic minorities. These disparities persist even when controlling for a wide variety of sociodemographic factors (Snowden, 2002). Therefore, it is imperative to understand how our implicit biases affect our ability to provide culturally competent care. Implicit biases color the way we connect with, address, and treat others.

Given that our implicit biases are part of our subconscious programming, they are often difficult to unearth. They are a part of the fabric of who we are at our core, and they develop as we develop. However, the good news is that these biases are still malleable. Because our brains are incredibly complex and plastic, we can gradually unlearn implicit biases through a variety of de-biasing techniques. The first step in this process is to develop awareness of our own implicit biases. We can take all the training in the world, routinely assess our organizations, and hire well-informed and diverse staff, but if we are not aware of how *we* show up in spaces, our organizations and clients will suffer. As practitioners, we are ambassadors for our values. Many of us entered our respective profession to effect change, to serve, or to heal. Authentic life application of these ideals requires commitment to personal development. Without self-awareness, we are running on subconscious programming. The desire to transform our connections, our workspaces, and ultimately our communities is built on the foundation that healing is possible. As in the first step in our ACTION-from-Trauma Approach, we cannot address what we do not **A**cknowledge. The following are some de-biasing strategies to develop this self-awareness:

1. Acknowledge that we all harbor implicit biases, and commit to a desire to evolve through them.
2. Take an Implicit Association Test (IAT) or equivalent, which provides you with a basic understanding of your implicit bias. It is a starting point for understanding how you show up in spaces. Table 11 provides a short list of these assessments.
3. Pay attention when stereotypical responses or assumptions come up.
4. Practice new tasks designed to break automatic associations:
   - Retrain your brain.
   - Actively doubt your objectivity.
   - Be mindful of snap judgments.
   - Oppose your stereotyped thinking.
   - Deliberately expose yourself to counter-stereotypical models and images.
   - Look for counter-stereotypes.
   - Remind yourself that you have implicit bias.
   - Engage in mindfulness exercises on a regular basis.
   - Engage in cross-difference relationships.
   - Shift perspectives.
   - Examine your personal blind spots using a tool like the Johari Window (Nalty, 2016).

Our lived experiences shape our worldview, and if you have lived on the planet, you have implicit biases. These implicit biases fuel policies, behaviors, norms, and attitudes that can inadvertently re-traumatize staff and clients. To create culturally competent trauma-informed care, we must actively work to assess our inner organization, as well as the greater organizational culture. No two people experience reality in the same way. In order to transform a system, we must commit to evolving through our implicit biases.

On the next page is a sample assessment tool that you can use to examine your own implicit biases using the Johari Window. This simple tool provides a useful demonstration that our perception of self is often at odds with how others perceive us.

PROVIDER WORKSHEET

THE JOHARI WINDOW*

Age Range: Adolescents and adults

Objective: To assist practitioners in improving communication, interpersonal relationships, self-awareness, and group dynamics

Description: The Johari Window is a simple self-awareness tool for organizing and inventorying personal characteristics from multiple perspectives. Created in 1955 by Jospeh Luft and Harry Ingram, the Johari Window contains a horizontal and a vertical axis. The horizontal axis describes our perception of self, while the vertical axis describes the group's (or a peer's) perception of us. Perceptions can be known or unknown along either axis, creating four distinct quadrants:

1. **Open Area:** Represents your perception of self
2. **Blind Area**: Represents any aspect that you do not know about yourself but that others within the group have become aware of (called your "blind spot")
3. **Hidden Area**: Represents aspects about yourself that you are aware of but might not want others to know
4. **Unknown Area:** Represents what is both unknown to you and to others

	Known to Self	**Unknown to Self**
Known to Others	Open Area	Blind Spot
Unknown to Others	Hidden Area (Façade)	Unknown

*Adapted from https://www.selfawareness.org.uk/news/understanding-the-johari-window-model

The Johari Window uses 56 adjectives as possible descriptions to emphasize behavior, empathy, and interpersonal development in each of these quadrants:

- Able
- Accepting
- Adaptable
- Bold
- Brave
- Calm
- Caring
- Cheerful
- Clever
- Complex
- Confident
- Dependable
- Dignified
- Empathetic
- Energetic
- Extroverted
- Friendly
- Giving
- Happy
- Helpful
- Idealistic
- Independent
- Ingenious
- Intelligent
- Introverted
- Kind
- Knowledgeable
- Logical
- Loving
- Mature
- Modest
- Nervous
- Observant
- Organized
- Patient
- Powerful
- Proud
- Quiet
- Reflective
- Relaxed
- Religious
- Responsive
- Searching
- Self-Assertive
- Self-Conscious
- Sensible
- Sentimental
- Shy
- Silly
- Spontaneous
- Sympathetic
- Tense
- Trustworthy
- Warm
- Wise
- Witty

Directions: The Johari Window activity is conducted in pairs. For optimal use, the tool requires partners to have some knowledge of each other. It is best suited for established teams as opposed to being used as an ice-breaker with a new group of employees or during orientation or onboarding.

After pairing off, select 6 adjectives from the provided list of 56 that best describe you. Ask your partner to select 6 adjectives that they believe describe you from the same list. Then plot the adjectives onto the quadrant template as follows:

1. Place adjectives that were selected by both you and your partner into the open quadrant.
2. Place adjectives that were selected by you (but not your partner) into the hidden quadrant.
3. Place adjectives that were not selected by you (but were selected by your partner) into the blind spot quadrant.
4. Place adjectives that were not selected by either you or your partner into the unknown quadrant.

Understanding the Results: We are often unaware of our behavior or how our behavior can impact others. The Johari Window can assist you in understanding how you show up in spaces and can allow you to discover aspects of yourself that you may not have known or appreciated in the past. The tool is not static, and the balance between the quadrants can change over time. For example, you can incrementally grow your "open area," or reduce your "blind spot" area, by seeking constructive, honest feedback. Similarly, sharing an aspect of yourself that you have previously kept hidden can assist in opening your "hidden area."

Personal Reflection: Self-reflection a critical step in understanding our implicit biases. Through the use of this tool and tools like it, we have an opportunity to appreciate ourselves through the eyes of others and to build new pathways of self-reflection and personal development. Take a moment to reflect on what you uncovered about yourself. In a quiet space, take a moment to capture your reflections here.

1. Was this your first time using this tool?

    ____ Yes ____ No

2. What did you discover about yourself?

    ____

    ____

3. Describe why you selected the six adjectives used to describe yourself.

    ____

    ____

4. Did you have difficulty selecting six adjectives to describe yourself? Why or why not?

    ____

    ____

5. How did you feel reviewing the six adjectives your partner selected to describe you?

    ____

    ____

6. How closely did your partner's perception of you match your perception of self?

____

____

7. Were you in agreement with the adjectives your partner selected to describe you? Why or why not?

____

____

8. What activities or actions could you take to lessen your "blind spot" quadrant?

____

____

9. What three activities will assist you in opening your "hidden" quadrant?

____

____

CONFLICT RESOLUTION

Even after learning and applying the framework of cultural competency, diversity, and inclusion, as well as understanding the role of implicit biases in our interactions with others, conflicts may arise. Therefore, conflict resolution is a key component toward ACTION. Conflict is often exacerbated in times of high stress and unrest, raising the need for a means to mitigate organizational conflict. Toxic spaces are full of unhealthy conflict, which compromises the integrity of our spaces. The health of a space depends on the health and well-being of its people. Employing methods to mitigate conflict is vital to creating and maintaining safe spaces, as well as to reducing the creation of a toxic work environment or hostile workplace.

Conflict is an inevitable part of the human-to-human experience. Navigating it with skill, compassion, and competency takes practice. Organizations can assist in mitigating conflict by first understanding its source. The use of conflict coaches, trained mediators, employee assistance programs, or ombudsmen can assist organizations in getting to the root cause of conflict, as well as in developing best practices that assist the organization in creating better outcomes.

ORGANIZATIONAL ASSESSMENT

Organizational transformation is an inside job. At the heart of effective organizational transformation are its people. Effective organizational cultures thrive on empathy and are sustained through reflection, assessment, communication, and a continuous commitment to process improvement. Proper diagnosis of organizational trauma and dysfunction is made using validated assessment tools and instruments (Nevis, 1987/2001). Organizations whose intent is on intervention, healing, recovery, and growth engage in a continuous process of self-reflection, assessment, and process improvement. It is crucial that we assess our organization's climate and culture routinely, specifically when caring for individuals impacted by structural trauma. When assessing an organization, we often think of its systems, but secondary trauma and organizational trauma are often intertwined, thus underscoring the need for full system assessment.

An organizational assessment follows a systems science approach to assess organizational dynamics, and it is accomplished in three phases: data collection, analysis, and action planning. There are several validated tools and frameworks used to assess organizational culture, climate, and implicit biases, as well as trauma-informed indicators. Table 11 provides a short list of these assessments.

Organizational Culture and Climate Assessment	Implicit Bias Assessment
Organizational Culture Assessment Instrument (OCAI)	Implicit Association Test (IAT)
Denison Organizational Culture Survey	Affect Misattribution Procedure (AMP)
Gallup Q12 Employee Engagement Survey	Implicit Relational Assessment Procedure (IRAP)
	Relational Responding Task (RRT)
Trauma-Informed Organizational Assessment	
Trauma-Informed Care Top Ten: A Checklist for Behavioral Health Organizations*	

Table 11. Tools to Assess Organizational Culture, Climate, and Implicit Biases

*Available at https://www.thenationalcouncil.org/wp-content/uploads/2013/05/Trauma-Top-Ten-Checklist.pdf?daf=375ateTbd56

TRAUMA-INFORMED ORGANIZATIONAL GOVERNANCE

Becoming a trauma-informed organization requires steady support from senior leaders (Menschner et al., 2016). Like all organizational change, organizational transformation is a top-down initiative, with leadership support required at all levels. This support is necessary to successfully implement trauma-informed governance, in which we can begin to move toward ACTION by defining an organization's trauma-informed mission, vision, and values. The organization's trauma-informed mission statement defines the organization's "why." This short, concise statement defines why the organization exists, what its overall goals are, and what type of service it delivers. The organization's vision statement defines the organization's aspirations and solidifies "what" the organization will achieve. Finally, its values reflect the organization's collective judgment. Values define and underscore "how" members of the organizational system interact with one another. A strategic implementation plan that aligns with the organization's mission, vision, and values puts ACTION into the trauma-informed care approach.

Next, the organization engages key stakeholders in the planning phases of this work. It is important to receive input from those impacted by the trauma we treat. This feedback is gathered in various ways, including stakeholder roundtable discussions, stakeholder sensing sessions, a stakeholder needs assessment, or individual stakeholder interviews. After assessing and reviewing key stakeholder responses and gathering trauma-informed community best practices, we create the policies and procedures that will govern implementation of trauma-informed protocols. Such policies and procedures should include monitoring strategies to create growth toward healing.

Creation of trauma-informed organizational governance ensures that the program has clear, concise instruction for consistent delivery of care that is inclusive for all. Standard operating procedures assist the organization in maintaining quality assurance and quality control over its trauma-informed care initiatives. It is also important to obtain feedback from key staff members who will be responsible for implementing the governance. After the organization creates trauma-informed governance, it moves into ACTION by training all staff on its mission, vision, values, trauma-informed policies, procedures, and governance. This must include neuroeducation, even if at the most basic level. Finally, after implementation, a commitment to continuous process improvement is required, which should begin with an annual trauma-informed culture and climate assessment and ACTION re-education on creating growth and neuroeducation. Table 12 provides a checklist for this plan of action.

Phase	Action	Intent
1	Engage in planning	• What are our organization's strengths, weaknesses, opportunities, and threats? • What is our trauma-informed mission? • Who are our stakeholders? • What resources are needed to implement this plan of action? • What is our time frame for program implementation?
2	Define the organization's trauma-informed mission, vision, and values	Mission, vision, and values are foundational in establishing trauma-informed care: • Mission is the organization's "why" • Vision is the "what" • Values is the "how"

3	Conduct key stakeholder needs assessment	• Trauma presents differently in the individuals we serve. When establishing a trauma-informed organization, it is imperative that we include stakeholders who have experienced the trauma we seek to treat. Their voices are valuable and critical in creating appropriate and successful interventions.
4	Create trauma-informed policies, procedures, and governance	• Trauma-informed policies, procedures, and governance establish best practices for maintaining cohesiveness of care and its implementation. • Seek feedback from key staff members prior to finalizing the trauma-informed policies, procedures, and governance. This feedback allows staff to have a stake in the policies and procedures they will implement. It also ensures connection between planning and application.
5	Train clinical and non-clinical staff on trauma-informed mission, vision, values, policies, procedures, and governance	• Disseminating the principles of trauma-informed governance to all the organization stakeholders ensures alignment with the organization's stated mission, vision, and values. • Training enhances staff skills, capabilities, and knowledge.
6	Conduct annual culture and climate assessment	• Assessment allows the organization to benchmark efforts and document progress in pursuit of their stated mission, vision, and values. • A trauma-informed assessment assists an organization in identifying its strengths, challenges, and areas for optimization. • Assessment is crucial to the program's continued success and ability.

Table 12. Trauma-Informed Plan of Action Checklist

CASE SCENARIO*

Review the following case study. Then attempt to apply some of the ACTION approaches discussed in this chapter.

Organization: Public School District
Setting: School-based

This particular public school district is located in a large, populous city. It has learners from kindergarten through 12th grade and has 111 schools in its portfolio. At the time of our assessment, 36 percent of its students demonstrated proficiency in mathematics, and 34 percent demonstrated proficiency in reading, with 42 percent on track to graduate in the year of our assessment. The school system had 4,113 teachers servicing 46,498 students. The poverty level for the district students was 22 percent. The school system had invested time and money into improving student performance by closing underutilized schools and reorganizing underperforming schools. The state superintendent's office and the school system took many steps to improve accountability and performance. At the request of district leadership, our team conducted an organizational climate assessment with the school's administrative staff six years post September 11, 2001, as the district was located near the epicenter of the attacks.

Due to its proximity to the events on 9/11, many of the administrative staff, support staff, teachers, and students were directly impacted by the events. At time of our assessment, about one-fifth of the district's teachers and a quarter of its principals had resigned, had retired, or were terminated. The school district's achievement shortfalls and systemic leadership mismanagement were constant topics of public discourse, both in the media and in the minds of many of its constituents. This public discourse—among many other challenges, such as the pressure of massive school reorganizations and budget cuts—assisted in fueling low morale, internal conflict, and uncertainly in the district offices. In turn, the district office saw an increase in grievances filed alleging a hostile work environment, discrimination, and unfair labor practices. The purpose of our district office organizational climate assessment was to get to the root of the concerns regarding low morale, discrimination, conflict, and hostility.

*Case study by Nikki Harley, MSOD

PROVIDER WORKSHEET

CASE ANALYSIS

In this chapter, we have reviewed background information on organizational trauma. After reading through the case study regarding the school district, use the following worksheet to analyze the case.

Task #1: Define the elements presented in the public school district case scenario that constitute organizational trauma.

____

____

____

____

____

Task #2: In a district leadership position, which tools would you utilize to assist in mitigating allegations of discrimination and a hostile or toxic work environment?

____

____

____

____

____

Task #3: What are the next steps? What would you recommend to ensure the school has addressed the noted challenges and traumagenic events impacting its work environment?

____

____

____

____

____

SELF-CARE STRATEGIES FOR THE TRAUMA-INFORMED PRACTITIONER

Using an ACTION-from-Trauma approach allows value-centric organizations to create, sustain, and promote a culture and climate in which wellness and well-being are intentional, comprehensive, and integrated into its values. Whole people arrive in our spaces. People with illnesses, worries, loves, obligations, commitments, dreams, and aspirations. The better equipped we are to honor the whole person, the more balanced, aligned, and productive our organizations become. Total well-being matters. We must nurture our own minds, bodies, and spirits as much as we nurture the individuals we serve. Well-being encompasses multiple domains, including emotional, environmental, financial, intellectual, occupational, physical, social, and spiritual domains (Swarbrick, 2006).

Thus far, we have defined social and cultural traumas and discussed their respective impact on treatment interventions. We have also discussed organizational trauma and its impacts. Now we will examine how we, as practitioners, show up in spaces. The true work of a practitioner is one of a healer, but in order for practitioners to create a pathway toward healing for others, we must first be willing to take care of ourselves. This requires empathy, vulnerability, authenticity, commitment, and reflection.

Creating organizations that work harmoniously in times of great stress requires team members who are resilient and centered. As practitioners, we serve people who have experienced any of the dimensions of trauma we have discussed. We also work in organizations and spaces that can cause or reactivate trauma. Over time, this traumatic exposure can cause us to experience secondary trauma, resulting in anxiety, depression, and PTSD, among other experiences. These times of high stress and crisis can lead to stress and burnout. Just as we have recognized the diverse manifestation of structural trauma in those we serve, organizations must recognize the symptoms of stress, burnout, and secondary trauma among its practitioners.

Organizations can assess and mitigate employee burnout through multiple system interventions. At the individual level, it is imperative to acknowledge and communicate your needs. Communicate with your coworkers, supervisors, and employees about job-related stress. In addition, there is a pervasive cultural pressure to keep pushing ourselves and to ignore our physical and emotional needs, which leads to burnout, stress, and depression. However, self-care is not just good for you, it vital for your well-being. It is necessary in order to balance your emotional, environmental, financial, intellectual, occupational, physical, social, and spiritual well-being (Figure 14).

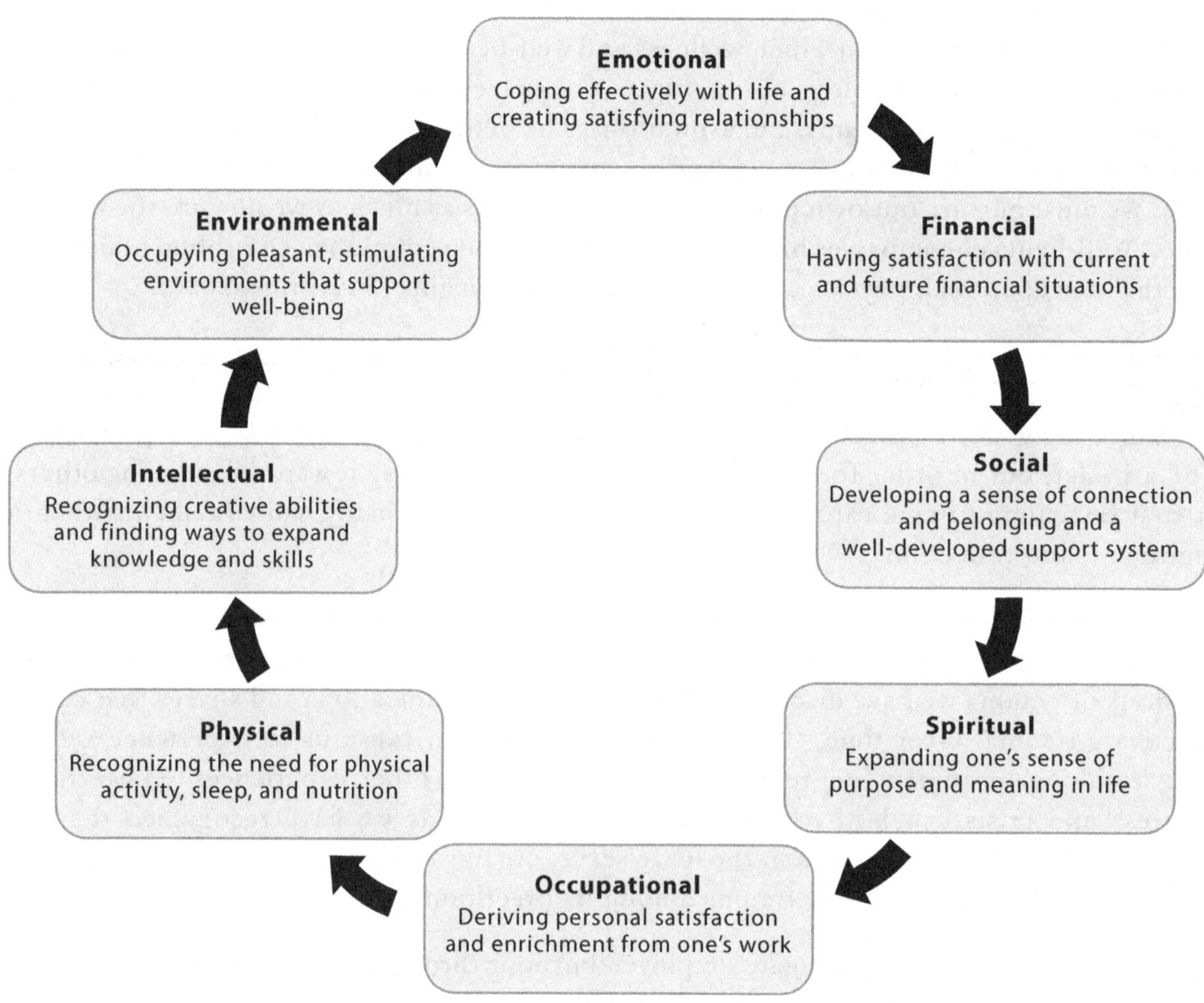

Figure 14. Domains of Well-Being*

On the next page is a worksheet you can use to assess your own well-being across these eight domains. The intent of this exercise is to assist you in establishing a baseline for your personal well-being while providing you with a foundation to move to sustained wellness.

*Adapted from Swarbrick (2006)

PROVIDER ACTIVITY

WELL-BEING ASSESSMENT*

Age Range: Adults

Objective: To assess well-being across these eight domains: emotional, environmental, financial, intellectual, occupational, physical, social, and spiritual

Directions: Rate the extent to which you agree with each of the following statements by placing an X in the corresponding column. For any statements that you somewhat agree with or disagree with, describe three practical action steps you will take to move this domain into full agreement. Make certain that each action step is SMART: specific, measurable, achievable, relevant, and time-bound. For any statements that you agree with, define three action steps you will take to ensure this domain remains in agreement.

Domains	Agree	Somewhat Agree	Disagree	Personal Plan of Action If you have rated this domain as *somewhat agree* or *disagree*, what are three actions you can take to move this domain into agreement? If you have rated this domain as *agree*, what three actions can you take to ensure this domain remains in agreement?
Emotional I am coping effectively with life and creating satisfying relationships.				1. 2. 3.
Environmental I occupy pleasant, stimulating environments (at work and at home) that support my well-being.				1. 2. 3.
Financial I am satisfied with my current and future financial situations and obligations.				1. 2. 3.

*Adapted from Swarbrick (2006)

Intellectual I recognize my creative abilities and have found ways to expand my knowledge and skills.				1. 2. 3.
Occupational I derive personal satisfaction and enrichment from my work or occupation.				1. 2. 3.
Physical I recognize the need for physical health and get optimal exercise, sleep, and nutrition.				1. 2. 3.
Social I have developed a sense of connection and belonging and have a well-developed support system.				1. 2. 3.
Spiritual I am expanding my sense of purpose and meaning in life.				1. 2. 3.

Reflection: Our well-being is influenced by many factors, some of which are outside of our control or sphere of influence. Our personal well-being is dynamic and constantly evolving, thus requiring continual assessment and reflection. Take a moment to reflect on your responses to this assessment.

1. Based on your assessment, which domains require immediate attention and nurture? In what ways?

____

____

____

2. For the domains that you rated as *agree*, describe their importance to your overall well-being. What personal practices do you currently implement to maintain alignment in those domains?

____

____

____

3. For those domains that you rated as *somewhat agree* or *disagree*, how long has each domain required attention (less than 6 months, 6–12 months, or greater than 12 months)?

4. For those domains that you rated as *somewhat agree* or *disagree*, do you have the skills, knowledge, and ability to align them into agreement? Why or why not?

5. For those domains that you rated as *somewhat agree* or *disagree*, what actions can you take to align them into agreement?

Creating Sanctuary

Given that we are often bombarded with our roles and responsibilities—multitasking and juggling many priorities and obligations—how do we cultivate safety in our lives? Where do we go to recharge, release, and refocus? We create sanctuary. A sanctuary is a place, space, or moment that is created just for you to reconnect and re-center. Creating sanctuary is an opportunity to take a moment to honor you. You define what sanctuary means to you. In this space, you can practice any exercises that allow you to re-center. In the previous chapters, we have provided activities and exercises that support our ACTION-from-Trauma approach. We summarize some of these strategies in Table 13.

Breathwork	Breathwork is a general term used to describe any type of therapy that utilizes breathing exercises to improve mental, physical, and spiritual health.
Yoga or mindful movement	The gentle movement associated with yoga helps develop body awareness and reduces over-reactivity to internal sensations. These practices recalibrate the threat detection system from the top down and bottom up, giving individuals with trauma control of their healing.
Mindfulness	Mindfulness activities can mitigate symptoms of PTSD by increasing activity in the prefrontal cortex and hippocampus and toning the amygdala. At its core, mindfulness is simply the basic human ability to be present. A simple mindfulness exercise involves the use of a stethoscope to center on the beauty of our heartbeat. For those who struggle with formal meditation or mindfulness practices, you can simply incorporate mindful awareness into your daily routines.
Gentle music	While music cannot cure PTSD, it has demonstrated positive results in helping to alleviate secondary symptoms of trauma, such as depression and insomnia (Blanaru et al., 2012).
Diet and exercise	Good nutrition and physical activity are important parts of leading a healthy and balanced lifestyle, which can dramatically assist in maintaining overall health and well-being.
Regular sleep	Lack of sleep can lead to insulin resistance, cardiovascular disease, mood swings, poor immune function, hormonal imbalances, and lowered life expectancy. Therefore, get on a regular sleep-wake schedule, and keep a journal by your bedside to capture any last-minute thoughts for the day. You can also perform light stretching or yoga before bed to prepare the body for sleep.

Table 13. Practical Ways for Practitioners to Re-Center

The following handout gives some additional ideas to create a sanctuary within your organization.

PROVIDER HANDOUT

CREATING SANCTUARY

Age Range: Adolescents and adults

Objective: To provide mindfulness strategies to increase self-awareness and decrease physical and psychological stress among the members of an organization

Directions: Consider the following strategies to develop opportunities for contextual mindful practices within your organization. This includes adapting the environment and providing moments within scheduled activities for mindfulness exercises:

- **Schedule mindful breaks:** Encourage members of your organization to identify a daily time when they can take a mindfulness break. For example, they can incorporate mindfulness into their lunch break by practicing mindful eating. For academic settings, schedule a time during the day, or even within a lesson, to stop and perform a mindfulness exercise.
- **Make a sensory room/space:** Identify an available room or space (e.g., a vacant office, an unused section of a classroom, or an empty cubicle) where you can create a sensory room. If possible, decrease artificial light in this space by using a floor lamp instead of overhead lighting or by purchasing calming lighting, such as a lava lamp. Provide comfortable seating, such as beanbag chairs, and place a docking station to allow the use of personal devices to play music. You can also consider using a diffuser for aromatherapy.
- **Create a virtual sensory space:** Seek out opportunities within the schedule to introduce mindfulness breaks. To do so, use a virtual meeting platform where you can set up a variety of virtual breakout "rooms." Within each room, provide specific sensory activities. For example, you can have a virtual room that provides a slideshow of scenic views, another virtual room that plays music, and another that offers stretching and yoga poses.
- **Take the meeting on the road:** Take a walk with the team if you plan to have a meeting with a small group.

Our clients' lived experiences demand our full attention, expertise, and empathy. Routine and adequate self-care is critical in ensuring we are able to meet and exceed the level of service, commitment, and attention our positions require. Your well-being and personal alignment are paramount for optimal client outcomes, personal happiness and well-being, and career longevity. Self-care is not a luxury in these unprecedented times; it is a vital commodity. By making a commitment to utilizing practical ways to re-center and align every day, you ensure that both you and your clients thrive.

CHAPTER 6

NOW IS THE TIME FOR ACTION

At the start of this book, we discussed the importance of expanding the concept of trauma-informed care to move into ACTION. In this chapter, we aim to encourage the development of an ACTION plan that includes specific action steps you can take. Society is now beginning to receive the message that traumatic experiences have the potential to penetrate every aspect of life. Now that we have begun to pay attention to the impact of trauma, there are still issues we need to address to move toward action. Here are some steps toward an ACTION plan:

- ☐ **Communication:** We must change our language and personal biases. Instead of neglecting our previous training, we must expand our view. Statements such as "He should be able to..." or "She just does not want to listen and chooses not to" must exit our vocabulary. Replace that language with statements of empathy, respect, gratitude, and growth.
- ☐ **Person first:** We must focus on the person first—not the trauma that happened to them. Individuals are resilient and have strengths that supersede trauma. Therefore, include strengths-based and evidence-based strategies in your work. While we have presented a multitude of activities in this book, make sure that your treatment plans are person- and family-centered as well.
- ☐ **Advocacy:** Attending expensive workshops and trainings is a beginning, not an ending. Reading this book is a start. The real work is in advocacy at every level. Advocate for your clients by acknowledging their unique needs and by aligning resources that fit those needs. Educate those who work with individuals with trauma. Advocate for resources to decrease the financial and social impacts of trauma. Establish mentorship programs and training for primary care, childcare, and eldercare providers.
- ☐ **Avoid re-traumatization:** Employ the use of de-escalation techniques versus the use of physical restraints. Many of the challenges individuals present with occur when they do not feel validated. Start by acknowledging their perspective and by recognizing the trauma lens of protection through which they view the world. Listen to what they have to say! Avoid making assumptions and judgments. Ask for and provide clarification by repeating and rephrasing statements. Apologize for any misunderstandings or misinterpretations. Provide choices rather than dictating rules.
- ☐ **Assess your knowledge of trauma:** Be aware of your personal experiences. As you work with clients, check in to see your level of acute stress. Utilize some of the techniques provided here to keep your mind-body connection healthy.
- ☐ **Establish a team:** Develop trauma stewardship, and establish a team of champions under a unified vision. Identify key individuals to be advocates for the family or client. Seek

buy-in, and provide mentorship for team members (Fette, Lambdin-Pattavina, & Weaver, 2019).

- ☐ **Promote physical activity:** Performing gross motor activities, such as sports, can improve positive outcomes and behaviors. Support the development of structured activities and access to such programs (Cahill, Egan, & Seber, 2020).
- ☐ **Address organizational trauma:** Complete organizational assessments for trauma-informed care. Develop a mission statement that includes inclusivity; cultural sensitivity and values around safety; trustworthiness and transparency; peer support and mutual self-help; collaboration and mutuality; empowerment, voice, and choice; and cultural, historical, and gender issues.
- ☐ **Incorporate a reflective practice:** With any clinical practice, it is necessary to incorporate a reflective practice on the services you provide. Be sure to revisit the events of therapy sessions by maintaining proper notes. Revisit your own thoughts and feelings during the session. Analyze what seemed to work and what did not. Consider other activities and approaches you could have taken to assist in revising treatment plans. In addition, revisit the Practitioner Readiness for Trauma Care Checklist from chapter 1 to make sure you are best supporting your clients' needs.

Now is the time for you to call others to ACTION!

Bibliography

For your convenience, the worksheets and forms from this book are available for download at www.pesi.com/TraumaInAction

Abdou, C. M., Fingerhut, A. W., Jackson, J. S., & Wheaton, F. (2016). Healthcare stereotype threat in older adults in the health and retirement study. *American Journal of Preventive Medicine, 50*(2), 191–198.

Alexander, J. C., Eyerman, R., Giesen, B., Smelser, N. J., & Sztompka, P. (2004). *Cultural trauma and collective identity.* Berkeley: University of California Press.

American Psychiatric Association. (2013). *Diagnostic and statistical manual of mental disorders* (5th ed.). Arlington, VA: Author.

Ayden, C. (2017). How to forget the unforgettable? On collective trauma, cultural identity, and mnemotechnologies. *Identity, 17*(3), 125–137.

Becker-Blease, K. A. (2017). As the world becomes trauma-informed, work to do. *Journal of Trauma & Dissociation, 18*(2), 131–138.

Benjet, C., Bromet, E., Karam, E. G., Kessler, R. C., McLaughlin, K. A., Ruscio, A. M., ... Koenen, K. C. (2016). The epidemiology of traumatic event exposure worldwide: Results from the World Mental Health Survey Consortium. *Psychological Medicine, 46*(2), 327–343.

Blanaru, M., Bloch, B., Vadas, L., Arnon, Z., Ziv, N., Kremer, I., & Haimov, I. (2012). The effects of music relaxation and muscle relaxation techniques on sleep quality and emotional measures among individuals with posttraumatic stress disorder. *Mental Illness, 4*(2), Article e13.

Blanding, D., & Solomon, D. (2020, March 30). *The coronavirus pandemic is fueling fear and hate across America.* Center for American Progress. Retrieved from https://www.americanprogress.org/issues/race/news/2020/03/30/482407/coronavirus-pandemic-fueling-fear-hate-across-america/

Bloom, S. L. (2007). *The Sanctuary Model® of trauma-informed organizational change.* The National Abandoned Infants Assistance Resources Center. Retrieved from http://www.sanctuaryweb.com/Portals/0/Bloom%20Pubs/2007%20Bloom%20The%20Sanctuary%20Model%20The%20Source%20Articles%20Sanctuary.pdf

Borg, C., Bedoin, N., Peyron, R., Bogey, S., Laurent, B., & Thomas-Antérion, C. (2013). Impaired emotional processing in a patient with a left posterior insula-SII lesion. *Neurocase, 19*(6), 592–603.

Bowles, B., Crupi, C., Pigott, S., Parrent, A., Wiebe, S., Janzen, L., & Köhler, S. (2010). Double dissociation of selective recollection and familiarity impairments following two different surgical treatments for temporal-lobe epilepsy. *Neuropsychologia, 48*(9), 2640–2647.

Cahill, S., Egan, B., & Seber, J. (2020). Activity- and occupation-based interventions to support mental health, positive behavior, and social participation for children and youth: A systematic review. *American Journal of Occupational Therapy, 74*(2), Article 7402180020.

Callaghan, B., Fields, A., Gee, D., Gabard-Durnam, L., Caldera, C., Humphreys, K., ... Tottenham, N. (2020). Mind and gut: Associations between mood and gastrointestinal distress in children exposed to adversity. *Development and Psychopathology, 32*(1), 309–328.

Carpenter, S. (2012, September). That gut feeling. *Monitor on Psychology, 43*(8). Retrieved from http://www.apa.org/monitor/2012/09/gut-feeling

Center on the Developing Child, Harvard University. (n.d.). *Brain architecture.* Retrieved from https://developingchild.harvard.edu/science/key-concepts/brain-architecture/#neuron-footnote

Centers for Disease Control and Prevention. (2020, June 25). *COVID-19 in racial and ethnic minority groups.* Retrieved from https://www.cdc.gov/coronavirus/2019-ncov/need-extra-precautions/racial-ethnic-minorities.html

Clancy, K., Ding, M., Bernat, E., Schmidt, N. B., & Li, W. (2017). Restless "rest": Intrinsic sensory hyperactivity and disinhibition in post-traumatic stress disorder. *Brain: A Journal of Neurology, 140*(7), 2041–2050.

Clark, G. F., & Kingsley, K. L. (2020). Occupational therapy practice guidelines for early childhood: Birth–5 years. *American Journal of Occupational Therapy, 74*(3), Article 7403397010.

Cook, J. M., Newman, E., & The New Haven Trauma Competency Group. (2014). A consensus statement on trauma mental health: The New Haven Competency Conference process and major findings. *Psychological Trauma: Theory, Research, Practice, and Policy, 6*(4), 300–307.

Cross, T. L., Bazron, B. J., Dennis, K. W., & Isaacs, M. R. (1989). *Towards a culturally competent system of care* (Vol. 1). Washington, DC: Georgetown University Child Development Center.

Darwin, C. (1872/2009). *The expression of the emotions in man and animals* (4th ed). London: John Murray.

Deiss, T., Meyers, R., Whitney, J., Bell, C., Tatarinova, T., Franckle, L., & Beaven, S. (2019). Physiological markers and reflex pattern progression in individuals with neurodevelopmental deficits utilizing the MNRI method. *Neuroscience and Medicine, 10*(1), 30–54.

Dunn, E. C., Nishimi, K., Powers, A., & Bradley, B. (2017). Is developmental timing of trauma exposure associated with depressive and post-traumatic stress disorder symptoms in adulthood? *Journal of Psychiatric Research, 84*, 119–127.

Eyerman, R. (2019). *Memory, trauma and identity.* New Haven, CT: Palgrave Macmillian.

Felitti, V. J., Anda, R. F., Nordenberg, D., Williamson, D. F., Spitz, A. M., Edwards, V., Koss, M. P., & Marks, J. S. (1998). Relationship of childhood abuse and household dysfunction to many of the leading causes of death in adults: The Adverse Childhood Experiences (ACE) study. *American Journal of Preventive Medicine, 14*(4), 245–258.

Fette, C., Lambdin-Pattavina, C., & Weaver, L. (2019). *Understanding and applying trauma-informed approaches across occupational therapy settings.* Retrieved from https://www.aota.org/-/media/Corporate/Files/Publications/CE-Articles/CE-Article-May-2019-Trauma.pdf

Fishbain, D. A., Pulikal, A., Lewis, J. E., & Gao, J. (2017). Chronic pain types differ in their reported prevalence of post-traumatic stress disorder (PTSD) and there is consistent evidence that chronic pain is associated with PTSD: An evidence-based structured systematic review. *Pain Medicine, 18*(4), 711–735.

Gibbs, V. D. (2017a). *Exploring disparities in underrepresented minority groups of children diagnosed with autism spectrum disorders using the biopsychosocial theoretical model* (Doctoral dissertation). Retrieved from Seton Hall University Dissertations and Theses (ETDs) (No. 2267).

Gibbs, V. D. (2017b). *Self-regulation & mindfulness: Over 82 exercises & worksheets for sensory processing disorder, ADHD & autism spectrum disorder.* Eau Claire, WI: PESI Publishing & Media.

Ginwright, S. (2018). *The future of healing: Shifting from trauma informed care to healing centered engagement.* Retrieved from http://kinshipcarersvictoria.org/wp-content/uploads/2018/08/OP-Ginwright-S-2018-Future-of-healing-care.pdf

Gorman, K. W., & Hatkevich, B. A. (2016). Role of occupational therapy in combating human trafficking. *American Journal of Occupational Therapy, 70*(6), Article 7006360010.

Guarino, K., Soares, P., Konnath, K., Clervil, R., & Bassuk, E. (2009). *Trauma-informed organizational toolkit.* Rockville, MD: Center for Mental Health Services, Substance Abuse and Mental Health Services Administration; The Daniels Fund; The National Child Traumatic Stress Network; The W.K. Kellogg Foundation. Retrieved from https://www.air.org/sites/default/files/downloads/report/Trauma-Informed_Organizational_Toolkit_0.pdf

Gupta, M. A., Jarosz, P., & Gupta, A. K. (2017). Posttraumatic stress disorder (PTSD) and the dermatology patient. *Clinics in Dermatology, 35*(3), 260–266.

Harley, E. K., Williams, M. E., Zamora, I., & Lakatos, P. P. (2014). Trauma treatment in young children with developmental disabilities: Applications of the Child-Parent Psychotherapy (CPP) model to the cases of "James" and "Juan." *Pragmatic Case Studies in Psychotherapy, 10*(3), 156–195.

Hebb, D. O. (1949). *The organization of behavior.* New York: John Wiley & Sons.

Hedges, D. W., & Woon, F. L. M. (2010). Premorbid brain volume estimates and reduced total brain volume in adults exposed to trauma with or without posttraumatic stress disorder: A meta-analysis. *Cognitive and Behavioral Neurology, 23*(2), 124–129.

Hemmings, S. M., Malan-Müller, S., van den Heuvel, L. L., Demmitt, B. A., Stanislawski, M. A., Smith, D. G., ... Lowry, C. A. (2017). The microbiome in posttraumatic stress disorder and trauma-exposed controls: An exploratory study. *Psychosomatic Medicine, 79*(8), 936–946.

Herman, J. (1997). *Trauma and recovery: The aftermath of violence—from domestic abuse to political terror.* New York: Basic Books.

Hirschberger, G. (2018). Collective trauma and the social construction of meaning. *Frontiers in Psychology*, 9, Article 1441.

Kane, A. V., Dinh, D. M., & Ward, H. D. (2015). Childhood malnutrition and the intestinal microbiome. *Pediatric Research, 77*(1–2), 256–262.

Kaplan, E. A. (2008). Global trauma and public feelings: Viewing images of catatrophe. *Consumption Markets & Culture, 11*(1), 3–24.

Kaur, H. (2020, May 8). *The coronavirus pandemic is hitting Black and Brown Americans especially hard on all fronts.* CNN. Retrieved from https://www.cnn.com/2020/05/08/us/coronavirus-pandemic-race-impact-trnd/index.html

Kellermann, N. P. (2013). Epigenetic transmission of holocaust trauma: Can nightmares be inherited? *The Israel Journal of Psychiatry and Related Sciences, 50*(1), 33–39.

Konicarova, J., & Bob, P. (2013). Principle of dissolution and primitive reflexes in ADHD. *Activitas Nervosa Superior, 55*(1/2), 74–78.

Kozlowska, K., Walker, P., McLean, L., & Carrive, P. (2015). Fear and the defense cascade: Clinical implications and management. *Harvard Review of Psychiatry, 23*(4), 263–287.

Krugers, H. J., Lucassen, P. J., Karst, H., & Joëls, M. (2010). Chronic stress effects on hippocampal structure and synaptic function: Relevance for depression and normalization by anti-glucocorticoid treatment. *Frontiers in Synaptic Neuroscience, 2*, Article 24.

Lee, J. (2020). Mental health effects of school closures during COVID-19. *The Lancet Child & Adolescent Health, 4*(6), Article 421.

Lee, Y. H., Park, B. N. R., & Kim, S. H. (2011). The effects of heat and massage application on autonomic nervous system. *Yonsei Medical Journal, 52*(6), 982–989.

Leitch, L. (2017). Action steps using ACEs and trauma-informed care: A resilience model. *Health & Justice 5*(1), 1–10.

MacLeod, C. M., Gopie, N., Hourihan, K. L., Neary, K. R., & Ozubko, J. D. (2010). The production effect: Delineation of a phenomenon. *Journal of Experimental Psychology: Learning, Memory, and Cognition, 36*(3), 671–685.

Maren, S. (2014). Fear of the unexpected: Hippocampus mediates novelty-induced return of extinguished fear in rats. *Neurobiology of Learning and Memory, 108*, 88–95.

Marsella, A. J., Johnson, J. L., Watson, P., & Gryczynski, J. (2008). Preface. In A. J. Marsella, J. L. Johnson, P. Watson, & J. Gryczynski (Eds.), *Ethnocultural perspectives on disaster and trauma: Foundations, issues, and applications* (pp. ix–xvi). New York: Springer.

Maslow, A. H. (1943). A theory of human motivation. *Psychological Review, 50*(4), 370–396.

McClure, V. S. (2017). *Infant massage: A handbook for loving parents* (4th ed.). New York: Bantam Books.

Menschner, C., Maul, A., & Center for Health Care Strategies. (2016, April). *Key ingredients for successful trauma-informed care implementation.* Retrieved from https://www.chcs.org/resource/key-ingredients-for-successful-trauma-informed-care-implementation/

Miller, L. J., Anzalone, M. E., Lane, S. J., Cermak, S. A., & Osten, E. T. (2007). Concept evolution in sensory integration: A proposed nosology for diagnosis. *American Journal of Occupational Therapy, 61*, 135–140.

Mueller-Pfeiffer, C., Schick, M., Schulte-Vels, T., O'Gorman, R., Michels, L., Martin-Soelch, C., … Hasler, G. (2013). Atypical visual processing in posttraumatic stress disorder. *NeuroImage: Clinical, 3*, 531–538.

Nalty, K. (2016, May). Strategies for confronting unconscious bias. *The Colorado Lawyer, 45*(5), 45–52.

National Child Traumatic Stress Network. (2016). *What is a trauma-informed child and family service system?* Retrieved from https://www.nctsn.org/resources/what-trauma-informed-child-and-family-service-system

National Child Traumatic Stress Network. (2017). *Complex trauma: In urban African-American children, youth, and families.* Retrieved from https://www.nctsn.org/sites/default/files/resources//complex_trauma_facts_in_urban_african_american_children_youth_families.pdf

National Children's Alliance. (2019). *CAC statistics.* Retrieved from http://www.nationalchildrensalliance.org/cac-statistics

National Network to End Domestic Violence. (n.d.). *Understanding the importance of trauma informed care.* Retrieved from https://nnedv.org/spotlight_on/understanding-importance-trauma-informed-care/

National Prevention Information Network. (n.d.). *Cultural competence in health and human services.* Retrieved from https://npin.cdc.gov/pages/cultural-competence

Nevis, E. C. (1987/2001). *Organizational consulting: A Gestalt approach.* Cleveland, OH: Gestalt Institute of Cleveland Press.

Office of Minority Health. (n.d.). *Profile: Black/African Americans.* Retrieved from https://minorityhealth.hhs.gov/omh/browse.aspx?lvl=3&lvlid=61

Oliveira, M. D. C., Barea, L. M., Horn, A. P. K., Ongaratti, B. R., Soares, J. O. D., Araujo, B., ... Pereira-Lima, J. F. S. (2020). Resolution of headache after reduction of prolactin levels in hyperprolactinemic patients. *Arquivos de Neuro-Psiquiatria, 78*(1), 28–33.

Pavlov, I. P. (1927). *Conditioned reflexes: An investigation of the physiological activity of the cerebral cortex.* London: Oxford University Press.

Pelt, A. C. (2011). *Glucocorticoids: Effects, action mechanisms, and therapeutic uses.* Hauppauge, NY: Nova Science.

Rakoff, V., Sigal, J. J., & Epstein, N. B. (1966). Children and families of concentration camp survivors. *Canada's Mental Health, 14*(4), 24–26.

Resource Sharing Project. (2016). *Organizational trauma and resilience.* National Sexual Assault Coalition. Retrieved from https://resourcesharingproject.org/sites/default/files/Organizational_Trauma_and_Resilience.pdf

Roberton, T., Carter, E. D., Chou, V. B., Stegmuller, A. R., Jackson, B. D., Tam, Y., ... Walker, N. (2020). Early estimates of the indirect effects of the COVID-19 pandemic on maternal and child mortality in low-income and middle-income countries: A modelling study. *The Lancet Global Health, 8*(7), e901–e908.

Ryan, T. J., Roy, D. S., Pignatelli, M., Arons, A., & Tonegawa, S. (2015). Engram cells retain memory under retrograde amnesia. *Science, 348*(6238), 1007–1013.

Sabel, B. A., Wang, J., Cárdenas-Morales, L., Faiq, M., & Heim, C. (2018). Mental stress as consequence and cause of vision loss: The dawn of psychosomatic ophthalmology for preventive and personalized medicine. *EPMA Journal, 9*(2), 133–160.

Salas, M. J. (2020, April 10). *The COVID-19 crisis is a trauma pandemic in the making.* Retrieved from https://psychcentral.com/blog/the-covid-19-crisis-is-a-trauma-pandemic-in-the-making/

Schoenfeld, T. J., McCausland, H. C., Morris, H. D., Padmanaban, V., & Cameron, H. A. (2017). Stress and loss of adult neurogenesis differentially reduce hippocampal volume. *Biological Psychiatry, 82*(12), 914–923.

Segal, Z. V., Williams, J. M. G., & Teasdale, J. D. (2001). *Mindfulness-based cognitive therapy for depression: A new approach to preventing relapse.* New York: Guilford Press.

Selye, H. (1974). *Stress without distress.* Philadelphia: Lippincott.

Shonkoff, J. P., Garner, A. S., Committee on Psychosocial Aspects of Child and Family Health, Committee on Early Childhood, Adoption, and Dependent Care, and Section on Developmental and Behavioral Pediatrics. (2012). The lifelong effects of early childhood adversity and toxic stress. *Pediatrics, 129*(1), e232–e246.

Silverman, H., Toropin, K., Sidner, S., & Perrot, L. (2020, May 18). *Navajo Nation surpasses New York state for the highest COVID-19 infection rate in the US.* CNN. Retrieved from https://www.cnn.com/2020/05/18/us/navajo-nation-infection-rate-trnd/index.html

Smith, W. H. (2010, February 16). *The impact of racial trauma on African Americans.* Paper developed for the Heinz Endowments African American Men and Boys Advisory Board. Retrieved from https://www.heinz.org/userfiles/impactofracialtraumaonafricanamericans.pdf

Snowden, L. R. (2002). Bias in mental health assessment and intervention: Theory and evidence. *American Public Health Association, 93*(2), 239–243.

Spectra Diversity. (2017, December 27). *Brain stuff: The neuroscience behind implicit bias.* Retrieved from https://www.spectradiversity.com/2017/12/27/unconscious-bias/

Staats, C., Capatosto, K., Wright, R. A., & Jackson, V. W. (2016). *State of the science: Implicit bias review.* Columbus, OH: The Kirwan Institute for the Study of Race and Ethnicity. Retrieved from https://kirwaninstitute.osu.edu/research/2016-state-science-implicit-bias-review

Substance Abuse and Mental Health Services Administration. (2014a). *SAMHSA's concept of trauma and guidance for a trauma-informed approach.* HHS Publication No. (SMA) 14-4884. Rockville, MD: Author.

Substance Abuse and Mental Health Services Administration. (2014b). *Trauma-informed care in behavioral health services.* Treatment Improvement Protocol (TIP) Series 57. HHS Publication No. (SMA) 13-4801. Rockville, MD: Author.

Swarbrick, M. (2006). A wellness approach. *Psychiatric Rehabilitation Journal, 29*(4), 311–314.

Tan, S. Y., & Yip, A. (2018). Hans Selye (1907–1982): Founder of the stress theory. *Singapore Medical Journal, 59*(4), 170–171.

Trent, M., Dooley, D. G., & Dougé, J. (2019). The impact of racism on child and adolescent health. *Pediatrics, 144*(2), Article e20191765.

United Nations Women. (2020, April 17). *Violence against women and girls data collection during COVID-19.* Retrieved from https://www.unwomen.org/en/digital-library/publications/2020/04/issue-brief-violence-against-women-and-girls-data-collection-during-covid-19

Venugopal, V. (2016). Understanding organizational trauma: A background review of types and causes. *Journal of Business and Management, 18*(10), 65–69.

Vivian, P., & Hormann, S. (2013). *Organizational trauma and healing.* North Charleston, SC: CreateSpace.

Wallwork, S. B., Grabherr, L., O'Connell, N. E., Catley, M. J., & Moseley, G. L. (2017). Defensive reflexes in people with pain—a biomarker of the need to protect? A meta-analytical systematic review. *Reviews in the Neurosciences, 28*(4), 381–396.

Wigert, B., & Agrawal, S. (2018, July 12). *Employee burnout, part 1: The 5 main causes.* Retrieved from https://www.gallup.com/workplace/237059/employee-burnout-part-main-causes.aspx

Wilson, J. P. (2008). Culture, trauma, and the treatment of post-traumatic syndromes: A global perspective. In A. J. Marsella, J. L. Johnson, P. Watson, & J. Gryczynski (Eds.), *Ethnocultural perspectives on disaster and trauma: Foundations, issues, and applications* (pp. 351–375). New York: Springer.

Xia, N., & Li, H. (2018). Loneliness, social isolation, and cardiovascular health. *Antioxidants & Redox Signaling, 28*(9), 837–851.

Yang, B., Wei, J., Ju, P., & Chen, J. (2019). Effects of regulating intestinal microbiota on anxiety symptoms: A systematic review. *General Psychiatry, 32*(2), Article e100056.

Yatchmenoff, D. K., Sundborg, S. A., & Davis, M. A. (2017). Implementing trauma-informed care: Recommendations on the process. *Advances in Social Work, 18*(1), 167–185.

Yehuda, R., Daskalakis, N. P., Bierer, L. M., Bader, H. N., Klengel, T., Holsboer, F., & Binder, E. B. (2016). Holocaust exposure induced intergenerational effects on FKBP5 methylation. *Biological Psychiatry, 80*(5), 372–380.

Yehuda, R., Engel, S. M., Brand, S. R., Seckl, J., Marcus, S. M., & Berkowitz, G. S. (2005). Transgenerational effects of posttraumatic stress disorder in babies of mothers exposed to the World Trade Center attacks during pregnancy. *The Journal of Clinical Endocrinology & Metabolism, 90*(7), 4115–4118.

Yochman, A., & Pat-Horenczyk, R. (2019). Sensory modulation in children exposed to continuous traumatic stress. *Journal of Child & Adolescent Trauma, 13*(1), 93–102.

Young, B. H., Ford, J. D., Ruzek, J. I., Friedman, M. J., & Gusman, F. D. (1998). *Disaster mental health services: A guidebook for clinicians and adminstrators.* White River Junction, VT: Department of Veterans Affairs, The National Center for Post-Traumatic Stress Disorder. Retrieved from https://www.hsdl.org/?view&did=441325

Zhuang, L., Chen, H., Zhang, S., Zhuang, J., Li, Q., & Feng, Z. (2019). Intestinal microbiota in early life and its implications on childhood health. *Genomics, Proteomics & Bioinformatics, 17*(1), 13–25.

Made in United States
North Haven, CT
26 January 2025